CW00337267

THE SUND

THE
SPORTING
DECADE
—1980s—

THE SUNDAY TIMES

THE SPORTING DECADE
— 1980s —

CHRIS DIGHTON

Macdonald
Queen Anne Press

A QUEEN ANNE PRESS BOOK

© Chris Dighton 1990
© Photographs Chris Smith 1990

First published in Great Britain in 1990 by
Queen Anne Press, a division of
Macdonald & Co (Publishers) Ltd
Orbit House
1 New Fetter Lane
London EC4A 1AR

A member of Maxwell Macmillan Pergamon Publishing Corporation

All photographs by Chris Smith

All rights reserved. No part of this publication may be reproduced, stored in a
retrieval system, or transmitted, in any form or by any means, without the prior
permission in writing of the publisher, nor be otherwise circulated in any form of
binding or cover other than that in which it is published and without a similar
condition including this condition being imposed on the subsequent purchaser.

British Library Cataloguing in Publication Data
Dighton, Chris
  Sunday Times: the sporting decade.
  1. Sporting events, history
  I. Title
  796.09

  ISBN 0–356–19209–1

Typeset by Butler & Tanner Ltd, Frome and London
Reproduced, printed and bound in Great Britain by
BPCC Hazell Books
Aylesbury, Bucks, England
Member of BPCC Ltd

CONTENTS

ACKNOWLEDGEMENTS

A great many thanks are owed to a lot of people who have helped see this project through. Those thanks not only go to the featured writers who so willingly contributed, but to the back-room sports team and all the other sports writers at *The Sunday Times* who chipped in with thoughts, advice and the necessary jogging of the memory. It is amazing how easy it is to overlook major events in a ten-year retrospective. Special mention must go to Steve Hutchings who provided life-saving computer expertise and to Carolyn Wigoder for typing skills. Last but not least a special mention for my wife, Helen, and children, Cassie, Luke, Lydia and Edward. Thank you for your patience. I will make it up to you some day!

FOREWORD

How will the eighties be remembered? For Ian Botham's exploits at Headingley and Edgbaston in 1981; for Seb Coe's two 1500m Olympic gold medals; for Martina Navratilova's six successive Wimbledon singles titles? Or perhaps the tragedies of Bradford, Heysel and Hillsborough? Or the disgrace of Ben Johnson, Lester Piggott and Mike Gatting?

Of course, it will be remembered for all of that. But when we sat down at *The Sunday Times* and tried to sum up the eighties we came up with one word that seemed to be at the root of it all: money.

The eighties will surely go down as the era when money, never quite happy with playing a supporting role, took centre stage. Television, using the power of money, tore up the fixture lists and rewrote them. They dictated the who, what, where and when of sport.

Sponsors, agents and South Africa also got in on the act. Money, or more precisely the refusal to spend it responsibly, left us with outmoded and dangerous stadiums and let the pernicious problem of football hooliganism fester. Rather the multi-million pound striker than the multi-million pound stadium.

This book offers no answers to this problem. Nor should it. It records what happened, and a series of essays from the writers of the Sports Department of *The Sunday Times* picks out the key moments or people that glorified or shamed the eighties.

An awful lot happened in those ten years to reshape our understanding of modern sport. Some of it good, much of it bad. But for all the bad, sport can always redeem itself on the field of play. And it is because awesome and inspirational achievements will always transcend knavery that sport succeeds as a medium of cultural fascination.

Higher, further, faster. It was ever thus. And so into the nineties.

Chris Nawrat
Sports Editor *The Sunday Times*

WHEN THE COLOUR OF MONEY TARNISHED OUR SPORTS HEROES BY STEPHEN JONES

THE most significant new event in the 1980s was the 973 metres. There were many contenders but James Mays, a mid-rank American, was supreme at the distance. He took the first 800 at rare pace, gradually faded and stopped, walked off the track and picked up his money. Simply, his job was artificially to rev up the pace of the glamorous middle-distance events to world-record schedule so the race's resident celebrity could break the record or, as happened almost always, fail to do so.

The pace had to be raised artificially because only one per race from the middle-distance galaxy would appear. Two or more could have cut out a bona fide pace, but protecting their pride and, more importantly, their market value, one would run the 1,500 while another hid in the mile or 1,000 metres or 3,000 metres, or behind a badly torn hamstring of the mind.

Athletics in essence is still the purest, best form of sport. I could even believe Ben Johnson if he said he took drugs in a drive to become the supreme sprinter rather than to make money, though even for that he is rightly set down as the disgrace of the last 10 years.

But the athletics circus revolted me in the 1980s because it blurred sport's keenest edges; it concentrated on money-making as much as winning. A tiny top stratum was pampered, even allowed to bottle out, if their members thought they might lose, thus violating the basic spirit of competition.

So the decade saw many forms of sporting excess. There was Sugar Ray Leonard and his old codgers' circus in boxing, the split in tennis, the cynicism of South Africa in buying in its sport, of cricket in making Test cricket boring through familiarity. There were self-pampering administrations in so many sports. When rugby, grappling with its own success, began the dramatic debate on its amateurism, the traditionalists' highest card was the grisly example of other sports.

The swirl of rapacity further glorified the individual and, in the hands of the sponsors, agents, organisers and the media, reduced even team sports to confrontations between two people. The Super Bowl was simply single combat: Marino versus Montana, Williams versus Elway, even though no team sport has been invented in which one player can bring success without foundations laid by his mates.

The celebrity cult meant that to have Aouita on his marks or Ballesteros on the tee or Higgins at the table or McEnroe knocking up, meant more than the overall quality of the event. Who cared who else was in the team or the event? Most sponsors didn't. ITV's caption before running events said: 'Among the competitors are ...' The rest, training and aspiring as fiercely as anyone, are the backdrop. Yet the swirl eventually engulfed.

Once it had bestowed money and fame and a sort of one-dimensional, pop-up soap status, it could turn savagely on its own kind. The fame meant that you could no longer shower away public attention in the dressing room and emerge unwatched. We wanted the full story, the skeletons and nasty smells.

The greatest sporting sadness of the 1980s is that some of the most brilliant sportspeople have been drastically reduced by some small weakness or foible of far less significance than their sporting greatness, but which obscures it.

Perhaps a considered history will restore them. It had better. How many people see Piggott as the tax-dodger, butt of the clever comedian in the striped tents in all those offensive corporate hospitality ghettos which every sport has installed? No longer the steely, wonderful jockey.

We now see Botham as the pot-smoking boorish clown, fodder for the old hams and whiners in cricket's commentary box; not the flourishing match-winner, in style and statistics the greatest ever.

Mary Decker is perceived as the weak-kneed, blubbing Yank scraped off the Los Angeles track after clashing with Zola Budd, that crude opportunist. Yet two years before, Decker achieved one of history's most courageous wins. She led Kazankina, the Russian, all round the 3,000 metres in the 1983 world championships. Kazankina almost smugly sprinted past on the straight, where you never come back. Decker dug deep, closed the gap and the Russian, shocked to her spikes, was literally staggered. Decker won. Some weakness.

Borg haunts himself in gossip columns, losing himself in bad businesses and as a low-charting pop singer and allegedly attempted suicide. Yet his true place in history is as the sublimely self-possessed king of Wimbledon.

They were all paid by sport, they were all hurt when sport's new seaminess came to collect the debt.

Who or what escaped? Golf did, gloriously maintaining its equilibrium. Even football maintained some of its egalitarianism. Several rose out of the dross, untainted: Chris Evert, Imran Khan, Bryan Robson, Ian Taylor, the hockey goalkeeper, John Rutherford, Adrian Moorhouse and, for distinguishing sport from its new trappings, Sharron Davies.

In one narrow sense everyone escaped because, when the starting gun sounded, everyone was forced to survive on sporting merit alone, and the upshot was sometimes wondrous. It was what happened before and after, as sport wheeled and dealed and became false, that was so unsportsmanlike.

1980

SOCCER: January 1

As they are to finish the decade, so they begin it. Liverpool the only real constant factor in ten years of change, drama and upheaval in world sport are top of the First Division. Their match against Stoke is postponed but that makes no difference. None of their rivals can make any impact on the Merseyside club's position at the top of the table.

CRICKET: The West Indies win their first ever Test match in Melbourne when they beat Australia by ten wickets. Australia make 156 and 259 while the West Indies score 397 and 22 for 0.

RUGBY UNION: January 4

The English Rugby Union join Wales, Scotland and Ireland in agreeing to a Lions tour of South Africa.

OLYMPICS: January 6

Saudi Arabia are the first country to withdraw from the Olympics over the Soviet invasion of Afghanistan. On January 20 Lord Killanin, President of the Olympic movement announces there is no likelihood of the Moscow venue for the Olympic Games being changed despite world condemnation of the Soviet invasion of Afghanistan.

CHESS: January 11

Nigel Short becomes Britain's youngest international master.

TENNIS: January 15

Chris Evert-Lloyd says she will retire from tennis after fulfilling obligations to play in five more events. It transpires that she will play for ten more years before bowing out at Wimbledon in 1989. The following day Wimbledon announces centre court seats will cost £4 and £5 this year, rising in price by £1 every three days. Entrance to the ground rises from £1.50 to £2.

RUGBY UNION: January 19

The Five Nations tournament opens with England convincingly beating Ireland 24–9 at Twickenham, where Tony Bond breaks a leg, and Wales beat France 18–9 in Cardiff.

ICE SKATING: January 24

Robin Cousins, from Bristol, wins the European Figure Skating Championships in Stockholm and goes on to collect Olympic gold in the Winter Games which start at Lake Placid on February 12. But he is denied a hat-trick of gold when he collects silver in the World Championships in West Germany on March 13. His success follows John Curry, and the world is soon to be enraptured by the talents of the British ice dance pair Jayne Torvill and Christopher Dean. In the Winter Olympics Ingmar Stenmark won the giant slalom gold while American Eric Heidan enjoyed Klondike fever with five speed skating golds.

BOXING: Maurice Hope, Britain's light-middleweight WBC champion visits a specialist after he is found to be suffering from a loose retina of the eye. Revolutionary laser treatment saves his career but Hope is to lose his title against Wilfred Benitez.

CRICKET: February 6

England lose a non-Ashes series against Australia 3–0 more infamous for Dennis Lillee and his aluminium bat saga. Lillee appeared at the crease with his revolutionary bat but was told it was out of order. The bat was flung angrily to the ground and Lillee was forced to use the willow. Fired up he managed to take 26 wickets in the series. Two days later Richard Hadlee took five for 34 in Dunedin as the West Indies are all out for 140. New Zealand go on to win the Test by one wicket.

SOCCER: February 13

Derek Shilson, a 25-year-old amateur footballer was ordered to pay £2,400 in damages for a foul tackle in a Sunday match between Frampton Athletic and Stapleton which left an opponent in hospital with a cartilage injury.

CRICKET: February 15

Bob Taylor equals Wasim Bari's world record of seven catches in an innings as England play India in Bombay.

RUGBY UNION: February 17

Welshman Paul Ringer, sent off in the previous day's international at Twickenham against England is banned from the game for eight weeks. England led and inspired by lock Bill Beaumont are on their way to their first Grand Slam since 1957, beating Wales 9–8, France in Paris for the first time in 16 years when they win 17–13 and Scotland at Murrayfield 30–18.

SOCCER: March 1

Bill 'Dixie' Dean dies at the Everton–Liverpool derby. Dean was 73 and scored 60 goals for Everton in the 1927–28 season.

OLYMPICS: March 12

The Government withdraws Foreign Office liaison help for the Moscow Olympics and public service workers will not be allowed special time off work to attend the games. Five days later a free vote in the House of Commons condemns the Soviet invasion of Afghanistan by 315–147 votes and urges British athletes not to go to the Olympics. However the British Olympic Association votes 18–5 to send a team to the Games.

SQUASH: March 17

Geoff Hunt won his seventh British Open title when he beat Qamar Zaman 9–3,9–3,1–9,9–1.

HORSE RACING: March

The Gold Cup is won by Tied Cottage which later fails a dope test when traces of theobromine are found in the animal's blood. The drug can be traced back to animal feed which has been blamed before for the 'doping' of animals.

BOXING: March 14

Jim Watt retains his world lightweight title when he stops Charlie Nash of Derry in the fourth round of their contest at the Kelvin Hall in Glasgow.

BOXING: March 16

Alan Minter wins the world middleweight title when he outpoints Vito Antufermo of the US. Minter is to knock him out in the eighth round of their return fight in June and is the first Briton to win a title in the US since 1912. Prone to cuts, his reign is to be short-lived and he is to lose his title on a September night when it is the behaviour of the hooligans rather than the skills of the boxers which make the headlines.

OLYMPICS: March 25

The Olympic ideal is shredded when the US decline to take part in the Moscow games in protest over the Soviet invasion of Afghanistan. Prime Minister Margaret Thatcher is against a British team taking part but the British Olympic Association leave the choice to individual sporting bodies who are committed to the games. However the British Equestrian Federation decide on April 7 not to send a team. The 1984 Olympics in Los Angeles are to suffer similar boycotts as tit-for-tat politicking rules the day and it is not until 1988 in troubled Seoul, ironically a nation suffering violent political upheaval on its streets, that at least the Olympic idea of all nations participating together is followed again.

RACING: March 29

Ben Nevis, priced at 40–1, wins the Grand National. He is one of four horses from the 30 starters to finish the race and is ridden by Baltimore merchant banker Mr Charles Fenwick. Ben Nevis is owned by his father-in-law.

BOXING: March 29

John Conteh put up a pitiful performance in his second fight for the WBC lightheavyweight title against Matthew Saad Muhammad. He was knocked out in four rounds and later he admitted that he had not even tried. That night signalled the end of the high-life for Conteh, who had seen his riches from the sport fast drain away and he was to fight only once more.

BOAT RACE: April 5

Apart from a dead heat in 1877 the Oxford-Cambridge boat race has its closest finish ever with Oxford winning by a canvas for their fifth successive victory.

TABLE TENNIS: April

John Hilton became Britain's first European men's singles champion. Ranked only number 3 in Britain he confounded the odds with the use of a bat with varying thicknesses of rubber. By 1987 Desmond Douglas proved he was Britain's finest player when he won the European title. He had been English national champion 10 times.

SAILING: April 23

David Scott Cowper, of Newcastle, in his 40ft yacht *Ocean Bond* beat Sir Francis Chichester's record for a single-handed sailing around the world by a day.

SOCCER: May 10

Arsenal contest their third successive Cup Final but are beaten by Second Division underdogs West Ham. Trevor Brooking scores the only goal of the game with a header in the 13th minute. A 100,000 crowd pay £729,000 to see the match and the players are told not to swap shirts on the pitch. In Scotland Celtic's George McCluskey scores the only goal of the match against Rangers in extra time. Crowd trouble at the final whistle leads to a police call for games between the old rivals to be played behind closed doors.

SOCCER: May 14

More misery for Arsenal when they lose the Cup Winners Cup Final on penalties. The score at full time in the game against Valencia was 0–0 but in a penalty do-or-die shoot out Graham Rix's effort is saved costing them the trophy.

4

SOCCER: May 17

After beating World Champions Argentina 3–1 at Wembley four days previously, England lose for the first time on Welsh soil for 25 years when they are comprehensively beaten 4–1 at Wrexham.

SOCCER: May 28

Nottingham Forest retain the European Cup when John Robertson scores the only goal of the game against SV Hamburg.

RACING: June 4

Willie Carson wins his second successive Derby when he steers the 7–1 shot Dick Hern-trained Henbit to victory over Master Willie and Rankin for the £166,820 first prize. Three days later Hern and Carson score the double win; they team up with Bireme to win The Oaks.

CRICKET: June 5–10

Some things never change. The West Indies took the summer's Test series with a victory in the first Test at Trent Bridge while the remaining matches were draws.

SOCCER: June 13

UEFA fines the FA £8,000 following riots in Turin during the European Championships. England draw 1–1 against Belgium, are beaten by Italy 1–0, and defeat Spain 2–1. West Germany win the tournament beating Belgium 2–1 in Rome.

BOXING: June 20

Roberto Duran beats Sugar Ray Leonard on points for the WBC Welterweight title but in the rematch in November Duran sensationally quits the fight in the eighth round saying 'No more, no more'. It is an extraordinary end to the fight but a prelude to a boxing quartet's path to fortune throughout the 80s. Leonard, Duran, Thomas Hearns and Marvin Hagler are to fight nine lucrative bouts throughout the decade.

TENNIS: June 23–July 5

Nine years after her only Wimbledon triumph Evonne Cawley, formerly Goolagong, beats Chris Lloyd 6–1, 7–6 to collect the winners' cheque of £18,000. Bjorn Borg wins his fifth successive men's title when he beats John McEnroe 1–6, 7–5, 6–3, 6–7, 8–6 for the £20,000 cheque. But Borg's era is closing in and the irresistible talent of McEnroe cannot be denied for much longer.

CRICKET: July 21

The Benson and Hedges Cup final was played on the Monday after rain washed out Saturday's play. Defending champions Essex were set a target of 209 by Northamptonshire but could manage only 203 from their 55 overs despite a swashbuckling 60 from Graham Gooch. Gate receipts were £144,472.50

OLYMPICS: July 19–August 3

Without America, West Germany and the Kenyans the Eastern bloc hold sway but remarkable feats of human endeavour hide the political issues. This is the era of Sebastian Coe and Steve Ovett. Coe, expected to win the 800m, is beaten by Ovett into silver while in the 1,500m, a distance over which Ovett had not been beaten in three years, Coe gets his revenge and Ovett runs in third. Daley Thompson became the first Briton to win the decathlon, an event he is to dominate, and Allan Wells won Britain's first 100m gold since Harold Abrahams in 1924. Wells nearly pulled off the sprint double but was edged out at the tape in the 200m by Italy's Pietro Mennea. In swimming Duncan Goodhew landed the 100m breaststroke gold.

BOXING: August 27

The menacing-looking Marvin Hagler destroys Britain's world middleweight champion Alan Minter in three rounds at Wembley. A battered and severely cut Minter is led from the fight in the third round but Hagler is not given a chance to acknowledge his victory and is forced to cower under his seconds as beer cans and coins rain down on the ring.

CRICKET: August 28–Sept 2

The Centenary Test ends in a draw after more than ten hours play is lost in the first three days because of rain. Graeme Wood and Kim Hughes score centuries for the Australians and Boycott hits an undefeated second innings century for England. The match was meant as a celebration but it left a bitter taste on the Saturday when MCC members, irritated by five pitch inspections, jostled the umpire David Constant in the Long Room. Police had to escort the umpires through the Long Room back to the field and the MCC apologised for the behaviour of its members. Hooliganism had invaded the holy of holies of cricket, a sombre prelude to the rest of the 1980s.

CRICKET: August 30–September 2

Middlesex beat Glamorgan by 72 runs to make sure of the County Championship.

CRICKET: August 31

Warwickshire beat Leicestershire by six wickets to take the Sunday League title and the first prize cheque of £6,500.

CRICKET: September 6

Middlesex complete the double when they beat Surrey by seven wickets to take the last Gillette Cup final. Surrey batted first scoring 201 all out while Middlesex scored 202 for three off 53.5 overs. Gate receipts were £142,242.50. Sponsors Gillette found to their horror that their name had become more synonymous with the cricket final than their product – razor blades.

BOXING: October

Muhammad Ali's remarkable career is finally coming to an end. At 38, he had been tempted out of retirement to take on Larry Holmes. Ali could not cope with Holmes and the referee stopped the fight in the 10th round. Ali was to fight Trevor Berbick a year later in the Bahamas and lose again. This time his career really was over and he admitted: 'This isn't going to bother me but I think it's too late to comeback.' For the rest of the 80s Ali, stricken by Parkinson's disease, surfaced at the big fights: once the proud lord of the ring, but now a stumbling, mumbling shadow of the fleet-footed, silver-tongued jester who had been The Greatest.

RUGBY LEAGUE: October 18

Great Britain draw 14–14 with New Zealand but expectations of going one better are dashed when on November 2 they lose the second match 12–8. However, a fortnight after that, pride sees them win 10–2 at Leeds and the series is salvaged.

BOXING: November 4

Six weeks after challenging world bantamweight Lupe Pintor for his title the Welsh contender Johnny Owen dies. He was knocked out by the Mexican in the 12th round of the fight staged in Los Angeles. Owen, dubbed the Merthyr Matchstick Man, was caught with a hook and crashed to the canvas unconscious. He never recovered consciousness.

BOXING: December

Frank Warren promoted his first show as a licensee of the British Boxing Board of Control in Bloomsbury. It was to be the first shot in his war with the cartel of Mickey Duff, Jarvis Astaire, Mike Barrett and Terry Lawless that effectively ran boxing in Britain. This dispute rumbled through the decade. Duff and Co. had virtually sewn up the BBC's coverage of boxing and Warren was to do much the same with ITV. By the end of the decade Warren not only smashed the cartel's monopoly, and through the courts curtailed the boxing board's arbitrary rule, he opened up boxing promotion and management to such a degree that as we enter the 1990s Barry Hearn is one of the most active entrepreneurs in boxing.

ROLL OF HONOUR

AMERICAN FOOTBALL: Superbowl: Pittsburgh Steelers 31 Los Angeles Rams 19.

CRICKET: County championship: Middlesex. John Player League: Warwickshire. Gillette Cup: Middlesex. Benson & Hedges Cup: Northants.

CYCLING: Tour de France: Joop Zoetemelk (Holland).

DARTS: World Championship: Eric Bristow.

GOLF: US Masters: Seve Ballesteros. US PGA: Jack Nicklaus. US Open: Jack Nicklaus. The Open (Muirfield): Tom Watson.

HORSE RACING: Flat:

1000 Guineas: Quick as Lightning. 2000 Guineas: Known Fact. The Derby: Troy (Jockey: Willie Carson. Trainer: Dick Hern). The Oaks: Bireme. St Leger: Light Cavalry. Champion jockey Willie Carson, 165 wins. Top trainer Dick Hern £831,964.

National Hunt: Grand National: Ben Nevis (Jockey: Mr Charlie Fenwick. Trainer: Tim Forster). Cheltenham Gold Cup: Master Smudge. Champion Hurdle: Sea Pigeon. Champion jockey Jonjo O'Neill, 115 wins. Top trainer Peter Easterby £218,258.

MOTOR RACING: Alan Jones (Australia) in a Williams-Ford. Constructors' Cup: Williams-Ford.

RUGBY LEAGUE: Challenge Cup: Hull Kingston Rovers. Championship: Bradford Northern.

RUGBY UNION: Grand Slam and Triple Crown: England. County Championship: Lancashire. John Player Cup: Leicester 21 London Irish 9. Schweppes Welsh Cup: Bridgend 15 Swansea 9.

SKIING: Overall champion, Men: Andreas Wenzel (Liechtenstein). Women: Hanni Wenzel (Liechtenstein).

SNOOKER: World Championship: Cliff Thorburn 18 Alex Higgins 16.

SOCCER: First Division Title: Liverpool (60pts). Runners-up: Manchester United. FA Cup winners: West Ham 1 Arsenal 0. League Cup Wolverhampton Wanderers 1 Nottingham Forest 0. Scotland: Premier League Title: Aberdeen (48pts). Runners-up: Celtic. Scottish Cup: Celtic 1 Rangers 0. Scottish League Cup: Dundee United 3 Aberdeen 0 (after replay 0–0). European Cup: Nottingham Forest 1 SV Hamburg 0. Cup Winners' Cup: Valencia 0 Arsenal 0 (Valencia won 5–4 on penalties). UEFA Cup: Borussia Munchengladbach beat Eintracht Frankfurt on away goals, (H)1–0 (A) 2–3. European Championship: West Germany 2 Belgium 1 (Rome).

SPEEDWAY: World Champion: Michael Lee (England). British League: Reading.

SQUASH: World Open Championship: Geoff Hunt.

TENNIS: Wimbledon, Men: Bjorn Borg (Sweden) bt John McEnroe (US) 1–6, 7–5, 6–3, 6–7, 8–6. Women: Evonne Cawley (Australia) bt Chris Evert-Lloyd (US) 6–1, 7–6. US Open: John McEnroe and Chris Evert-Lloyd. French Open: Bjorn Borg, Chris Evert-Lloyd. Australian Open: Brian Teacher (US), Hana Mandlikova (Cze). Davis Cup: Czechoslovakia. Wightman Cup: US beat Britain 5–2.

YACHTING: America's Cup: *Freedom* (US) skipper Dennis Conner.

FOOTBALL LEAGUE 1979–80

DIVISION 1

		Home					Away					
	P	W	D	L	F	A	W	D	L	F	A	Pts
1 Liverpool	42	15	6	0	46	8	10	4	7	35	22	60
2 Man U	42	17	3	1	43	8	7	7	7	22	27	58
3 Ipswich T	42	14	4	3	43	13	8	5	8	25	26	53
4 Arsenal	42	8	10	3	24	12	10	6	5	28	24	52
5 Nottingham F	42	16	4	1	44	11	4	4	13	19	32	48
6 Wolverhampton W	42	9	6	6	29	20	10	3	8	29	27	47
7 Aston Villa	42	11	5	5	29	22	5	9	7	22	28	46
8 Southampton	42	14	2	5	53	24	4	7	10	12	29	45
9 Middlesbrough	42	11	7	3	31	14	5	5	11	19	30	44
10 WBA	42	9	8	4	37	23	2	11	8	17	27	41
11 Leeds U	42	10	7	4	30	17	3	7	11	16	33	40
12 Norwich C	42	10	8	3	38	30	3	6	12	20	36	40
13 Crystal Palace	42	9	9	3	26	13	3	7	11	15	37	40
14 Tottenham H	42	11	5	5	30	22	4	5	12	22	40	40
15 Coventry C	42	12	2	7	34	24	4	5	12	22	42	39
16 Brighton & HA	42	8	8	5	25	20	3	7	11	22	37	37
17 Manchester C	42	8	8	5	28	25	4	5	12	15	41	37
18 Stoke C	42	9	4	8	27	26	4	6	11	17	32	36
19 Everton	42	7	7	7	28	25	2	10	9	15	26	35
20 Bristol C	42	6	6	9	22	30	3	7	11	15	36	31
21 Derby C	42	9	4	8	36	29	2	4	15	11	38	30
22 Bolton W	42	5	11	5	19	21	0	4	17	19	52	25

DIVISION 2

		Home					Away					
	P	W	D	L	F	A	W	D	L	F	A	Pts
1 Leicester C	42	12	5	4	32	19	9	8	4	26	19	55
2 Sunderland	42	16	5	0	47	13	5	7	9	22	29	54
3 Birmingham C	42	14	5	2	37	16	7	6	8	21	22	53
4 Chelsea	42	14	3	4	34	16	9	4	8	32	36	53
5 QPR	42	10	9	2	46	25	8	4	9	29	28	49
6 Luton T	42	9	10	2	36	17	7	7	7	30	28	49
7 West Ham	42	13	2	6	37	21	7	5	9	17	22	47
8 Cambridge U	42	11	6	4	40	23	3	10	8	21	30	44
9 Newcastle U	42	13	6	2	35	19	2	8	11	18	30	44
10 Preston NE	42	8	10	3	30	23	4	9	8	26	29	43
11 Oldham Ath	42	12	5	4	30	21	4	6	11	19	32	43
12 Swansea C	42	13	1	7	31	20	4	8	9	17	33	43

		Home					Away					
	P	W	D	L	F	A	W	D	L	F	A	Pts
13 Shrewsbury T	42	12	3	6	41	23	6	2	13	19	30	41
14 Orient	42	7	9	5	29	31	5	8	8	19	23	41
15 Cardiff C	42	11	4	6	21	16	5	4	12	20	32	40
16 Wrexham	42	13	2	6	26	15	3	4	14	14	34	38
17 Notts C	42	4	11	6	24	22	7	4	10	27	30	37
18 Watford	42	9	6	6	27	18	3	7	11	12	28	37
19 Bristol R	42	9	8	4	33	23	2	5	14	17	41	35
20 Fulham	42	6	4	11	19	28	5	3	13	23	46	29
21 Burnley	42	5	9	7	19	23	1	6	14	20	50	27
22 Charlton Ath	42	6	6	9	25	31	0	4	17	14	47	22

DIVISION 3

		Home					Away					
	P	W	D	L	F	A	W	D	L	F	A	Pts
1 Grimsby T	46	18	2	3	46	16	8	8	7	27	26	62
2 Blackburn R	46	13	5	5	34	17	12	4	7	24	19	59
3 Sheffield W	46	12	6	5	44	20	9	10	4	37	27	58
4 Chesterfield	46	16	5	2	46	16	7	6	10	25	30	57
5 Colchester U	46	10	10	3	39	20	10	2	11	25	36	52
6 Carlisle U	46	13	6	4	45	26	5	6	12	21	30	48
7 Reading	46	14	6	3	43	19	2	10	11	23	46	48
8 Exeter C	46	14	5	4	38	22	5	5	13	22	46	48
9 Chester	46	14	6	3	29	18	3	7	13	20	39	47
10 Swindon T	46	15	4	4	50	20	4	4	15	21	43	46
11 Barnsley	46	10	7	6	29	20	6	7	10	24	36	46
12 Sheffield U	46	13	5	5	35	21	5	5	13	25	45	46
13 Rotherham U	46	13	4	6	38	24	5	6	12	20	42	46
14 Millwall	46	14	6	3	49	23	2	7	14	16	36	45
15 Plymouth Arg	46	13	7	3	39	17	3	5	15	20	38	44
16 Gillingham	46	8	9	6	26	18	6	5	12	23	33	42
17 Oxford U	46	10	4	9	34	24	4	9	10	23	38	41
18 Blackpool	46	10	7	6	39	34	5	4	14	23	40	41
19 Brentford	46	10	6	7	33	26	5	5	13	26	47	41
20 Hull C	46	11	7	5	29	21	1	9	13	22	48	40
21 Bury	46	10	4	9	30	23	6	3	14	15	36	39
22 Southend U	46	11	6	6	33	23	3	4	16	14	35	38
23 Mansfield T	46	9	9	5	31	24	1	7	15	16	34	36
24 Wimbledon	46	6	8	9	34	38	4	6	13	18	43	34

DIVISION 4

			Home				Away					
	P	W	D	L	F	A	W	D	L	F	A	Pts
1 Huddersfield T	46	16	5	2	61	18	11	7	5	40	30	66
2 Walsall	46	12	9	2	43	23	11	9	3	32	24	64
3 Newport Co	46	16	5	2	47	22	11	2	10	36	28	61
4 Portsmouth	46	15	5	3	62	23	9	7	7	29	26	60
5 Bradford C	46	14	6	3	44	14	10	6	7	33	36	60
6 Wigan Ath	46	13	5	5	42	26	8	8	7	34	35	55
7 Lincoln C	46	14	8	1	43	12	4	9	10	21	30	53
8 Peterborough U	46	14	3	6	39	22	7	7	9	19	25	52
9 Torquay U	46	13	7	3	47	25	2	10	11	23	44	47
10 Aldershot	46	10	7	6	35	23	6	6	11	27	30	45
11 AFC Bournemouth	46	8	9	6	32	25	5	9	9	20	26	44
12 Doncaster R	46	11	6	6	37	27	4	8	11	25	36	44
13 Northampton T	46	14	5	4	33	16	2	7	14	18	50	44
14 Scunthorpe	46	11	9	3	37	23	3	6	14	21	52	43
15 Tranmere R	46	10	4	9	32	24	4	9	10	18	32	41
16 Stockport Co	46	9	7	7	30	31	5	5	13	18	41	40
17 York C	46	9	6	8	35	34	5	5	13	30	48	39
18 Halifax T	46	11	9	3	29	20	2	4	17	17	52	39
19 Hartlepool U	46	10	7	6	36	28	4	3	16	23	36	38
20 Port Vale	46	8	6	9	34	24	4	6	13	22	46	36
21 Hereford U	46	8	7	8	22	21	3	7	13	16	31	36
22 Darlington	46	7	11	5	33	26	2	6	15	17	48	35
23 Crewe Alex	46	10	6	7	25	27	1	7	15	10	41	35
24 Rochdale	46	6	7	10	20	28	1	6	16	13	51	27

SCOTTISH LEAGUE 1979–80

PREMIER DIVISION

		Home					Away				
	P	W	D	L	F	A	W	D	L	F	A	Pts
1 Aberdeen	36	10	4	4	30	18	9	6	3	38	18	48
2 Celtic	36	13	3	2	44	17	5	8	5	17	21	47
3 St Mirren	36	11	5	2	37	23	4	7	7	19	26	42
4 Dundee U	36	9	7	2	23	6	3	6	9	20	24	37
5 Rangers	36	11	5	2	29	16	4	2	12	21	30	37
6 Morton	36	9	4	5	24	16	5	4	9	27	30	36
7 Partick T	36	6	8	4	24	22	5	6	7	19	25	36
8 Kilmarnock	36	7	6	5	19	19	4	5	9	17	33	33
9 Dundee	36	9	3	6	33	30	1	3	14	14	43	26
10 Hibernian	36	6	4	8	23	31	0	2	16	6	36	18

DIVISION 1

		Home					Away				
	P	W	D	L	F	A	W	D	L	F	A	Pts
1 Hearts	39	13	6	1	33	18	7	7	5	25	21	53
2 Airdrieonians	39	14	2	4	46	21	7	7	5	32	26	51
3 Ayr U	39	11	5	4	37	22	5	7	7	27	29	44
4 Dumbarton	39	10	4	5	34	22	9	2	9	25	29	44
5 Raith R	39	8	7	5	30	22	6	8	5	29	24	43
6 Motherwell	39	9	7	3	32	17	7	4	9	27	31	43
7 Hamilton A	39	11	5	3	39	20	4	5	11	21	39	40
8 Stirling Albion	39	7	6	7	23	19	6	7	6	17	21	39
9 Clydebank	39	9	6	5	32	21	5	2	12	26	36	36
10 Dunfermline Ath	39	7	7	5	23	24	4	6	10	16	33	35
11 St Johnstone	39	5	5	9	28	32	7	5	8	29	42	34
12 Berwick R	39	5	8	7	36	31	3	7	9	21	33	31
13 Arbroath	39	7	5	7	31	32	2	5	13	19	47	28
14 Clyde	39	3	6	10	22	34	3	7	10	21	35	25

DIVISION 2

	P	W	D	L	F	A	W	D	L	F	A	Pts
			Home						*Away*			
1 Falkirk	39	11	7	2	34	12	8	5	6	31	23	50
2 East Stirling	39	10	3	6	28	20	11	4	5	27	20	49
3 Forfar Ath	39	9	6	5	35	27	10	2	7	28	24	46
4 Albion R	39	11	5	3	46	21	5	7	8	27	35	44
5 Queen's Park	39	8	5	6	32	21	8	4	8	27	26	41
6 Stenhousemuir	39	10	1	8	32	22	6	8	6	24	29	41
7 Brechin C	39	9	4	6	35	23	6	6	8	26	36	40
8 Cowdenbeath	39	9	7	4	33	24	5	5	9	21	28	40
9 Montrose	39	8	5	7	37	35	6	5	8	23	28	38
10 East Fife	39	9	6	5	26	21	3	3	13	19	36	33
11 Stranraer	39	7	4	8	26	25	5	4	11	25	40	32
12 Meadowbank T	39	7	2	11	17	29	5	6	8	25	41	32
13 Queen of the South	39	6	6	8	29	29	5	3	11	22	40	31
14 Alloa	39	8	4	7	32	28	3	3	14	12	36	29

SCHWEPPES CHAMPIONSHIP

	P	W	L	D	Bt	Bl	Pts
						Bonus	
1 Middlesex (14)	22	10	2	10	58	80	258
2 Surrey (3)	22	10	4	8	51	74	245
3 Nottinghamshire (9)	22	6	5	11	42	64	178
4 Sussex (4)	22	4	3	15	60	60	168
5 Somerset (8)	21	3	5	13	56	70	168
6 Yorkshire (7)	22	4	3	15	51	64	163
7 Gloucestershire (10)	21	4	5	12	39	74	161
8 Essex (1)	22	4	3	15	48	64	160
9 ⎧ Derbyshire (16)	20	4	3	13	47	62	157
⎩ Leicestershire (6)	22	4	2	16	45	58	157
11 Worcestershire (2)	21	3	7	11	54	61	151
12 Northamptonshire (11)	22	5	4	13	41	47	148
13 Glamorgan (17)	21	4	4	13	43	57	148
14 Warwickshire (15)	22	3	4	15	55	54	145
15 Lancashire (13)	20	4	3	13	26	58	132
16 Kent (5)	22	2	8	12	36	59	119
17 Hampshire (12)	22	1	10	11	34	56	102

1979 positions in brackets.

Leicestershire and Somerset were awarded 6 points in drawn matches when the scores were level.

JOHN PLAYER LEAGUE

		P	W	L	Tie	NR	Pts
1	Warwickshire (17)	16	11	4	1	0	46
2	Somerset (1)	16	11	5	0	0	44
3	Middlesex (4)	16	10	5	0	1	42
4	Leicestershire (6)	16	9	6	0	1	38
5	Surrey (12)	16	8	6	0	2	36
6	Derbyshire (7)	16	8	7	0	1	34
	Northamptonshire (12)	16	8	7	0	1	34
	Worcestershire (3)	16	8	7	0	1	34
9	Sussex (12)	16	6	6	0	4	32
10	Gloucestershire (8)	16	7	8	0	1	30
11	Hampshire (10)	16	6	8	0	2	28
	Kent (2)	16	6	8	1	1	28
13	Lancashire (10)	16	6	9	0	1	26
14	Essex (6)	16	6	10	0	0	24
	Nottinghamshire (8)	16	6	10	0	0	24
	Yorkshire (4)	16	6	10	0	0	24
17	Glamorgan (12)	16	4	10	0	2	20

1979 positions in brackets.

OLYMPIC GAMES: MOSCOW
LEADING MEDAL WINNERS

	G	S	B	Tot
Soviet Union	80	69	46	195
East Germany	47	37	42	126
Bulgaria	8	16	17	41
Cuba	8	7	5	20
Italy	8	3	4	15
Hungary	7	10	15	32
Romania	6	6	13	25
France	6	5	3	14
Great Britain	5	7	9	21
Poland	3	14	15	32
Sweden	3	3	6	12
Finland	3	1	4	8
Czechoslovakia	2	3	9	14
Yugoslavia	2	3	4	9
Australia	2	2	2	9

SNOOKER by CLIVE EVERTON

THE EIGHTIES was the Decade of Davis. The Age of Steve began in November 1980 when he overwhelmed Alex Higgins 16–6 for the first of his six UK titles; it may have ended with him losing to Stephen Hendry, prospectively the player of the 90s, in the 1989 UK final, but this was his era.

He won six world titles, two Benson & Hedges Masters, twelve assorted ranking tournaments, more than 20 substantial non-ranking events and even when he was not winning, he was still the man to beat. His were the standards by which other players defined themselves. While Higgins remained snooker's folk hero, Davis became a megastar, Britain's most highly paid and easily recognisable sportsman.

While Higgins extracted sporadic glory from his long strug- gle against self-destruction, notably the 1982 world title, Davis advertised everything from milk and baked beans to slippers and watches, accruing an immense fortune through his own unremitting dedication and the lively acumen of British sport's entrepreneur of the 80s, Barry Hearn.

Davis won so often and usually so comfortably that his rare defeats come more readily to mind, though images of chilling excellence survive from assorted prime time slaughters like his 9–0 whitewash of Dennis Taylor in the 1981 Jameson International final and similar drubbings of Mike Hallett and Dean Reynolds respectively in the 1988 Benson & Hedges Masters and 1989 Rothmans Grand Prix finals.

Not all that often did he prevail in close finishes – he usually won before it got close – though he did hold on to beat Jimmy White 18–16 in the 1984 world final after leading 12–4 and did emerge at 2.14 am a 10–9 winner over Dennis Taylor in the 1985 Rothmans final.

It had been his defeat by Taylor on the last black of the last frame of the 1985 Embassy World Championship which had provided the BBC with 18.5m midnight viewers, the largest- ever British television audience for a sporting event and snook- er's most indelible memory of the 80s.

Davis led 8–0; Taylor won 18–17 after an epic 68 minute deciding frame. It was a curious echo of Davis' 16–15 defeat by Higgins in the 1983 UK final after leading 7–0. Through the first hairline crack in his omnipotence his confidence drained away, a syndrome which also came into play, albeit in a slightly different way, when he lost 18–12 to the 150–1 outsider, Joe Johnson, in the 1986 world final after surmounting what appeared to be his two most difficult hurdles in Jimmy White and Cliff Thorburn.

As the 1981 world champion, Davis made one mistake he never repeated, exhausting himself so thoroughly with a relentless schedule of travelling and off table engagements that he lost 10–1 to Tony Knowles in the first match in defence of his title.

Perhaps making the first televised 147 break (15 reds, 15 blacks and all the colours) in the Lada Classic in January that year when still heavily jet lagged assisted the self-delusion that he could not burn himself out.

Most seasons, he had relatively quiet patches but even at his worst he was difficult to beat. His average game was usually enough and his best, like his breaks of 108, 131 and 104 in the 1988 Fidelity International, the first time anyone had made three centuries in three frames in competition, was irresistible.

Thorburn, the first world champion of the 80s, made the first and still only 147 break in the 63-year history of the World Championship in 1983 and won three Benson & Hedges Masters titles. Never was his nickname The Grinder better exemplified than in the 1983 championship. His 13–12 victory over Terry Griffiths took him until 3.51 am. In the two more epic struggles Kirk Stevens and Knowles also took him the distance and he had nothing left for Davis in the final. This popular Canadian achieved notoriety for failing a drug test – for cocaine – in the 1989 British Open. He was fined £10,000, docked two world ranking points and banned from two tournaments.

Drugs had first become an issue in snooker during the 1985 British Open final in which Silvino Francisco, in beating Stevens 12–9, alleged that his opponent was 'as high as a kite' on drugs.

This allegation was reported by a national newspaper. The WPBSA, nervous of the commercial damage that might accrue through any linkage with drugs, instituted a drugs testing programme. Meanwhile, they arraigned Francisco on a charge of bringing the game into disrepute.

The WPBSA, originally a players' trade union for a low profile sport, was already floundering as a governing body. It was soon out of its depth legally. Compelled to quash Francisco's punishment of a £6,000 fine with two world ranking points docked, seen as all the more disproportionate once Stevens had admitted that he was 'helplessly addicted' to cocaine, it appointed Gavin Lightman QC as a one-man disciplinary tribunal. Francisco was fined £2,000 but extracted damages and costs from Rex Williams, then WPBSA chairman, and John Virgo, then vice chairman, in an out-of-court libel settlement for remarks they had made about the affair.

The Sports Council's drug testing grants and facilities had been enlisted for the new tests but problems arose with the potentially performance-enhancing beta blockers which were on its banned list of substances. It emerged that several players, including Williams, were taking them, albeit for what appeared to be sound medical reasons. Because the WPBSA would not accept the Sports Council's banned list in its entirety, aid and facilities were withdrawn. The WPBSA set up an alternative anti-drugs programme which inevitably carried less credibility.

In the early 80s with hundreds of television hours to offer, snooker could hardly go wrong but the WPBSA made no contingency provisions, lost sponsors with alarming frequency and engaged in a war it could not win against Hearn, who had added to his eight-man management stable a variety of promotional interests and ambitions.

Initially, Hearn exploited the way the WPBSA was run as a consortium of vested interests but ended by trying to reform it, appreciating that snooker could not be taken seriously without a governing body which commanded respect. His troupe made pathfinding tours to the Far East, notably Hong Kong and China, the Middle East, notably Dubai, and even to Brazil and the United States. He was in the thick of most worthwhile ventures outside the circuit of WPBSA ranking events, of which there were ten annually by the end of the decade.

Overseas, snooker expanded rapidly, particularly in mainland Europe, where it was unknown at the start of the decade. When the 18-year-old White took the 1980 world amateur title, only 15 countries were represented. By 1989 there were 25. At the start of the 80s, it was news if a woman made a 50 break;

by the end, Alison Fisher, Stacey Hillyard and Kim Shaw had all made centuries in competition and Fisher was regarded as by far the finest player the women's game had yet seen.

Higgins made the most memorable clearance of the decade, 69, to snatch the penultimate frame on the black, as he recovered from two down with three to play to beat White in the 1982 world semi-final. While Higgins went on to beat Ray Reardon for the title White remained the greatest player of the 80s never to win the title.

The most notorious incident of the decade, Higgins's head butting of the WPBSA's tournament director, Paul Hatherell, at the 1986 UK Open, was among the offences for which he was fined £12,000 and suspended from five events.

Doug Mountjoy, 24th in the world rankings and falling, made the comeback of the decade at the age of 46, rebuilding his entire game with his devoted coach Frank Callan and winning the Tennents UK Open and the Mercantile Classic in succession.

In 1980 Cliff Thorburn took a first prize of £15,000 from the Embassy World Championship; Davis's in 1989 was £105,000. Davis's first UK title in 1980 was worth £6,000, Hendry's in 1989 brought him £100,000.

England striker Gary Lineker in action.

Seb Coe wins the 1,500 metres at the 1984 Los Angeles Olympics.

1981

ICE SKATING: February 6

First reward for the magic of Jayne Torvill and Christopher Dean as they land the European ice dancing gold with their startlingly original routine which is to captivate all those who see it.

CRICKET: February

In the Benson & Hedges World Series Cup in Melbourne New Zealand need six to win off the last ball. Australian captain Greg Chappell tells his brother Trevor to bowl it underarm to make sure the runs cannot be scored. In the furore afterwards New Zealand's Prime Minister, Robert Muldoon, calls it an 'act of cowardice' and cricket commentator and former Australian skipper Richie Benaud describes it as 'the most gutless thing I have ever seen on a cricket field'. There is to be more trouble for cricket when the second Test in Guyana on England's West Indies trip is called off after Robin Jackman is called into the side as a replacement for the injured Bob Willis. The row is over Jackman's connections with South Africa. England go on to lose the third Test, played after the sudden death of assistant-manager and coach Ken Barrington, and the series 2–0.

MOTOR CYCLING: March 23

Isle of Man master Mike Hailwood is killed in a car crash. He was 40. Hailwood won nine world championships and 14 Tourist Trophies in the Isle of Man road race.

ATHLETICS: March 29

London stages its first marathon and the running boom takes off. American Dick Beardsley joins hands with Inge Simonsen to share the win. Joyce Smith collects the women's trophy.

RACING: April 4

Horse and rider, Aldaniti and Bob Champion, overcome remarkable odds to win the Grand National. Aldaniti had suffered years of tendon trouble and a broken hock bone, while Champion was back in the saddle having been given only eight months to live when cancer was diagnosed in 1979. The 10–1 shot beat 38 runners for the prize of £51,324. Second home was Spartan Missile followed by Royal Mail.

BOAT RACE: April 4

Sue Brown became the first woman cox in the history of the boat race when she steered Oxford to their fifth successive win. In the same race Boris Rankov became the first don and oarsman from a women's college, St Hugh's, to take part in the race. The next year he became the first man to win five boat races as Oxford extended their winning sequence to 1985. Arguments broke out over the composition of crews, and in 1984 Oxford fielded four internationals in their eight which included two Australians, two Canadians and an American cox. The row was over colleges admitting oarsmen purely to bolster the eight, which some people felt was contrary to the spirit of the event.

BOXING: April 12

The legendary heavyweight Joe Louis died on April 12. He was 66. The Brown Bomber won the world heavyweight crown in 1937 when he stopped Jim Braddock. He was 23 and in the next 12 years he defended the title 25 times before retiring in 1949 with little to show from the $5m he had earned. He made two abortive comebacks, being beaten by Ezzard Charles and knocked out by Rocky Marciano.

SNOOKER: April 20

Steve Davis wins his first world championship and £20,000 when he beats Doug Mountjoy 18–12 in the final at The Crucible Theatre in Sheffield. It was the jewel in the crown for Davis who had also won the English professional title and three other classic tournaments. Along with his manager Barry Hearn he is to dominate snooker throughout the 80s. Hearn's power in the game increases as he creates the Matchroom stable featuring the world's leading players and later he starts to move into boxing. For the defeated Mountjoy there was the consolation of £12,000 plus another £5,000 for the highest break of the tournament and in the championship's history. He made a 142 clearance in the semi-final where he beat Ray Reardon 16–10.

SOCCER: May 9

Tottenham and Manchester City draw 1–1 in the Cup Final. Tommy Hutchinson scores both goals. Amazingly he is still playing league football into his 40s and makes his European debut for Swansea City in September 1989. The match is replayed at Wembley five days later with Spurs' Argentine player Ricardo Villa scoring twice, his second a long weaving run through the

City defence for one of the Cup Final's most memorable goals. In Scotland Rangers beat Dundee United 4–1, also in a replay; the first match ended 0–0.

SOCCER May 27

British domination of the European Cup continues when Liverpool beat Real Madrid at the Parc des Princes in Paris. Alan Kennedy scores the only goal of the game with just under ten minutes of the match remaining. In a portent of tragedy to come Paris riot police baton charged fans who had been throwing missiles at them outside the ground.

RACING: June 3

The Derby is won by Shergar. The Aga Khan's horse romps home by 10 lengths to record the biggest margin of victory this century. A short priced favourite at 10/11, Walter Swinburn is in the saddle in a race worth £149,000. Second home is Glint of Gold followed by Scintillating Air. Eighteen ran and Michael Stoute was the winning trainer. Shergar was to be kidnapped in February 1983 and a ransom demand of £2m made. The horse was never seen again.

TENNIS: June 22–July 4

The Borg era ends. McEnroe, vanquished a year earlier, wins in four sets 4–6, 7–6, 7–6, 6–4 to end Borg's run of 42 successive single Wimbledon matches without defeat and collect £21,600. Borg had beaten Ivan Lendl a month earlier in the French championships but was to lose to McEnroe again in the US Open Championship later in the year. It was the fourth time he had been a beaten finalist in America and it was a competition he failed to win. Despite two attempted comebacks in 1982 and 1984 Borg went into virtual exile running clothing and perfume companies in his name. He was to catapult back into the public eye after he nearly died following a mysterious overdose in 1989. In the women's final Chris Evert-Lloyd beat an overawed Hana Mandlikova 6–2, 6–2 and collected £19,440.

CRICKET: July 21

This was the year that Ian Botham seemed capable of walking on water. He resigned the England captaincy in the first week of July, a failure. In the next month playing under Mike Brearley, who had been recalled to the captaincy, he became the most treasured national institution. He walked out to bat at Leeds with England in a parlous state: three wickets left, needing 92 to escape an innings defeat against Australia and bookmakers offering 500–1 against an England victory. Botham scored 149 not out, England set Australia 130 to win and bowled them out for 111, Bob Willis firing on all cylinders taking eight for 43. It was only the second time in Test history that a team following on had won a match. Then Botham did it again at Edgbaston. Australia, wanting 142 to win, were 105 for five when Botham took five wickets for one run in 28 balls and England won by 29 runs. In the fifth Test he hit 118, an innings that earned him the description of a modern Jessop. England, who probably should have lost the series 3–1, had retained the Ashes 3–1. And so the myth of Botham the superman was born. It was only at the end of the decade when Botham's miraculous powers waned that English cricket realised that it was not always possible to convert impossible positions into stunning victories; wretched defeats became more the norm. A rejuvenated England set out for India that winter in a tour dogged by controversy. The tour nearly did not take place because of the South African connections of Geoffrey Boycott and Geoff Cook. Amid firecrackers and ever present umpiring controversies England lost the first Test. In the third Test Geoff Boycott passed Gary Sobers' record Test total of 8,032 runs. He played in only one more Test and his status as the greatest run-getter in Test history was to be short-lived. Sunil Gavaskar became the first batsman to reach 10,000 runs, finishing with 10,122 at an average of 51.12 in 125 Tests.

ATHLETICS: August 28

The end of an astonishing 10 days in which Sebastian Coe and Steve Ovett broke the world mile record three times. First Coe running in Zurich clips 0.3secs off Ovett's record of 3min 48.53secs. A week later and not to be outdone Ovett recaptures the record when he trims 0.13secs off it at Koblenz. Two days later and Coe repossesses it at Heysel in Brussels with a time of 3min 47.53secs.

SOCCER: November 18

England beat Hungary 1–0 at Wembley with a Paul Mariner goal to qualify for the World Cup in Spain. Scotland lost 2–1 to Portugal in Lisbon but had already qualified. Northern Ireland beat Israel 1–0 and also reached the finals. The following night Wales beat Czechoslovakia at Cardiff 1–0.

CHESS: November 20

Anatoly Karpov wins the world chess championship in Italy.

RUGBY LEAGUE: December 6

Seven goals from Woods help Great Britain to a 37–0 win over France but two weeks later the position is reversed when France beat them 19–2 in Marseilles.

ROLL OF HONOUR

AMERICAN FOOTBALL: Superbowl: Oakland Raiders 27 Philadelphia Eagles 10.

ATHLETICS: World Cup, Men: Europe 147pts, East Germany 130 pts, United States 127pts. Women: East Germany 120.5pts, Europe 110pts, USSR 98pts. European Cup, Men: East Germany. Women: East Germany.

CRICKET: County championship: Nottinghamshire. John Player League: Essex. NatWest Trophy: Derbyshire. Benson & Hedges Cup: Somerset.

CYCLING: Tour de France: Bernard Hinault (France).

DARTS: World Championship: Eric Bristow.

GOLF: US Masters: Tom Watson. US PGA: Larry Nelson. US Open: David Graham (Aus). The Open (Sandwich): Bill Rogers. Ryder Cup (Walton Heath): Europe 9.5 US 18.5.

HOCKEY: World Cup, Women: West Germany.

HORSE RACING: Flat: 1000 Guineas: Fairy Footsteps. 2000 Guineas: To-Agori-Mou. The Derby: Shergar (Jockey: Walter Swinburn. Trainer: Michael Stoute). The Oaks: Blue Wind. St Leger: Cut Above. Champion jockey Lester Piggott 179 wins. Top trainer Michael Stoute £723,786.

National Hunt: Grand National: Aldaniti (Jockey: Bob Champion. Trainer: Josh Gifford). Cheltenham Gold Cup: Little Owl. Champion Hurdle: Sea Pigeon. Champion jockey John Francome, 105 wins. Top trainer Peter Easterby £236,867.

MOTOR RACING: Nelson Piquet (Brazil) in a Brabham-Ford. Constructors' Cup: Williams-Ford.

RUGBY LEAGUE: Challenge Cup: Widnes. Championship: Hull Kingston Rovers.

RUGBY UNION: Grand Slam: France. Triple Crown: Not won. County Championship: Northumberland. John Player Cup: Leicester 22 Gosforth 15. Schweppes Welsh Cup: Cardiff 14 Bridgend 6.

SKIING: Overall champion, Men: Phil Mahre (US). Women: Marie-Therese Nadig (Switzerland).

SNOOKER: World Championship: Steve Davis 18 Doug Mountjoy 12.

SOCCER: First Division Title: Aston Villa (60pts). Runners-up: Ipswich Town. FA Cup winners: Tottenham 3 Manchester City 2 (after replay 1–1). League Cup: Liverpool 2 West Ham 1 (after replay 1–1). Scotland: Premier League Title: Celtic (56pts). Runners-up: Hearts. Scottish Cup: Rangers 4 Dundee United 1 (after replay 0–0). Scottish League Cup: Dundee United 3 Dundee 0. European Cup: Liverpool 1 Real Madrid 0. Cup Winners' Cup: Dynamo Tbilisi 2 Carl Zeiss Jena 1. UEFA Cup: Ipswich Town beat AZ 67 Alkmaar 5–4 on agg. (H) 3–0 (A) 2–4.

SPEEDWAY: World Champion: Bruce Penhall (US). British League: Cradley Heath.

SQUASH: World Open Championship, Men: Jahangir Khan (Pakistan). Women: Rhonda Thorne (Australia).

TABLE TENNIS: World Championship, Men: Guo Yue-Hua (China). Women: Tong Ling (China).

TENNIS: Wimbledon: Men: John McEnroe (US) bt Bjorn Borg (Sweden) 4–6, 7–6, 7–6, 6–4; Women: Chris Evert-Lloyd (US) bt Hana Mandlikova (Cze) 6–2, 6–2. US Open: John McEnroe and Tracy Austin (US). French Open: Bjorn Borg, Hana Mandlikova. Australian Open: Johan Kriek (S. Africa), Martina Navratilova (US). Davis Cup: United States. Wightman Cup: US beat Britain 7–0.

YACHTING: Admiral's Cup: Britain.

FOOTBALL LEAGUE 1980–81

DIVISION 1

		Home					Away					
	P	W	D	L	F	A	W	D	L	F	A	Pts
1 Aston Villa	42	16	3	2	40	13	10	5	6	32	27	60
2 Ipswich T	42	15	4	2	45	14	8	6	7	32	29	56
3 Arsenal	42	13	8	0	36	17	6	7	8	25	28	53
4 WBA	42	15	4	2	40	15	5	8	8	20	27	52
5 Liverpool	42	13	5	3	38	15	4	12	5	24	27	51
6 Southampton	42	15	4	2	47	22	5	6	10	29	34	50
7 Nottingham F	42	15	3	3	44	20	4	9	8	18	24	50
8 Manchester U	42	9	11	1	30	14	6	7	8	21	22	48
9 Leeds U	42	10	5	6	19	19	7	5	9	20	28	44
10 Tottenham H	42	9	9	3	44	31	5	6	10	26	37	43
11 Stoke C	42	8	9	4	31	23	4	9	8	20	37	42
12 Manchester C	42	10	7	4	35	25	4	4	13	21	34	39
13 Birmingham C	42	11	5	5	32	23	2	7	12	18	38	38
14 Middlesbrough	42	14	4	3	38	16	2	1	18	15	45	37
15 Everton	42	8	6	7	32	25	5	4	12	23	33	36
16 Coventry C	42	9	6	6	31	30	4	4	13	17	38	36
17 Sunderland	42	10	4	7	32	19	4	3	14	20	34	35
18 Wolverhampton W	42	11	2	8	26	20	2	7	12	17	35	35
19 Brighton & HA	42	10	3	8	30	26	4	4	13	24	41	35
20 Norwich C	42	9	7	5	34	25	4	0	17	15	48	33
21 Leicester C	42	7	5	9	20	23	6	1	14	20	44	32
22 Crystal Palace	42	6	4	11	32	37	0	3	18	15	46	19

DIVISION 2

		Home					Away					
	P	W	D	L	F	A	W	D	L	F	A	Pts
1 West Ham U	42	19	1	1	53	12	9	9	3	26	17	66
2 Notts Co	42	10	8	3	26	15	8	9	4	23	23	53
3 Swansea C	42	12	5	4	39	19	6	9	6	25	25	50
4 Blackburn R	42	12	8	1	28	7	4	10	7	14	22	50
5 Luton T	42	10	6	5	35	23	8	6	7	26	23	48
6 Derby Co	42	9	8	4	34	26	6	7	8	23	26	45
7 Grimsby T	42	10	8	3	21	10	5	7	9	23	32	45
8 QPR	42	11	7	3	36	12	4	6	11	20	34	43
9 Watford	42	13	5	3	34	18	3	6	12	16	27	43
10 Sheffield W	42	14	4	3	38	14	3	4	14	15	37	42
11 Newcastle U	42	11	7	3	22	13	3	7	11	8	32	42
12 Chelsea	42	8	6	7	27	15	6	6	9	19	26	40
13 Cambridge U	42	13	1	7	36	23	4	5	12	17	42	40

		Home					Away					
	P	W	D	L	F	A	W	D	L	F	A	Pts
14 Shrewsbury T	42	9	7	5	33	22	2	10	9	13	25	39
15 Oldham Ath	42	7	9	5	19	16	5	6	10	20	32	39
16 Wrexham	42	5	8	8	22	24	7	6	8	21	21	38
17 Orient	42	9	8	4	34	20	4	4	13	18	36	38
18 Bolton W	42	10	5	6	40	27	4	5	12	21	39	38
19 Cardiff C	42	7	7	7	23	24	5	5	11	21	36	36
20 Preston NE	42	8	7	6	28	26	3	7	11	13	36	36
21 Bristol C	42	6	10	5	19	15	1	6	14	10	36	30
22 Bristol R	42	4	9	8	21	24	1	4	16	13	41	23

DIVISION 3

		Home					Away					
	P	W	D	L	F	A	W	D	L	F	A	Pts
1 Rotherham U	46	17	6	0	43	8	7	7	9	19	24	61
2 Barnsley	46	15	5	3	46	19	6	12	5	26	26	59
3 Charlton Ath	46	14	6	3	36	17	11	3	9	27	27	59
4 Huddersfield T	46	14	6	3	40	11	7	8	8	31	29	56
5 Chesterfield	46	17	4	2	42	16	6	6	11	30	32	56
6 Portsmouth	46	14	5	4	35	19	8	4	11	20	28	53
7 Plymouth Arg	46	14	5	4	35	18	5	9	9	21	26	52
8 Burnley	46	13	5	5	37	21	5	9	9	23	27	50
9 Brentford	46	7	9	7	30	25	7	10	6	22	24	47
10 Reading	46	13	5	5	39	22	5	5	13	23	40	46
11 Exeter C	46	9	9	5	36	30	7	4	12	26	36	45
12 Newport Co	46	11	6	6	38	22	4	7	12	26	39	43
13 Fulham	46	8	7	8	28	29	7	6	10	29	35	43
14 Oxford U	46	7	8	8	20	24	6	9	8	19	23	43
15 Gillingham	46	9	8	6	23	19	3	10	10	25	39	42
16 Millwall	46	10	9	4	30	21	4	5	14	13	39	42
17 Swindon	46	10	6	7	35	27	3	9	11	16	29	41
18 Chester	46	11	5	7	25	17	4	6	13	13	31	41
19 Carlisle U	46	8	9	6	32	29	6	4	13	24	41	41
20 Walsall	46	8	9	6	43	43	5	6	12	16	31	41
21 Sheffield U	46	12	6	5	38	20	2	6	15	27	43	40
22 Colchester U	46	12	7	4	35	22	2	4	17	10	43	39
23 Blackpool	46	5	9	9	19	28	4	5	14	26	47	32
24 Hull C	46	7	8	8	23	22	1	8	14	17	49	32

DIVISION 4

		P	W	D	L	F	A	W	D	L	F	A	Pts
			Home					*Away*					
1	Southend U	46	19	4	0	47	6	11	3	9	32	25	67
2	Lincoln C	46	15	7	1	44	11	10	8	5	22	14	65
3	Doncaster R	46	15	4	4	36	20	7	8	8	23	29	56
4	Wimbledon	46	15	4	4	42	17	8	5	10	22	29	55
5	Peterborough U	46	11	8	4	37	21	6	10	7	31	33	52
6	Aldershot	46	12	9	2	28	11	6	5	12	15	30	50
7	Mansfield T	46	13	5	5	36	15	7	4	12	22	29	49
8	Darlington	46	13	6	4	43	23	6	5	12	22	36	49
9	Hartlepool U	46	14	3	6	42	22	6	6	11	22	39	49
10	Northampton T	46	11	7	5	42	26	7	6	10	23	41	49
11	Wigan Ath	46	13	4	6	29	16	5	7	11	22	39	47
12	Bury	46	10	8	5	38	21	7	3	13	32	41	45
13	Bournemouth	46	9	8	6	30	21	7	5	11	17	27	45
14	Bradford C	46	9	9	5	30	24	5	7	11	23	36	44
15	Rochdale	46	11	6	6	33	25	3	9	11	27	45	43
16	Scunthorpe U	46	8	12	3	40	31	3	8	12	20	38	42
17	Torquay U	46	13	2	8	38	26	5	3	15	17	37	41
18	Crewe Alex	46	10	7	6	28	20	3	7	13	20	41	40
19	Port Vale	46	10	8	5	40	23	2	7	14	17	47	39
20	Stockport Co	46	10	5	8	29	25	6	2	15	15	32	39
21	Tranmere R	46	12	5	6	41	24	1	5	17	18	49	36
22	Hereford U	46	8	8	7	29	20	3	5	15	9	42	35
23	Halifax T	46	9	3	11	28	32	2	9	12	16	39	34
24	York C	46	10	2	11	31	23	2	7	14	16	43	33

SCOTTISH LEAGUE 1980–81

PREMIER DIVISION

		P	W	D	L	F	A	W	D	L	F	A	Pts
			Home					*Away*					
1	Celtic	36	12	3	3	47	18	14	1	3	37	19	56
2	Aberdeen	36	11	4	3	39	16	8	7	3	22	10	49
3	Rangers	36	12	3	3	33	10	4	9	5	27	22	44
4	St Mirren	36	9	6	3	28	20	9	2	7	28	27	44
5	Dundee U	36	8	5	5	34	24	9	4	5	32	18	43
6	Partick T	36	6	6	6	17	17	4	4	10	15	31	30
7	Aidrieonians	36	6	5	7	19	25	4	4	10	17	30	29
8	Morton	36	7	2	9	24	28	3	6	9	12	30	28
9	Kilmarnock	36	3	5	10	14	31	2	4	12	9	34	19
10	Hearts	36	3	4	11	10	27	3	2	13	17	44	18

DIVISION 1

		Home					Away					
	P	W	D	L	F	A	W	D	L	F	A	Pts
1 Hibernian	39	14	4	2	38	9	10	5	4	29	15	57
2 Dundee	39	14	4	2	42	18	8	4	7	22	22	52
3 St Johnstone	39	12	3	5	31	21	8	8	3	33	24	51
4 Raith R	39	11	7	1	26	11	9	3	8	23	21	50
5 Motherwell	39	14	5	1	41	20	5	6	8	24	31	49
6 Ayr U	39	11	5	3	34	17	6	6	8	25	25	45
7 Hamilton A	39	9	5	6	39	27	6	2	11	22	30	37
8 Dumbarton	39	8	5	6	23	22	5	6	9	26	28	37
9 Falkirk	39	7	4	8	24	29	6	4	10	15	23	34
10 Clydebank	39	8	6	5	31	25	2	7	11	17	34	33
11 East Stirling	39	4	10	6	20	24	2	7	10	21	32	29
12 Dunfermline Ath	39	6	3	11	17	28	4	4	11	24	30	27
13 Stirling Albion	39	4	6	9	13	21	2	5	13	5	27	23
14 Berwick R	39	5	6	8	18	27	0	6	14	13	55	22

DIVISION 2

		Home					Away					
	P	W	D	L	F	A	W	D	L	F	A	Pts
1 Queen's Park	39	9	9	2	30	19	7	9	3	32	24	50
2 Queen of the S	39	7	8	4	31	29	9	6	5	35	24	46
3 Cowdenbeath	39	12	3	4	35	20	6	6	8	28	28	45
4 Brechin C	39	10	7	3	29	18	5	7	7	23	28	44
5 Forfar Ath	39	9	3	7	34	32	8	6	6	29	25	43
6 Alloa	39	10	4	6	29	25	5	8	6	32	29	42
7 Montrose	39	9	4	6	31	24	7	4	9	35	31	40
8 Clyde	39	10	6	4	45	31	4	6	9	23	32	40
9 Arbroath	39	3	9	8	20	29	10	3	6	38	25	38
10 Stenhousemuir	39	4	7	8	27	32	9	4	7	36	26	37
11 East Fife	39	6	9	4	21	21	4	6	10	23	32	35
12 Albion R	39	9	3	8	37	41	4	6	9	22	31	35
13 Meadowbank T	39	6	2	11	17	35	5	5	10	25	29	29
14 Stranraer	39	4	5	11	20	41	3	3	13	16	42	22

SCHWEPPES CHAMPIONSHIP

					Bonus		
	P	W	L	D	Bt	Bl	Pts
1 Nottinghamshire (3)	22	11	4	7	56	72	304
2 Sussex (4)	22	11	3	8	58	68	302

		P	W	L	D	Bt	Bl	Pts
						Bonus		
3	Somerset (5)	22	10	2	10	54	65	279
4	Middlesex (1)	22	9	3	10	49	64	267
5	Essex (8)	22	8	4	10	62	64	254
6	Surrey (2)	22	7	5	10	52	72	236
7	Hampshire (17)	22	6	7	9	43	65	205
8	Leicestershire (9)	22	6	6	10	45	58	199
9	Kent (16)	22	5	7	10	51	58	189
10	Yorkshire (6)	22	5	9	8	41	66	187
11	Worcestershire (11)	22	5	9	8	44	52	172
12	Derbyshire (9)	22	4	7	11	51	57	172
13	Gloucestershire (7)	22	4	3	15	51	55	170
14	Glamorgan (13)	22	3	10	9	50	69	167
15	Northamptonshire (12)	22	3	6	13	51	67	166
16	Lancashire (15)	22	4	7	11	47	57	164
17	Warwickshire (14)	22	2	11	9	56	47	135

1980 positions in brackets

Worcestershire and Lancashire totals include 12 points for win in match reduced to one innings.

JOHN PLAYER LEAGUE

		P	W	L	T	NR	Pts
1	Essex (14)	16	12	3	0	1	50
2	Somerset (2)	16	11	5	0	0	44
	Warwickshire (1)	16	10	4	0	2	44
4	Derbyshire (6)	16	10	5	0	1	42
5	Sussex (9)	16	8	5	0	3	38
6	Hampshire (11)	16	8	7	0	1	34
7	Kent (11)	16	7	7	1	1	32
	Surrey (5)	16	7	7	0	2	32
	Yorkshire (11)	16	6	6	0	4	32
10	Glamorgan (17)	16	6	8	0	2	28
	Lancashire (13)	16	6	8	1	1	28
	Nottinghamshire (14)	16	6	8	0	2	28
	Worcestershire (6)	16	7	9	0	0	28
14	Leicestershire (4)	16	5	9	0	2	24
15	Middlesex (3)	16	4	9	0	3	22
16	Gloucestershire (10)	16	3	9	0	4	20
17	Northamptonshire (6)	16	4	11	0	1	18

1980 positions in brackets.

TENNIS *by SUE MOTT*

John Patrick McEnroe was already a familiar figure in 1980 and it was not entirely a pretty sight. Hair clenched fiercely in a red headband and brows furrowed in a furious scowl, his stomping, cursing, spellbinding brand of tennis had already caused many a spluttered gin and tonic in the hallowed boxes of Wimbledon.

But as it turned out, we'd seen nothing yet.

First came the glory. A five-set final against Bjorn Borg in which a breathtaking tie-break was set like a jewel in the cathedral gloom of the Centre Court. McEnroe's luminous tennis won the tie-break 18–16 but he lost the match to the Swede who had already won Wimbledon four times in a row.

Then came the gore. The unsightly ructions that were to sour McEnroe's reputation for a decade and, ironically, install him as the most tempestuously charismatic idol of his era.

Born in West Germany but made in New York, he symbolised the pressures and the passions of a sport that underwent an industrial revolution. A game with bats and balls had suddenly become an international multi-million dollar-spinning business empire.

Back in 1980 Martina Navratilova was still plump with a penchant for cream buns and burgers. The age of 'eating to win' was unheard of. Chris Evert had won nine Grand Slam singles titles with metronomic groundstrokes not meticulous dieting and lifting weights. Steffi Graf was eleven.

Hamilton Jordan was still working for peanuts as Jimmy Carter's chief of staff in the White House but ten years later he was earning an annual salary of $500,000 for organising the new men's international circuit, the ATP Tour, a sponsored, televised and glossily packaged deal run by the players themselves.

A decade ago tennis racquets were still made of wood, Ivan Lendl's smile was still wooden and agents were something through which the players booked their holidays in Monte Carlo.

But the writing was on the wall. Anyone fluent in the future's graffiti would have read: 'Power ... Money ... Andre Agassi's pink-painted finger nail.' They were all inevitable developments in the coming decade.

Finesse and subtlety on the tennis court were already becoming rarities in 1980. Apart from McEnroe, poised at number two in the world, the men's top ten were power merchants programmed to strike the ball with maximum venom and velocity. The advent of high-tech racquets has taken the power game a stage further. Man-made materials like Kevlar, boron and ceramics, developed by NASA during the space shuttle missions, allow Boris Becker to serve the sporting equivalent of meteorites.

Manuel Santana, the 1966 Wimbledon champion and one of the most graceful players of the modern era, has spoken of his beloved style of tennis as a lost art. 'McEnroe is the last of the beautiful champions', he said of the last man to win a Grand Slam title with a wooden racquet.

But beauty is in the eye of the beholders and the players have yet to see anything ugly about the green clusters of dollar bills that are waved under their questing noses.

Some, like ever-training Lendl, have tried to earn their millions by embarking on radical fitness regimes worthy of the astronauts who took racquet technology for a test-drive.

Lendl was a perennial bridesmaid until 1984 when McEnroe unaccountably faltered in the French Open final on his way to carving his first masterpiece in clay. Lendl was reprieved at two sets and 2–4 down and went on to win his first major title. It was, in the words of Wojtek Fibak, Lendl's mentor, the making of a 'killer robot'.

But the emergence of Lendl was not the only respite from the McEnroe/Connors axis of aggravated behaviour. The Swedes, post-Borg, were models of decorum, sweetness and unspectacular love-lives. Mats Wilander won seven Grand Slam titles yet retained the soubriquet Modest Mats. Stefan Edberg became Wimbledon champion in 1988 and could still enter a Kensington pizza parlour without fear of being mobbed.

But far more acceptable to gossip columnists was the rise of the German twinset, Boris Becker and Steffi Graf. Arrogance and eminence combined, they dominated their rivals at Wimbledon and, in the case of Graf, at almost every other tennis venue round the globe.

But the sportswoman of the decade remains, indisputably, Martina Navratilova. Eight times Wimbledon singles champion and the winner of 15 Grand Slam singles titles, she imperiously swept into a league above Evert, no matter how many Chrissie-lovers would tearfully protest.

Her rivalry with Graf remains a promise unfulfilled, so masterful has the younger woman become. But for dragging the sedate (and occasionally sedating) women's game into a new era of exciting, ultra-fit professionalism, Navratilova richly deserves her place on the roll-call of All Time Greats.

The only pity is that so few young women followed her aggressive serve-volleying example. A bombardment of groundstrokes delivered from a baseline bunker is now the order of the day. The sighting of a female natural volleyer is about as likely as spotting a dodo.

Less rare, even nine years after the infamous 'Pits of the world' conversation that McEnroe shared with Wimbledon officials, are demands for the American's trial and banishment from the sporting stage.

This seems to misunderstand the nature of the beast, both tennis and the man himself. Despite the inharmonious moments, McEnroe's extravagant presence has spanned the decade and the sport would have been infinitely poorer without him.

For ten years he has been the author of mayhem, beauty and the exaggerated response. Where else would we get so much from one pallid, outrageously-talented, self-tormented package?

Charlton Heston, the American film actor, once left the Royal Box at Wimbledon because he could not bear to see McEnroe embarrass his country. 'That's all right', said McEnroe, 'people walk out of his movies too.'

Graeme Souness and Mick Robinson celebrate Liverpool's European Cup final win against Roma, 1984.

Lester Piggott, twice champion flat race jockey at the beginning of the decade.

1982

SNOOKER: *January 11*

Steve Davis makes the first televised maximum break of 147 in the Lada Classic at the Civic Hall in Oldham. His opponent, John Spencer, could only sit and watch.

CRICKET: *March 19*

The Test and County Cricket Board bans the 15 players who went to South Africa on a rebel tour direct from India, for three years. Amongst those disqualified from Test cricket are Graham Gooch, Geoffrey Boycott, Derek Underwood and John Emburey. Boycott, who had played a major part in organising the tour, had returned to England in controversial circumstances. As England struggled against India in Calcutta, Boycott went off in the middle of the Test match to play golf. He was to justify going to South Africa as just another business decision, an increasing tendency to make the game sound like a nine-to-five job.

SNOOKER: *April 19–May 2*

Defending champion Steve Davis loses 10–1 in the first round of the World Championship to Tony Knowles. Alex Higgins, after a 16–15 semi-final win over Jimmy White beats Ray Reardon in the final, 18–15. The controversial Irishman, the self-styled 'people's champion' is never to reach such heights again and his career is hit by a series of rows and public domestic scenes.

SOCCER: *May 22*

Spurs play in their second successive Cup Final which goes to a replay when they are held 1–1 by Queen's Park Rangers. Gate receipts are a record £918,000. But five days later a Glenn Hoddle penalty is enough to give them the cup. In Scotland Aberdeen beat Rangers 4–1 after extra time.

SOCCER: *May 28*

Barcelona pay £5m to Boca Juniors and Argentinos Juniors for Diego Maradona.

RACING: *June 2*

Golden Fleece, trained by Vincent O'Brien and ridden by Pat
Eddery, beats a field of 18 horses to win The Derby from Touching
Wood and third placed Silver Hawk. For winning owner Robert
Sangster the victory was worth £146,720.

CRICKET: *June 10–15*

England beat India in the first of the summer's three Tests.
England inspired by 126 from Derek Randall won by seven
wickets.

WORLD CUP: *June 13–July 11*

World champions Argentina open the competition in Spain and
lose 1–0 to Belgium. England's first game in Bilbao is against
France. Robson with two goals and Mariner with one seal a 3–1
victory. England then beat Czechoslovakia 2–0. Mariner and
Francis score. In their final match of the group they beat Kuwait
1–0, Francis scoring the only goal. England top Group 4 followed
by France, Czechoslovakia and Kuwait. Northern Ireland draw
0–0 with Yugoslavia, draw 1–1 with Honduras, thanks to an
Armstrong goal, then beat Spain with Armstrong scoring again.
They top Group 5 followed by Spain, Yugoslavia and Honduras.
In Group 6 Scotland open their campaign against New Zealand
with a 5–2 win. Goals were scored by Dalglish, Wark 2, Robertson
and Archibald. Three days later they are crushed 4–1 by Brazil in
Seville with Narey getting their only goal of the match. Their last
match is against the USSR and they draw 2–2, with Jordan and
Souness scoring but it is not enough to see them through to the
next stage of the finals. They finish third with Brazil top, USSR
second and New Zealand bottom. The tournament keeps to a
round-robin format for the next stage. England, now playing in
Madrid draw 0–0 with West Germany and Spain while the
Germans beat the Spanish 2–1. A lack of goals in this stage has
sent England to the airport with World Cup thoughts only for
1986. Northern Ireland, after their sensational first round performance draw 2–2 with Austria, both their goals coming from
Hamilton. But they are hammered by France 4–1, Armstrong
scoring the goal. They finish bottom of their group. The semi-
finals follow a knockout format. Rossi scores twice as Italy
beat Poland 2–0 and France draw 3–3 with West Germany only
to lose on penalties 5–4. The final is played in Madrid on July
11 and despite missing a penalty Italy beat West Germany
3–1. Rossi, the tournament's top scorer with six, Tardelli and
Altobelli score for Italy while Breitner gets the German consolation goal.

TENNIS: June 21–July 4

Jimmy Connors upsets Wimbledon champion John McEnroe 3–6, 6–3, 6–7, 7–6, 6–4 and by winning the championship collects £41,667 – almost double the winner's prize money of the previous year. For the women the money was also raised to £37,500 as Martina Navratilova beat Chris Evert-Lloyd 6–1, 3–6, 6–2 and embarked on an incredible sequence which saw her take six successive Wimbledon singles titles.

CRICKET: July 9

Ian Botham, hero of the previous year's Ashes series, hits the highest Test score of his career, 208, against India at The Oval as England show no signs of missing the rebels banned earlier in the year.

GOLF: July 19

Tom Watson wins The Open at Royal Troon and becomes only the fifth man to win The Open and the US Open in the same year. It was his fourth Open win, all of them achieved on Scottish courses.

CRICKET: July 24

Somerset won the Benson & Hedges Cup by nine wickets after dismissing Nottinghamshire for 130 in 50.1 overs.

CRICKET: July 29–August 1

England beat Pakistan by 113 runs at Edgbaston in the first of a three Test series, Derek Randall scoring a second innings century. But in the second Test at Lord's a double century from Mohsin Khan condemns England to a ten wicket defeat for Pakistan's second ever victory over England. The third Test at Headingley ends in an England victory by three wickets.

CRICKET: August 29

Sussex, pioneering experts of the one-day game, beat Middlesex at Hove by 23 runs to capture the Sunday League title and set a record number of wins, 14, in taking the trophy for the first time.

SWIMMING: August 29

American Ashby Harper, 65, becomes the oldest person to swim the English Channel.

CRICKET: September 4

Surrey beat Warwickshire by nine wickets to lift the NatWest trophy after Warwickshire were all out for 158 in 57.2 overs. Alan Butcher with 86 for Surrey steered them to victory in 33.4 overs.

ATHLETICS: September 8

Daley Thompson carries on in his own inimitable way beating allcomers in the decathlon at the European Games in Athens.

CRICKET: September 14

Middlesex beat Worcestershire by ten wickets to win the County Championship, the competition they have headed throughout the season. The match also marked the retirement of Mike Brearley from First Class cricket. Brearley's farewell was appropriately English on a misty September morning with Worcester cathedral in the background. He had, as ever, timed it beautifully. This was the fourth championship he had led Middlesex to in 11 years as captain. In the previous 89 years Middlesex had only won three championships but under him they also won the Gillette Cup twice, and had been finalists and runners-up in other competitions. As an international captain his record was second only to the legendary Don Bradman. In 31 Tests England had won 18 and lost four. Of the nine series only one was lost and one drawn, with seven wins. That England missed Brearley became evident in the winter in Australia when they lost the second and third Tests by wide margins, but some of the old magic seemed to return when England won a pulsating Test at Melbourne by three runs, one of the narrowest margins in Ashes history. The New Year was to show that the miracles of 1981 could not be repeated so easily. The age of the superman had been replaced by the age of the illusionist.

RUGBY LEAGUE: October 30

At the end of September the Australian team arrived in Britain to become the first country to win all their tour games, a feat they extended to the second leg of their trip to France. The best British clubs were swept aside, League Champions Leigh 44–4, Leeds 31–4 and Hull KR 30–10. The three Tests were won 40–4, 27–6 and 32–8 and in Britain they totalled 97 tries against seven. In France they scored 69 against two. By 1985, when Wigan beat Hull in the Challenge Cup final and 11 of the 30 players in the squads for the game were ineligible for Great Britain some people were complaining that overseas players were stifling home talent. But the truth was that they were raising the standard of British rugby league. The game had slimmed down its administration, increased its popularity with spectators and sponsors, and marketed itself as fast and exciting. The emergence of players such as Martin Offiah and Ellery Hanley helped build that image. The proof was there in 1988 when Great Britain scored their first victory over the Australians for 10 years. Then on January 5, 1989, rugby league landed its biggest coup of all when Widnes tempted Jonathan Davies, the outstanding Llanelli and Wales fly-half, to sign-up. It was one in the eye for rugby union.

MOTOR RACING: December

A sad year in which the talented Gilles Villeneuve was killed during practice for the Belgian Grand Prix at Zolder in April ends with the death of the legendary Mr Lotus, Colin Chapman, from a heart attack. He was 54. Chapman, a brilliant innovator won world championships for Lotus with Jim Clark (1963, 1965), Graham Hill (1968), Jochen Rindt (1970), Emerson Fittipaldi (1974) and Mario Andretti in 1978.

CRICKET: December 30

England win the fourth Test in Melbourne by one of the narrowest margins in Ashes history. It is another psychological blow to the Australians after the battering they received at the hands of Ian Botham the previous summer.

ROLL OF HONOUR

AMERICAN FOOTBALL: Superbowl: San Francisco 49ers 26 Cincinnati Bengals 21.

ATHLETICS: Commonwealth Games: Held in Brisbane, Australia. Canada 44 gold medals, England 27, Australia 25.

CRICKET: County championship: Middlesex. John Player League: Sussex. NatWest Trophy: Surrey. Benson & Hedges Cup: Somerset.

CYCLING: Tour de France: Bernard Hinault (France).

DARTS: World Championship: Jocky Wilson.

GOLF: US Masters: Craig Stadler. US PGA: Ray Floyd. US Open: Tom Watson. The Open (Royal Troon): Tom Watson.

HOCKEY: World Cup, Men: Pakistan.

HORSE RACING: Flat:

1000 Guineas: On the House. 2000 Guineas: Zino. The Derby: Golden Fleece (Jockey: Pat Eddery. Trainer: Vincent O'Brien). The Oaks: Time Charter. St Leger: Touching Wood. Champion jockey Lester Piggott. Top trainer Henry Cecil £872,614.

National Hunt: Grand National: Grittar (Jockey: Mr Dick Saunders. Trainer: Frank Gilman). Cheltenham Gold Cup: Silver Buck. Champion Hurdle: For Auction. Champion jockey John Francome and Peter Scudamore, 120 winners. Top trainer Michael Dickinson £296,028.

MOTOR RACING: Keke Rosberg in a Williams-Ford. Constructors' Cup: Ferrari.

RUGBY LEAGUE: Challenge Cup: Hull. Championship: Widnes.

RUGBY UNION: No Grand Slam. Triple Crown: Ireland. County Championship: Lancashire. John Player Cup: Gloucester

12 Moseley 12 (shared). Schweppes Welsh Cup: Cardiff 12 Bridgend 12. Cardiff won on tries count.

SKIING: Overall champion, Men: Phil Mahre (US). Women: Erika Hess (Switzerland).

SNOOKER: World Championship: Alex Higgins 18 Ray Reardon 15.

SOCCER: First Division Title: Liverpool (87pts). Runners-up: Ipswich Town. FA Cup winners: Tottenham 1 Queen's Park Rangers 0 (after replay 1–1). Milk Cup: Liverpool 3 Tottenham 1. Scotland: Premier League Title: Celtic (55pts). Runners-up: Aberdeen. Scottish Cup: Aberdeen 4 Rangers 1. Scottish League Cup: Rangers 2 Dundee United 1. European Cup: Aston Villa 1 Bayern Munich 0. Cup Winners' Cup: Barcelona 2 Standard Liege 1. UEFA Cup: IFK Gothenburg beat SV Hamburg 4–0 on agg. (H) 3–0. (A) 1–0. World Cup: Italy 3 West Germany 1 (Madrid). Poland 3 France 2 for third place.

SPEEDWAY: World Champion: Bruce Penhall (US). British League: Belle Vue.

SQUASH: World Open Championship: Jahangir Khan (Pakistan).

TENNIS: Wimbledon: Jimmy Connors (US) bt John McEnroe (US) 3–6, 6–3, 6–7, 7–6, 6–4. Women: Martina Navratilova (US) bt Chris Evert-Lloyd (US) 6–1, 3–6, 6–2. US Open: Jimmy Connors and Chris Evert-Lloyd. French Open: Mats Wilander (Sweden), Martina Navratilova (US). Australian Open: Johan Kriek (S. Africa), Chris Evert-Lloyd. Davis Cup: United States. Wightman Cup: US beat Britain 6–1.

FOOTBALL LEAGUE 1981–82

DIVISION 1

	P	W	D	L	F	A	W	D	L	F	A	Pts
1 Liverpool	42	14	3	4	39	14	12	6	3	41	18	87
2 Ipswich T	42	17	1	3	47	25	9	4	8	28	28	83
3 Manchester U	42	12	6	3	27	9	10	6	5	32	20	78
4 Tottenham H	42	12	4	5	41	26	8	7	6	26	22	71
5 Arsenal	42	13	5	3	27	15	7	6	8	21	22	71
6 Swansea C	42	13	3	5	34	16	8	3	10	24	35	69
7 Southampton	42	15	2	4	49	30	4	7	10	23	37	66
8 Everton	42	11	7	3	33	21	6	6	9	23	29	64
9 West Ham U	42	9	10	2	42	29	5	6	10	24	28	58
10 Manchester C	42	9	7	5	32	23	6	6	9	17	27	58
11 Aston Villa	42	9	6	6	28	24	6	6	9	27	29	57
12 Nottingham F	42	7	7	7	19	20	8	5	8	23	28	57
13 Brighton & HA	42	8	7	6	30	24	5	6	10	13	28	52
14 Coventry C	42	9	4	8	31	24	4	7	10	25	38	50
15 Notts Co	42	8	5	8	32	33	5	3	13	29	36	47
16 Birmingham	42	8	6	7	29	25	2	8	11	24	36	44
17 WBA	42	6	6	9	24	25	5	5	11	22	32	44
18 Stoke C	42	9	2	10	27	28	3	6	12	17	35	44
19 Sunderland	42	6	5	10	19	26	5	6	10	19	32	44
20 Leeds U	42	6	11	4	23	20	4	1	16	16	41	42
21 Wolverhampton W	42	8	5	8	19	20	2	5	14	13	43	40
22 Middlesbrough	42	5	9	7	20	24	3	6	12	14	28	39

DIVISION 2

	P	W	D	L	F	A	W	D	L	F	A	Pts
1 Luton T	42	16	3	2	48	19	9	10	2	38	27	88
2 Watford	42	13	6	2	46	16	10	5	6	30	26	80
3 Norwich C	42	14	3	4	41	19	8	2	11	23	31	71
4 Sheffield W	42	10	8	3	31	23	10	2	9	24	28	70
5 QPR	42	15	4	2	40	9	6	2	13	25	34	69
6 Barnsley	42	13	4	4	33	14	6	6	9	26	27	67
7 Rotherham U	42	13	5	3	42	19	7	2	12	24	35	67
8 Leicester C	42	12	5	4	31	19	6	7	8	25	29	66
9 Newcastle U	42	14	4	3	30	14	4	4	13	22	36	62
10 Blackburn R	42	11	4	6	26	15	5	7	9	21	28	59
11 Oldham Ath	42	9	9	3	28	23	6	5	10	22	28	59
12 Chelsea	42	10	5	6	37	30	5	7	9	23	30	57

		Home					Away					
	P	W	D	L	F	A	W	D	L	F	A	Pts
13 Charlton Ath	42	11	5	5	33	22	2	7	12	17	43	51
14 Cambridge U	42	11	4	6	31	19	2	5	14	17	34	48
15 Crystal Palace	42	9	2	10	25	26	4	7	10	9	19	48
16 Derby Co	42	9	8	4	32	23	3	4	14	21	45	48
17 Grimsby T	42	5	8	8	29	30	6	5	10	24	35	46
18 Shrewsbury T	42	10	6	5	26	19	1	7	13	11	38	46
19 Bolton W	42	10	4	7	28	24	3	3	15	11	37	46
20 Cardiff C	42	9	2	10	28	32	3	6	12	17	29	44
21 Wrexham	42	9	4	8	22	22	2	7	12	18	34	44
22 Orient	42	6	8	7	23	24	4	1	16	13	37	39

DIVISION 3

		Home					Away					
	P	W	D	L	F	A	W	D	L	F	A	Pts
1 Burnley	46	13	7	3	37	20	8	10	5	29	25	80
2 Carlisle U	46	17	4	2	44	21	6	7	10	21	29	80
3 Fulham	46	12	9	2	44	22	9	6	8	33	29	78
4 Lincoln C	46	13	7	3	40	16	8	7	8	26	24	77
5 Oxford U	46	10	8	5	28	18	9	6	8	35	31	71
6 Gillingham	46	14	5	4	44	26	6	6	11	20	30	71
7 Southend U	46	11	7	5	35	23	7	8	8	28	28	69
8 Brentford	46	8	6	9	28	22	11	5	7	28	25	68
9 Millwall	46	12	4	7	36	28	6	9	8	26	34	67
10 Plymouth Arg	46	12	5	6	37	24	6	6	11	27	32	65
11 Chesterfield	46	12	4	7	33	27	6	6	11	24	31	64
12 Reading	46	11	6	6	43	35	6	5	12	24	40	62
13 Portsmouth	46	11	10	2	33	14	3	9	11	23	37	61
14 Preston NE	46	10	7	6	25	22	6	6	11	25	34	61
15 Bristol R*	46	12	4	7	35	28	6	5	12	23	37	61
16 Newport Co	46	9	10	4	28	21	5	6	12	26	33	58
17 Huddersfield T	46	10	5	8	38	25	5	7	11	26	34	57
18 Exeter C	46	14	4	5	46	33	2	5	16	25	51	57
19 Doncaster R	46	9	9	5	31	24	4	8	11	24	44	56
20 Walsall	46	10	7	6	32	23	3	7	13	19	32	53
21 Wimbledon	46	10	6	7	33	27	4	5	14	28	48	53
22 Swindon T	46	9	5	9	37	36	4	8	11	18	35	52
23 Bristol C	46	7	6	10	24	29	4	7	12	16	36	46
24 Chester	46	2	10	11	16	30	5	1	17	20	48	32

* Bristol Rovers had 2 points deducted for fielding an unregistered player.

DIVISION 4

		Home					Away					
	P	W	D	L	F	A	W	D	L	F	A	Pts
1 Sheffield U	46	15	8	0	53	15	12	7	4	41	26	96
2 Bradford C	46	14	7	2	52	23	12	6	5	36	22	91
3 Wigan Ath	46	17	5	1	47	18	9	8	6	33	28	91
4 AFC Bournemouth	46	12	10	1	37	15	11	9	3	25	15	88
5 Peterborough U	46	16	3	4	46	22	8	7	8	25	35	82
6 Colchester U	46	12	6	5	47	23	8	6	9	35	34	72
7 Port Vale	46	9	12	2	26	17	9	4	10	30	32	70
8 Hull C	46	14	3	6	36	23	5	9	9	34	38	69
9 Bury	46	13	7	3	53	26	4	10	9	27	33	68
10 Hereford U	46	10	9	4	36	25	6	10	7	28	33	67
11 Tranmere R	46	7	9	7	27	25	7	9	7	24	31	60
12 Blackpool	46	11	5	7	40	26	4	8	11	26	34	58
13 Darlington	46	10	5	8	36	28	5	8	10	25	34	58
14 Hartlepool U	46	9	8	6	39	34	4	8	11	34	50	55
15 Torquay U	46	9	8	6	30	25	5	5	13	17	34	55
16 Aldershot	46	8	7	8	34	29	5	8	10	23	39	54
17 York C	46	9	5	9	45	37	5	3	15	24	54	50
18 Stockport Co	46	10	5	8	34	28	2	8	13	14	39	49
19 Halifax T	46	6	11	6	28	30	3	11	9	23	42	49
20 Mansfield T*	46	8	6	9	39	39	5	4	14	24	42	47
21 Rochdale	46	7	9	7	26	22	3	7	13	24	40	46
22 Northampton	46	9	5	9	32	27	2	4	17	25	57	42
23 Scunthorpe U	46	7	9	7	26	35	2	6	15	17	44	42
24 Crewe Alex	46	3	6	14	19	32	3	3	17	10	52	27

* Mansfield Town had 2 points deducted for fielding an ineligible player.

SCOTTISH LEAGUE 1981–82

PREMIER DIVISION

		Home					Away					
	P	W	D	L	F	A	W	D	L	F	A	Pts
1 Celtic	36	12	5	1	41	16	12	2	4	38	17	55
2 Aberdeen	36	12	4	2	36	15	11	3	4	35	14	53
3 Rangers	36	10	5	3	34	16	6	6	6	23	29	43
4 Dundee U	36	10	4	4	40	14	5	6	7	21	24	40
5 St Mirren	36	8	4	6	30	23	6	5	7	19	29	37
6 Hibernian	36	8	7	3	23	14	3	7	8	15	26	36

		Home					Away					
	P	W	D	L	F	A	W	D	L	F	A	Pts
7 Morton	36	9	6	3	20	12	0	6	12	11	42	30
8 Dundee	36	7	2	9	28	34	4	2	12	18	38	26
9 Partick T	36	4	5	9	19	23	2	5	11	16	36	22
10 Airdrieonians	36	5	4	9	24	36	0	4	14	7	40	18

DIVISION 1

		Home					Away					
	P	W	D	L	F	A	W	D	L	F	A	Pts
1 Motherwell	39	12	7	0	41	17	14	2	4	51	19	61
2 Kilmarnock	39	6	12	2	25	11	11	5	3	35	18	51
3 Hearts	39	12	2	5	33	19	9	6	5	32	18	50
4 Clydebank	39	12	3	5	33	27	7	5	7	28	26	46
5 St Johnstone	39	12	3	4	44	29	5	5	10	25	31	42
6 Ayr U	39	12	6	1	39	20	3	6	11	17	30	42
7 Hamilton A	39	10	3	6	20	16	6	5	9	32	33	40
8 Queen's Park	39	11	5	4	32	17	2	5	12	9	24	36
9 Falkirk	39	8	8	4	26	19	3	6	10	23	33	36
10 Dunfermline Ath	39	3	9	7	24	31	8	5	7	22	25	36
11 Dumbarton	39	10	1	9	25	30	3	8	8	24	31	35
12 Raith R	39	5	2	13	13	32	6	5	8	18	27	29
13 East Stirling	39	4	6	9	20	35	3	4	13	18	42	24
14 Queen of the S	39	2	5	13	25	50	2	5	12	19	43	18

DIVISION 2

		Home					Away					
	P	W	D	L	F	A	W	D	L	F	A	Pts
1 Clyde	39	11	6	2	35	16	13	5	2	44	22	59
2 Alloa	39	9	6	4	33	25	10	6	4	33	17	50
3 Arbroath	39	12	5	2	34	16	8	5	7	28	34	50
4 Berwick R	39	14	4	2	46	15	6	4	9	20	23	48
5 Brechin C	39	9	5	5	28	19	9	5	6	33	24	46
6 Forfar Ath	39	11	6	3	35	12	4	9	6	24	23	45
7 East Fife	39	7	5	8	23	24	7	4	8	25	27	37
8 Stirling Albion	39	9	5	6	25	18	3	6	10	14	26	35
9 Cowdenbeath	39	8	6	6	34	26	3	7	9	17	31	35
10 Montrose	39	8	4	8	28	31	4	4	11	21	43	32
11 Albion R	39	8	3	8	28	28	5	2	13	24	46	31
12 Meadowbank T	39	8	6	6	34	29	2	4	13	15	33	30
13 Stenhousemuir	39	6	5	8	22	28	5	1	14	19	37	28
14 Stranraer	39	5	1	13	22	44	2	5	13	14	41	20

SCHWEPPES CHAMPIONSHIP 1982

		P	W	L	D	Bonus Bt	Bl	Pts
1	Middlesex (4)	22	12	2	8	59	74	325
2	Leicestershire (8)	22	10	4	8	57	69	286
3	Hampshire (7)	22	8	6	8	48	74	250
4	Nottinghamshire (1)	21	7	7	7	44	65	221
5	Surrey (6)	22	6	6	10	56	62	214
6	Somerset (3)	22	6	6	10	51	66	213
7	Essex (5)	22	5	5	12	57	75	212
8	Sussex (2)	22	6	7	9	43	68	207
9	Northamptonshire (15)	22	5	3	14	61	54	195
10	Yorkshire (10)	21	5	1	15	48	51	179
11	Derbyshire (12)	22	4	3	15	45	64	173
12	Lancashire (16)	22	4	3	15	.48	55	167
13	Kent (9)	22	3	4	15	55	63	166
14	Worcestershire (11)	22	3	5	14	43	54	141
15	Gloucestershire (13)	22	2	9	11	46	55	133
16	Glamorgan (14)	22	1	8	13	43	60	119
17	Warwickshire (17)	22	0	8	14	58	53	111

1981 positions in brackets.

Worcestershire total includes 12 points for a win in a match reduced to one innings.

JOHN PLAYER LEAGUE 1982

		P	W	L	Tie	NR	Pts
1	Sussex (5)	16	14	1	0	1	58
2	Middlesex (15)	16	11	4	0	1	46
3	Leicestershire (14)	16	9	6	0	1	38
4	Kent (7)	16	9	7	0	0	36
5	Essex (1)	16	9	7	0	0	36
	Hampshire (6)	16	8	6	2	0	36
	Nottinghamshire (10)	16	8	6	1	1	36
8	Northamptonshire (17)	16	8	7	0	1	34
9	Somerset (2)	18	8	8	0	0	32
10	Glamorgan (10)	16	6	7	0	3	30
	Lancashire (10)	16	6	7	1	2	30
12	Derbyshire (4)	16	6	9	0	1	26
	Surrey (7)	16	6	9	1	0	26

		P	W	L	Tie	NR	Pts
14	Gloucestershire (16)	16	5	9	0	2	24
15	Worcestershire (10)	16	5	10	0	1	22
16	Yorkshire (7)	16	3	10	1	2	18
17	Warwickshire (3)	16	3	11	0	2	16

1981 positions in brackets.

Kent finished in fourth place over Essex, Hampshire and Nottingham by virtue of their greater nuimber of away wins. This criteria applied only for the first four placings.

CRICKET by ROBIN MARLAR

DR W G GRACE was cricket in the Victorian age. In the speeded-up twentieth century, reigns, especially one as long as that monarch's, are replaced by decades and Ian Botham's spell as Mr Cricket was confirmed in the eyes of the Great British public in the space of just a month, a miraculous month from July 16 to August 17 1981 during which in an unprecedented run England dramatically won three Tests against Australia.

It was a heady period. There had been the first stirring for freedom in Eastern Europe, the governments of Reagan and Thatcher were then growing in popularity and in England in that same month Prince Charles married the beautiful princess and Buckingham Palace acquired the look of the fairy-tale castle for which all Britons perpetually hunger.

Capping, within days, England's extraordinary success on the cricket field, Messrs Coe and Ovett began to smash athletic records like so much china.

Botham was extraordinary. He brought to this national party the same mysterious background that distinguishes the giants of mythology. He came up, curiously, from Summerzet where the cider apples grow but there was north country in his voice thanks to his breeding and, unlike the conventional country bumpkin, he was already a London-trained sophisticate, quite able to accept the accolades and not grow big-headed as all the greatest actors on the capital's stage have learned to do. It is worth lingering on his particular deeds in that month, each one truly Herculean.

At Leeds England were gone, lost beyond recovery, the bookies' odds against an England victory so grotesquely huge that they tempted Australian cricketers, Lillee and Marsh, to an ill-fated punt just for a lark, a lark that was to stain characters as these sportsmen were eventually revealed to have backed the opposition and then collected as their own team lost.

From 135 for seven after following on, Botham, always steering, sometimes slogging, carried England to 356 whereupon Australia were bowled out for next to nothing giving England their most improbable ever victory by a mere 18 runs.

Thence to Birmingham where England were again failing only for Botham to destroy the Australians' final innings with a spell in which he took five wickets for one run in 29 deliveries. He bowled like a man possessed, capable of dismissing the deity and all the archangels on that unforgettable afternoon.

Next the Test match caravan moved to Manchester where England built up a useful if not obviously winning lead of 99 runs on the first innings, only to have to stare at a scoreboard reading 104 for five at the second attempt which gave them every chance of plucking defeat from the jaws of victory in the series. Botham hit 118 in just over two hours of the most exhilarating cricket any Englishman had seen or was ever likely to see, including no fewer than six sixes, a record for Anglo-Australian Tests.

The Australians fought, none more so than Border who was to become their hero deeper into the decade when he carried off the World Cup in India from under England's nose, but even his century was never other than a rearguard and England's winning margin was this time three figures rather than two.

Unlike Hercules Botham could not have done what he did single-handedly but this modern giant had helpers. Brearley, the grey-haired captain, not only managed Botham to glory but also helped to inspire the moody spirit within England's only fast bowler of the eighties, Willis, who experienced his most famous hour. He roared down the Headingley hill, as the lion in the Wizard of Oz could never do, and thus tormented some talented visitors from the real world Oz, bowling for once perfectly as every part of his machinery, physical and mental, operated in tune as never before, the combination irresistible, the figures outstanding at 8–43.

Thereafter England's bolt seemed mostly shot in the years which followed and the world stage was dominated by the West Indies who were all but unbeatable, and seriously challenged only by the Pakistanis under their most famous cricketing mogul, the great Imran Khan. The West Indians seemed able to defy the ancient lore of ebb and flow and their own Caribbean well of talent yielded fast bowlers, not just run-of-the-mill merchants but magnificent men, some tall, some short, by the bucketful.

To be able to bring on a Marshall to take the place of a Holding and feel confident that an Ambrose or a Bishop would emerge to succeed the Marshall was a demonstration of cricketing prowess indeed. Nor is this all. Powerful greedy batsmen like Greenidge, defying every surgeon's prediction of disability, carried on like many an Old Man of the Sea. Richardson not so much followed Richards as joined him on the pedestal and in the matter of leadership, so often vexatious to the African spirit, Lloyd's massive mantle eventually came to fit Richards, his chosen successor. England never looked like taking a Test off these masters of the game and Australia could do so but rarely.

True there were some allegedly crabbed critics who disliked aspects of West Indian cricket, the threat of their speed directed at the batsmen's upper body and often translated into physical injury, their ability to slow the game down with fast bowling runs to such an extent that not only were they unbeatable but also, because of their sameness, unwatchable. In committee rooms their backers refused to enforce a speeding up.

On the other hand it was thanks to Caribbean initiatives that by the end of the decade the pernicious South African question which had so bedevilled the game for 20 years was eventually resolved. One aspect, the popularity of Test matches, came under increasing scrutiny as crowds disappeared from their most popular haunts, first in Pakistan then in India, as the popularity of the one-day game increased dramatically at the expense of the longer matches beloved by the players but games seen by some as too leisurely for the increasingly frenetic lives of the middle-classes who provided cricket's spectator background everywhere in the world.

Thus the eighties ended with renewed concentration on financial matters which became increasingly identified with television fees and the game's appeal on the box in the corner of the living room. Instant cricket was bad for player development, too, everyone argued, especially in England where the spring of talent was by the end of the decade revealed to have run almost dry. In the awful sixties the teachers of the eighties were taught that competitive team games are elitist and sexist, a vicious message that cricket alone has no power to expunge in the nineties.

Niki Lauda, 1984 World Champion, in thoughtful mood.

Roma fans at the 1984 European Cup final against Liverpool.

CRICKET: January 7

The first cracks in the optimism generated by the miraculous Ashes series of 1981 began to show as Australia drew the fifth Test to win the series 2–1 and thereby regain the Ashes for the first time since 1977. England also failed to reach the the finals of the one-day World Series Cup against Australia and New Zealand and the first doubts about the captaincy of Bob Willis began to surface. He clearly did not have the leadership qualities of a Brearley who pulled all the disparate talents together.

RACING: February 9

1981 Derby winner Shergar is kidnapped in Ireland and a demand for £2m is made. The horse is never seen again.

AMERICAN FOOTBALL: January

Washington Redskins beat Miami Dolphins 27–17 at Super Bowl XVII. Enthusiasm for the sport, which has been kindled by regular Sunday evening coverage on Channel 4, exploded with the first complete live showing of a Super Bowl on British television. Since then, the sport's popularity in Britain has boomed with regular coverage of the events in America plus a serious British competition sponsored by an American brewer. Players started to become household names, thanks mainly to William 'The Fridge' Perry, a man-mountain who was used as a battering ram by the Chicago Bears. Perry's star came and went but other big names established their own British followings, such as Dan Marino and Joe Montana, the driving force of the San Francisco 49ers, the most successful team of the 1980s.

RUGBY LEAGUE: February 20

Joe Lydon with a try and three goals helps Great Britain to a 20–5 win over France.

SKIING: February

It was a chance to relive the glorious 70s for Austrian Franz Klammer when he won the men's downhill skiing World Cup in

1983 for the first time in four years while Switzerland's Ingemar Stenmark was also making a return to the winner's podium after a break of a year when he won the slalom. Klammer had won the downhill from 1975 until 1978 while Stenmark had been king of the slalom from 1975 until 1981. But for both men it was a swansong. Stenmark had won his 63rd World Cup victory a month earlier, surpassing the record held by Austrian Annemarie Moser-Proll and returned in 1984 to win the giant slalom but it was to be the turn of a new generation. Pirmin Zurbriggen won the downhill and giant slalom in 1988 and repeated his success in the downhill the following year. He also won the super-giant slalom from 1987 onwards. Luxembourg's Marc Girardelli won the slalom in 1984, won it again in 1985 along with the giant slalom and then took the downhill title in 1989, winning in each of the four disciplines, the super-giant slalom, the giant slalom, downhill and slalom. Italian Alberto Tomba won the slalom and giant slalom in 1988. Queen of the slopes was Switzerland's Michela Figini who was overall champion in 1985 and 1988 winning along the way the downhill in 1985 and from 1987 to 1989. She also shared the giant slalom title in 1985 with East German Marina Kiehl. Figini's performances were the most dominating in the sport since Austrian Annemarie Moser-Proll's reign from 1971 until 1979. Switzerland Erika Hess won three slalom titles from 1981 to 1983 and Marie-Therese Nadig won the downhill in 1980 and 1981.

SOCCER: February 26

Pat Jennings, the former Tottenham and now Arsenal goalkeeper becomes the first player in England to appear in over 1,000 first class matches. He had played for Northern Ireland in the previous summer's World Cup.

RUGBY LEAGUE: March 6

Great Britain beat France 17–5.

RACING: March 17

Michael Dickinson saddled the first five past the post in the Cheltenham Gold Cup. His victory parade was led by Bregawn ridden by Graham Bradley, Captain John with jockey David Goulding, Wayward Lad ridden by Jonjo O'Neill, Silver Buck with Robert Earnshaw, and Ashley House with Dermot Browne in the saddle. At this point in the season he had been saddling one winner from every two horses sent out.

GOLF: April 11

Severiano Ballesteros wins the Green Jacket for the second time when he captures the Masters title.

ATHLETICS: April 17

The booming popularity of the London marathon continues with the event won by Briton Michael Gratton and Grete Waitz of Norway being the first woman home.

SNOOKER May 2

Steve Davis makes amends for last year's first round defeat by beating Canadian Cliff Thorburn 18–6 in the final of the World Championship. At least Thorburn had the satisfaction of compiling the first 147 maximum break in the World Championships in Sheffield when he played Terry Griffiths.

SOCCER: May 21

For the third year running the Cup Final goes to a replay. Brighton, already relegated to the Second Division, make the most of their day out against Manchester United. They take an early lead, find themselves 2–1 down then equalise near the end. They miss a good chance in extra time so five days later return to Wembley for the replay. This time they are outplayed as Robson 2, Whiteside and Muhren make it 4–0. In Scotland Aberdeen beat Rangers 1–0 as Black scores in extra time.

BOXING: May 31

Jack Dempsey dies. The great American heavyweight who lost his title in 1926 to Gene Tunney retired from the ring in 1940 to open a restaurant having made an estimated $10m from the sport.

RACING: June 1

The Geoffrey Wragg trained Teenoso gives Lester Piggott his ninth Derby win. The 9/2 favourite beat Carlingford Castle and Shearwalk.

TENNIS: June 20–July 3

Wimbledon opens with John McEnroe, the previous year's losing finalist, involved in a characteristic argument with the umpire. In the final McEnroe beat Chris Lewis 6–2, 6–2, 6–2, to collect the £66,600 first prize. The unseeded New Zealander was the surprise of the tournament and had beaten Kevin Curren in an epic five set semi-final. The women's title went to Martina Navratilova who was starting to make it her personal property. She beat Andrea Jaeger 6–0, 6–3 to win £60,000. There is something for Britain to cheer as John Lloyd partners Australian Wendy Turnbull to the mixed doubles championship over Steve Denton and Billie Jean King, 6–7, 7–6, 7–5.

CRICKET: June 25

India upset the favourites, the West Indies, to win the Prudential World Cup at Lord's. India made 183 all out in 53.4 overs, a total which looked meagre but three wickets from Madan Lal and three from Amarnath skittled the West Indies out for 140. The West Indies have never again dominated one-day cricket – they failed to reach the semi-finals in 1987 – even if this one-day setback was compensated as the decade wore on by their increasing dominance of Test cricket. England, after coming through the zonal matches were beaten in the semi-final by India at Old Trafford. England made 213 in 60 overs while India scored 217 in 54.4 overs. In the other semi-final the West Indies beat Pakistan by eight wickets.

CRICKET: July 14–18

Second innings centuries from Graeme Fowler, Chris Tavare and Ian Botham earn England a 189 run Test victory over New Zealand, after England had been bowled out in the first innings for 209 and New Zealand for 196. But in the second Test at Headingly, ten days later, New Zealand won by five wickets for their first Test victory in England. It was their 29th attempt in 52 years. The foundations for the win were laid by a first innings 93 from John Wright and 84 from Bruce Edgar. England won the third Test at Lord's by 127 runs, Gower scoring a century, and the fourth Test in Nottingham by 165 runs where Lamb and Botham both scored 100s. But while England in the end won the series comfortably the margin could not disguise the growing problems of the England cricket team. Too much of a club, not enough of a team, it was suggested.

GOLF: July 17

Tom Watson retains The Open title at Royal Birkdale. He finishes with 275 and is followed into the clubhouse by compatriots Hale Irwin (276) and Andy Bean (276).

CRICKET: July 23

Essex turned victory into defeat in the Benson & Hedges Cup after restricting Middlesex to 196 for eight from 55 overs. At 185 for five and with four overs remaining Essex seemed assured of victory but sensationally collapsed to 192 all out with five balls remaining.

ATHLETICS: August 14

The inaugural World Championships are held in Helsinki devoid of political wrangling. Daley Thompson adds the gold to his collection of European and Olympic medals while Steve Cram beats both Steve Ovett and Sebastian Coe for the 1,500m title. American Carl Lewis wins three golds, the 100m, the long jump and in the 4 × 100m relay. Mary Decker of the US takes 1,500m and 3,000m golds while Czech Jarmila Kratochvilova also does the double in 400m and 800m.

CRICKET: September 3

Somerset scored 193 from 50 overs to win the NatWest Cup from Kent who were taunted by Vic Marks. Marks took 3 for 30 as Kent were all out for 169 in 47.1 overs.

CRICKET: September 10, 12, 13

Essex drew with Yorkshire at Chelmsford to win the County Championship, pipping Middlesex by 16 points. They won £14,000 for their endeavours.

CRICKET: September 11

Two points from a no results match at Essex were enough to give Yorkshire the Sunday League title and £13,000. They finished on the same number of points as Somerset but five away wins compared to three for the West country team earned them the trophy. But the sweetness of this victory was tainted by the fact they were bottom of the county championship for the first time ever. They had only one win all season, and that was away from home.

SAILING: September 26

After 132 years the New York Yacht Club had to unbolt the America's Cup from the floor of their clubhouse and hand it over to somebody else. The battle for the trophy captivated the world as the yacht *Australia II*, 3–1 down in the best of seven competition squared the series at 3–3. It was the first time the race had reached the decider and *Australia II* skippered by John Bertrand trailed until the fifth of the six-leg final race. He then overhauled Dennis Conner in *Liberty* to seal a sensational victory by 49 seconds and become a national hero. The prize had not been won without controversy. *Australia II* had a winged keel which was hidden from rival crews by a special covering – that did not stop other crews trying to discover the secret and the reason for *Australia II*'s speed. Victory also meant the Australians would stage the next America's Cup challenge in home waters at Fremantle but by 1989 the excitement and thrill of the competition had been reduced to farce as competitors stretched the definition of a 12m yacht – the qualification for the race – to incredible lengths. This resulted in a series of legal and courtroom battles which left those observers who had been so thrilled by Bertrand's victory disinterested.

CRICKET: October 21

The blood-letting that followed Yorkshire's miserable county season was even by their standards amazing. Boycott who had been offered a testimonial for the 1984 season was sacked and this provoked a Yorkshire revolt which saw the committee defeated and Boycott reinstated by January 1984.

SOCCER: November 16

England win 4–0 in Luxembourg but are out of the European Championships because of Denmark's 2–0 win in Greece which gives them the group by a point. English fans riot. Norman Whiteside scores in Hamburg as Northern Ireland beat West Germany, Wales lose 1–0 in Bulgaria and Eire destroy Malta 8–0 in Dublin. Scotland lose 2–1 to East Germany and none of the teams from Great Britain qualify for the finals in France.

CRICKET: December 29

In Madras Sunil Gavaskar scored 236 not out against the West Indies. This was his 30th Test hundred, one more than Don Bradman's record of 29 which had stood for 35 years. Gavaskar promptly gave his bat to Dujon, the West Indian wicket-keeper who had asked for it, and received a car as his reward from the grateful Indians. Gavaskar's career record of 34 Test centuries still stands and just as unique is his success in using cricket to further a flourishing business career.

ROLL OF HONOUR

AMERICAN FOOTBALL: Superbowl: Washington Redskins 27 Miami Dolphins 17.

ATHLETICS: European Cup, Men: East Germany. Women: East Germany.

CRICKET: County championship: Essex. John Player League: Yorkshire. NatWest Trophy: Somerset. Benson & Hedges Cup: Middlesex.

CYCLING: Tour de France: Laurent Fignon (France).

DARTS: World Championship: Keith Deller.

GOLF: US Masters: Seve Ballesteros (Spain). US PGA: Hal Sutton. US Open: Larry Nelson. The Open (Royal Birkdale): Tom Watson. Ryder Cup (PGA National GC, Florida): Europe 13.5 US 14.5.

HOCKEY: World Cup, Women: Holland.

HORSE RACING: Flat:

1000 Guineas: Ma Biche. 2000 Guineas: Lomond. The Derby: Teenoso (Jockey: Lester Piggott. Trainer: Geoffrey Wragg). The Oaks: Sun Princess. St Leger: Sun Princess. Champion jockey Willie Carson, 159 wins. Top trainer Dick Hern £549,598.

National Hunt: Grand National: Corbiere (Jockey: Ben De Haan.

Trainer: Mrs Jenny Pitman). Cheltenham Gold Cup: Bregawn. Champion Hurdle: Gaye Brief. Champion jockey John Francome, 106 wins. Top trainer Michael Dickinson, £358,837.

MOTOR RACING: Nelson Piquet (Brazil) in a Brabham-BMW. Constructors' Cup: Ferrari.

RUGBY LEAGUE: Challenge Cup: Featherstone Rovers. Championship: Widnes.

RUGBY UNION: No Grand Slam or Triple Crown. Joint leaders: France and Ireland. County Championship: Gloucester. Pilkington Cup: Bristol 28 Leicester 22. Schweppes Welsh Cup: Pontypool 18 Swansea 6.

SKIING: Overall champion, Men: Phil Mahre (US). Women: Tamara McKinney (US).

SNOOKER: World Championship: Steve Davis 18 Cliff Thorburn (Canada) 6.

SOCCER: First Division Title: Liverpool (82pts). Runners-up: Watford. FA Cup Winners: Manchester United 4 Brighton 0 (after replay 2–2). Milk Cup: Liverpool 2 Manchester United 1. Scotland: Premier League Title: Dundee United (56pts). Runners-up: Celtic. Scottish Cup: Aberdeen 1 Rangers 0. Scottish League Cup: Celtic 2 Rangers 1. European Cup: SV Hamburg 1 Juventus 0. European Cup Winners' Cup: Aberdeen 2 Real Madrid 1. UEFA Cup: Anderlecht beat Benfica 2–1. (H) 1–0 (A) 1–1.

SPEEDWAY: World Champion: Egon Muller (West Germany). British League: Cradley Heath.

SQUASH: World Open Championship, Men: Jahangir Khan (Pakistan). Women: Vicki Cardwell (Australia).

TABLE TENNIS: World Championship, Men: Guo Yue-Hua (China). Women: Cao Yan-Hua (China).

TENNIS: Wimbledon: Men: John McEnroe (US) beat Chris Lewis (NZ) 6–2, 6–2, 6–2. Women: Martina Navratilova (US) beat Andrea Jaeger (US) 6–0, 6–3. US Open: Jimmy Connors (US), Martina Navratilova. French Open: Yannick Noah (France), Chris Evert-Lloyd (US). Australian Open: Mats Wilander (Sweden), Martina Navratilova. Davis Cup: Australia. Wightman Cup: US beat Britain 6–1.

YACHTING: America's Cup: *Australia II* (Australia) skipper John Bertrand. Admiral's Cup: West Germany.

FOOTBALL LEAGUE 1982–83

DIVISION 1

		Home					Away					
	P	W	D	L	F	A	W	D	L	F	A	Pts
1 Liverpool	42	16	4	1	55	16	8	6	7	32	21	82
2 Watford	42	16	2	3	49	20	6	3	12	25	37	71
3 Manchester U	42	14	7	0	39	10	5	6	10	17	28	70
4 Tottenham H	42	15	4	2	50	15	5	5	11	15	35	69
5 Nottingham F	42	12	5	4	34	18	8	4	9	28	32	69
6 Aston Villa	42	17	2	2	47	15	4	3	14	15	35	68
7 Everton	42	13	6	2	43	19	5	4	12	23	29	64
8 West Ham U	42	13	3	5	41	23	7	1	13	27	39	64
9 Ipswich T	42	11	3	7	39	23	4	10	7	25	27	58
10 Arsenal	42	11	6	4	36	19	5	4	12	22	37	58
11 WBA	42	11	5	5	35	20	4	7	10	16	29	57
12 Southampton	42	11	5	5	36	22	4	7	10	18	36	57
13 Stoke C	42	13	4	4	34	21	3	5	13	19	43	57
14 Norwich C	42	10	6	5	30	18	4	6	11	22	40	54
15 Notts Co	42	12	4	5	37	25	3	3	15	18	46	52
16 Sunderland	42	7	10	4	30	22	5	4	12	18	39	50
17 Birmingham C	42	9	7	5	29	24	3	7	11	11	31	50
18 Luton T	42	7	7	7	34	33	5	6	10	31	51	49
19 Coventry C	42	10	5	6	29	17	3	4	14	19	42	48
20 Manchester C	42	9	5	7	26	23	4	3	14	21	47	47
21 Swansea C	42	10	4	7	32	29	0	7	14	19	40	41
22 Brighton & HA	42	8	7	6	25	22	1	6	14	13	46	40

DIVISION 2

		Home					Away					
	P	W	D	L	F	A	W	D	L	F	A	Pts
1 QPR	42	16	3	2	51	16	10	4	7	26	20	85
2 Wolverhampton W	42	14	5	2	42	16	6	10	5	26	28	75
3 Leicester C	42	11	4	6	36	15	9	6	6	36	29	70
4 Fulham	42	13	5	3	36	20	7	4	10	28	27	69
5 Newcastle U	42	13	6	2	43	21	5	7	9	32	32	67
6 Sheffield W	42	9	8	4	33	23	7	7	7	27	24	63
7 Oldham Ath	42	8	10	3	38	24	6	9	6	26	23	61
8 Leeds U	42	7	11	3	28	22	6	10	5	23	24	60
9 Shrewsbury T	42	8	9	4	20	15	7	5	9	28	33	59
10 Barnsley	42	9	8	4	37	28	5	7	9	20	27	57
11 Blackburn R	42	11	7	3	38	21	4	5	12	20	37	57

		P	W	D	L	F	A	W	D	L	F	A	Pts
			Home					*Away*					
12	Cambridge U	42	11	7	3	26	17	2	5	14	16	43	51
13	Derby Co	42	7	10	4	27	24	3	9	9	22	34	49
14	Carlisle U	42	10	6	5	44	28	2	6	13	24	42	48
15	Crystal Palace	42	11	7	3	31	17	1	5	15	12	35	48
16	Middlesbrough	42	8	7	6	27	29	3	8	10	19	38	48
17	Charlton Ath	42	11	3	7	40	31	2	6	13	23	55	48
18	Chelsea	42	8	8	5	31	22	3	6	12	20	39	47
19	Grimsby T	42	9	7	5	32	26	3	4	14	13	44	47
20	Rotherham U	42	6	7	8	22	29	4	8	9	23	39	45
21	Burnley	42	10	4	7	38	24	2	4	15	18	42	44
22	Bolton W	42	10	2	9	30	26	1	9	11	12	35	44

DIVISION 3

		P	W	D	L	F	A	W	D	L	F	A	Pts
			Home					*Away*					
1	Portsmouth	46	16	4	3	43	19	11	6	6	31	22	91
2	Cardiff C	46	17	5	1	45	14	8	6	9	31	36	86
3	Huddersfield T	46	15	8	0	56	18	8	5	10	28	31	82
4	Newport Co	46	13	7	3	40	20	10	2	11	36	34	78
5	Oxford U	46	12	9	2	41	23	10	3	10	30	30	78
6	Lincoln C	46	17	1	5	55	22	6	6	11	22	29	76
7	Bristol R	46	16	4	3	55	21	6	5	12	29	37	75
8	Plymouth Arg	46	15	2	6	37	23	4	6	13	24	43	65
9	Brentford	46	14	4	5	50	28	4	6	13	38	49	64
10	Walsall	46	14	5	4	38	19	3	8	12	26	44	64
11	Sheffield U	46	16	3	4	44	20	3	4	16	18	44	64
12	Bradford C	46	11	7	5	41	27	5	6	12	27	42	61
13	Gillingham	46	12	4	7	37	29	4	9	10	21	30	61
14	AFC Bournemouth	46	11	7	5	35	20	5	6	12	24	48	61
15	Southend U	46	10	8	5	41	28	5	6	12	25	37	59
16	Preston NE	46	11	10	2	35	17	4	3	16	25	52	58
17	Millwall	46	12	7	4	41	24	2	6	15	23	53	55
18	Wigan Ath	46	10	4	9	35	33	5	5	13	25	39	54
19	Exeter C	46	12	4	7	49	43	2	8	13	32	61	54
20	Orient	46	10	6	7	44	38	5	3	15	20	50	54
21	Reading	46	10	8	5	37	28	2	9	12	27	51	53
22	Wrexham	46	11	6	6	40	26	1	9	13	16	50	51
23	Doncaster R	46	6	8	9	38	44	3	3	17	19	53	38
24	Chesterfield	46	6	6	11	28	28	2	7	14	15	40	37

DIVISION 4

		Home					Away					
	P	W	D	L	F	A	W	D	L	F	A	Pts
1 Wimbledon	46	17	4	2	57	23	12	7	4	39	22	98
2 Hull C	46	14	8	1	48	14	11	7	5	27	20	90
3 Port Vale	46	15	4	4	37	16	11	6	6	30	18	88
4 Scunthorpe U	46	13	7	3	41	17	10	7	6	30	25	83
5 Bury	46	15	4	4	43	20	8	8	7	31	26	81
6 Colchester U	46	17	5	1	51	19	7	4	12	24	36	81
7 York C	46	18	4	1	59	19	4	9	10	29	39	79
8 Swindon T	46	14	3	6	45	27	5	8	10	16	27	68
9 Peterborough U	46	13	6	4	38	23	4	7	12	20	29	64
10 Mansfield T	46	11	6	6	32	26	5	7	11	29	44	61
11 Halifax T	46	9	8	6	31	23	7	4	12	28	43	60
12 Torquay U	46	12	3	8	38	30	5	4	14	18	35	58
13 Chester	46	8	6	9	28	24	7	5	11	27	36	56
14 Bristol C	46	10	8	5	32	25	3	9	11	27	45	56
15 Northampton T	46	10	8	5	43	29	4	4	15	22	46	54
16 Stockport Co	46	11	8	4	41	31	3	4	16	19	48	54
17 Darlington	46	8	5	10	27	30	5	8	10	34	41	52
18 Aldershot	46	11	5	7	40	35	1	10	12	21	47	51
19 Tranmere R	46	8	8	7	30	29	5	3	15	19	42	50
20 Rochdale	46	11	8	4	38	25	0	8	15	17	48	49
21 Blackpool	46	10	8	5	32	23	3	4	16	23	51	49
22 Hartlepool U	46	11	5	7	30	24	2	4	17	16	52	48
23 Crewe Alex	46	9	5	9	35	32	2	3	18	18	39	41
24 Hereford U	46	8	6	9	19	23	3	2	18	23	56	41

SCOTTISH LEAGUE 1982–83

PREMIER DIVISION

		Home					Away					
	P	W	D	L	F	A	W	D	L	F	A	Pts
1 Dundee U	36	13	4	1	57	18	11	4	3	33	17	56
2 Celtic	36	12	3	3	44	18	13	2	3	46	18	55
3 Aberdeen	36	14	0	4	46	12	11	5	2	30	12	55
4 Rangers	36	9	6	3	32	16	4	6	8	20	25	38
5 St Mirren	36	8	5	5	30	18	3	7	8	17	33	34
6 Dundee	36	8	3	7	29	28	1	8	9	13	25	29
7 Hibernian	36	3	11	4	21	17	4	4	10	14	34	29
8 Motherwell	36	9	3	6	28	27	2	2	14	11	46	27
9 Morton	36	4	4	10	14	26	2	4	12	16	48	20
10 Kilmarnock	36	3	7	8	17	31	0	4	14	11	60	17

DIVISION 1

		Home					Away				
	P	W	D	L	F	A	W	D	L	F	A	Pts
1 St Johnstone	39	17	1	2	34	10	8	4	7	25	27	55
2 Hearts	39	13	4	3	46	20	9	6	4	33	18	45
3 Clydebank	39	8	5	6	32	27	12	5	3	40	22	50
4 Partick T	39	9	6	4	31	23	11	3	6	35	22	49
5 Airdrieonians	39	7	3	9	27	27	9	4	7	35	19	39
6 Alloa Ath	39	8	7	5	31	21	6	4	9	21	31	39
7 Dumbarton	39	6	7	6	26	32	7	3	10	24	27	36
8 Falkirk	39	8	2	9	20	22	7	4	9	25	33	36
9 Raith R	39	8	3	8	32	29	5	5	10	32	34	34
10 Clyde	39	8	2	10	32	38	6	4	9	23	28	34
11 Hamilton A	39	7	6	7	27	32	4	6	9	27	34	34
12 Ayr U	39	9	4	7	29	26	3	4	12	16	35	32
13 Dunfermline Ath	39	5	9	6	19	30	2	8	9	20	39	31
14 Queen's Park	39	3	6	10	24	39	3	5	12	20	41	23

DIVISION 2

		Home					Away				
	P	W	D	L	F	A	W	D	L	F	A	Pts
1 Brechin C	39	13	5	2	46	17	8	8	3	31	21	55
2 Meadowbank T	39	13	2	4	37	20	10	6	4	27	25	54
3 Arbroath	39	14	4	2	45	23	7	3	9	33	28	49
4 Forfar Ath	39	8	9	2	31	16	10	3	7	27	22	48
5 Stirling A	39	12	5	2	35	17	6	5	9	22	24	46
6 East Fife	36	8	5	6	35	20	8	6	6	33	23	43
7 Queen of the S	39	8	6	6	44	30	9	2	8	31	35	42
8 Cowdenbeath	39	10	4	5	35	25	3	8	9	19	28	38
9 Berwick R	39	6	7	6	25	30	7	3	10	22	30	36
10 Albion R	39	10	2	8	29	23	4	4	11	26	43	34
11 Stenhousemuir	39	4	8	8	22	33	3	7	9	21	33	29
12 Stranraer	39	6	4	10	21	32	4	3	12	25	47	27
13 East Stirling	39	4	4	12	20	38	3	5	11	21	41	23
14 Montrose	39	5	2	12	18	33	3	4	13	19	53	22

SCHWEPPES CHAMPIONSHIP 1983

	P	W	L	D	Bonus Bt	Bonus Bl	Pts
1 Essex (7)	24	11	5	8	69	79	324
2 Middlesex (1)	23	11	4	8	60	72	308
3 Hampshire (3)	24	10	2	12	62	71	289
4 Leicestershire (2)	24	9	3	12	52	81	277
5 Warwickshire (17)	24	10	3	11	52	64	276
6 Northamptonshire (9)	24	7	4	13	63	77	252
7 Kent (13)	24	7	4	13	68	70	250
8 Surrey (5)	24	7	4	13	65	70	247
9 Derbyshire (11)	24	7	5	12	46	65	219
10 Somerset (6)	24	3	7	14	57	75	180
11 Sussex (8)	23	3	10	10	50	72	170
12 { Gloucestershire (15)	23	3	8	12	56	61	165
12 { Lancashire (12)	24	3	4	17	56	61	165
14 Nottinghamshire (4)	24	3	10	11	39	62	149
15 Glamorgan (16)	24	2	10	12	45	64	141
16 Worcestershire (14)	24	2	11	11	43	54	129
17 Yorkshire (10)	23	1	5	17	45	64	125

1982 positions in brackets.

Hampshire and Derbyshire totals each include 12 points for a win in a match reduced to one innings.

JOHN PLAYER LEAGUE 1983

	P	W	L	Tie	NR	Pts
1 Yorkshire (16)	16	10	3	0	3	46
2 Somerset (9)	16	10	3	0	3	46
3 Kent (4)	16	8	3	0	5	42
4 Sussex (1)	16	9	5	0	2	40
5 Hampshire (5)	16	9	6	0	1	38
6 { Derbyshire (12)	16	7	5	0	4	36
6 { Essex (5)	16	7	5	0	4	36
8 { Lancashire (10)	16	5	5	1	5	32
8 { Middlesex (2)	16	7	7	0	2	32
10 Glamorgan (10)	16	6	8	0	2	28
11 { Leicestershire (3)	16	4	7	0	5	26
11 { Surrey (12)	16	4	7	0	5	26
11 { Worcestershire (15)	16	4	7	3	2	26

		P	W	L	Tie	NR	Pts
14	Gloucestershire (14)	16	4	8	0	4	24
	Northamptonshire (8)	16	5	10	0	1	22
15	Nottinghamshire (5)	16	4	9	1	2	22
	Warwickshire (17)	16	4	9	1	2	22

1982 positions in brackets.

Yorkshire finished in first place over Somerset by virtue of their greater number of away wins. This criteria applied only for the first four placings.

RUGBY UNION by Stephen Jones

RUGBY WAS pursued by a relentless and even malevolent force throughout the decade – itself. The single greatest problems for the game lay in coming to terms with its own expansion and success and that process caused pain.

The game worldwide strode on. By 1989, it was being played regularly in around 113 countries; internationals and top domestic rugby in the eight member countries of the International Rugby Board – England, Wales, Scotland, Ireland, South Africa, New Zealand, France and Australia – attracted enormous public interest, and sponsorship. For example, the 10 games of the Five Nations championship in Europe became the most popular sporting attraction in the country, bar none. A monstrous black market for tickets was created. Company sponsorships of rugby became so popular that, for example, the Rugby Football Union in England drew up short lists over 10 multinationals for their major competitions and events.

Yet in all this there was a dramatic and final drift away from the old concept of the sport – a few mates banding together for fun, and possibly to win, and all as a recreation and escape from the daily grind. For the leading players in the major countries, it was almost as if their daily lives, their family and work, became the release and the sport itself provided the pressure.

The game now had to produce winners throughout – leagues came in and expanded massively so that we knew the best club in the district, county, country. The world cup concept finally arrived so that we knew the best country in the world. The inaugural tournament, a marvellous success, took place in Australia and New Zealand in 1987. For the first time, rugby began to dabble in self-promotion, instead of allowing its essential basic goodnesses to spread unheralded.

Of course, the myriad lower orders of the game continued on much as before – but suddenly, the top players in the various international squads and leading clubs were asked to sacrifice and to sacrifice again. By 1990, they often had to train six days per week, to spend increasing and even frightening amounts of time away from home and job.

And the upshot of the whole process was utterly inevitable – pressure on the game's first principle, amateurism. By 1990 there was still no significant demand from any section of the game that players should be paid direct; but in the last two years of the decade, the pressures growing alarmingly, there was a powerful lobby in the game, which included the vast majority of the best players, that the amateur laws should finally be dismantled and that players should be allowed to retain the proceeds of the ancillary activities – from books and articles, speeches and personal appearances.

The players and their families realised that they were being pushed beyond the limits of what could be expected of an amateur sportsman. There was also the ultra-commercialism of sport and the outside world to hasten the process. In fact, there were indeed proposals that by the end of 1990 the laws relating to amateurism would be eased.

The chief opponent of easing and therefore the main upholder of a kind of neo-Victorian amateurism, was the RFU. This was ironic in that it was chiefly the authorities themselves who drove the players to the limit by increasing the number of pressure games and the demands; chiefly the Unions who had lost the sympathy of the players years before by ruthlessly crushing aspirations – players lived for years with the image of the top rugby official in the front of an aircraft while the team cram in the back; of a rugby official with more tickets for the big matches than the players – all these prepared players mentally for the day when they would demand a slice of the action.

However, at the end of the 1980s the players themselves, the foundation of the massive revenues flowing in to the RFU and the other Unions, were still occasionally travelling cattle class – one England captain could not take his wife to watch him captain his country in Paris because he could not afford to and no-one else would pay. The Welsh national team, on tour in New Zealand in 1988, had to sleep wearing jerseys and track-suits because their nameless, faceless motel was cold and unheated.

Of course, amateurism has served rugby wonderfully well. It is the staple, the foundation of the fierce and forgiving greatness of the whole pursuit. But in the commercial world, in the era of leagues and the World Cup, the relaxation of the amateur laws became inevitable; pockets of opposition could not halt a tide.

When the training was over and before the bickering about rewards began, there were some dazzling occasions. The World Cup was a pyrotechnic experience and, fittingly, it was won by New Zealand. This was an apt tribute to the greatest team in the world at the time and, in fact, only a harbinger of greater things. New Zealand lost a match in France before the tournament but they were not to lose again in the decade.

By 1989 they were probably the most ruthlessly efficient team the world has seen. In particular, the old rivalry between the All Blacks and Wales had been devalued as the Welsh went down to four crashing defeats inside three years. As Welsh rugby suffered and almost sank – they lost twice in the decade to Romania – there were signs that England's revival, long promised and often dashed, was approaching.

New Zealand set the tactical guidelines too. They took the games away from giant, immovable scrummaging forwards and invested power with faster, sleeker players and in a scientific fitness programme. Their dedication and commitment were astonishing. Other countries matched them for individuals – Serge Blanco, the great French full-back, spanned the decade with rich talents; David Campese, the unorthodox and brilliant Australia wing, was probably the most charismatic figure in the game; towards the end of the decade, Jeremy Guscott, a young Bath centre, promised to take over that mantle in the 1990s and he took a full part in the first stirrings of a British revival when he played for the successful 1989 Lions in Australia.

Yet the only team which would have run New Zealand close for team effort took the field only for furtive scratch matches. South Africa remained nominally inside the fold because of the continuing membership of the International Rugby Board, but the whole question of South African contacts hammered rugby's image. Several times, clandestine tourist parties were formed to tour and the two most important – a New Zealand Cavaliers team in 1985 and a World XV tour in 1989 – did provide some international competition for the legions of the sports-starved.

The International Board themselves were unreasonably lenient on South Africa and allowed them to remain in membership even when an Everest of circumstantial evidence confirmed the worldwide rumours that at least some of the 'rebel' visitors were bought in. It was a graphic illustration of the lack of leadership, the under-the-counter dealing, the secretive non-revealing nature of the Board. The only hope is that the eight member unions disband the Board in its present form and install a democratic, accountable and dynamic organisation. The only good news was that rugby flourished in spite of its governors.

Indeed, it forged ahead of itself.

Worm's-eye view in the Champion Hurdle at Cheltenham.

Hang gliding off Beachy Head, 1985.

RUGBY LEAGUE: *January 29*
Great Britain, playing in Avignon, beat France 12–0.

ICE SKATING: *February 14*
Jayne Torvill and Christopher Dean spellbind crowd and judges to win the Olympic gold for ice dancing. All nine judges gave them a maximum score for artistic impression after witnessing their Bolero routine. Only the world championships beckon before they turn professional.

RUGBY UNION: *February*
Scotland win their first Triple Crown since 1938 and in the process win the 100th Calcutta Cup match when they beat England 18–6 at Murrayfield. They also take the Grand Slam.

RUGBY LEAGUE: *February 17*
Five goals from Hobbs earn Great Britain a 10–0 win over France in Leeds.

BADMINTON: *February*
England's women team won the silver medal in the Uber Cup finals in Kuala Lumpur, earning them the honour as second best in the world. But money poured into the sport by China, South Korea, Indonesia and the USSR makes the likelihood of Britain reaching such a position again highly unlikely.

BOAT RACE: *March 18*
Oxford set the record time of 16min 45secs as they beat Cambridge.

ATHLETICS: *April 16*
South African Zola Budd, the waif-like schoolgirl who runs barefoot and broke Mary Decker's 5,000m record in January, is given a British passport and will run for her adopted country in the Olympics in Los Angeles. It took just 13 days for Budd to be granted British citizenship but taking into account what was to happen in Los Angeles, perhaps even she might have wished it had turned out differently.

SNOOKER: April 23–May 7

Steve Davis retains his World Championship crown when he beats Jimmy White 18–16 in the final in Sheffield.

RACING: May 1

John Francome retires having ridden 1,138 winners beating Stan Mellor's jump benchmark of 1,035. He rode his 1,000th winner in February.

OLYMPICS: May 8

The Soviet Union withdraws from the Los Angeles Olympic Games. The move is put down to a fear over security arrangements for their competitors and has been expected for four years since the Americans boycotted Moscow.

SOCCER: May 19

Everton settle the Cup Final against Watford within 90 minutes for the first time in four seasons thanks to goals from Sharp and Andy Gray. In Scotland Aberdeen completed the League and Cup double when they beat Celtic 2–1 in a bad tempered match. Six players were booked and Celtic's Roy Aitken was sent off. The match was settled in extra time. Black and McGhee scored for Aberdeen and Paul McStay hit the Celtic goal.

SOCCER: May 23

Spurs win the UEFA Cup after beating Anderlecht on penalties. Both games ended in 1–1 draws.

SOCCER: May 30

Liverpool and Roma draw 1–1 in the European Cup in Italy's Olympic Stadium. Liverpool take the trophy after winning the penalty shoot-out 4–2.

CRICKET: May 31

Viv Richards hits the highest one-day international score at Old Trafford when he takes an undefeated 189 off England, still the highest score in a one-day match. And so began the summer of the blackwash. The sun shone, the golden Boy of English cricket, David Gower was captain but the West Indies still created a record by becoming the first touring team to have a 100 per cent record in a full Test series: 5–0. They lost only a solitary one-day international, otherwise were undefeated. England never recovered from Old Trafford as brave young Englishmen came to do battle and retired hurt with broken bones never again to play Test cricket: Andy Lloyd of Warwickshire, Paul Terry of Hampshire. One old campaigner, Pat Pocock, recalled to Test cricket took refuge in the helmet and a form of aerial gymnastics to ward off Malcolm Marshall.

RACING: June 6

Secreto wins the Derby by a short head from El Gran Senor with Mighty Flutter third. Seventeen horses were in the running for the prize of £227,680.

RUGBY LEAGUE: June 9

The opening match of Great Britain's tour to Australia is lost 25–8 in Sydney and there is only a slight improvement two weeks later when the teams meet in Brisbane. This time Britain lose 18–6.

SOCCER: June 27

France win the European Championship in Paris when they beat Spain 2–0. Platini, with his ninth goal of the tournament, scored in the second half but it was not until injury time that Bellone put the result beyond doubt. France had easily been the team of the tournament but on the day of the final French fear of defeat seemed to be passed on to the players who threatened to freeze on the big occasion.

TENNIS: June 25–July 8

It is a repeat for Wimbledon as McEnroe retains his title against Jimmy Connors, 6–1, 6–1, 6–2 and Martina Navratilova defeats Chris Evert-Lloyd 7–6, 6–2. McEnroe earned £100,000, up £34,000 on the previous year and Navratilova collected an extra £30,000 when she pocketed her cheque for £90,000. Astonishingly all defending champions were successful. John Lloyd and Wendy Turnbull won the mixed doubles, Navratilova and Pam Shriver the women's doubles and McEnroe, partnered by Peter Fleming, the men's doubles.

RUGBY LEAGUE: July 7

Great Britain struggle on but the margin of defeat is much the same as they lose the series to Australia after going down 20–7 in Sydney. A week later they continue their tour in New Zealand but the mantle of defeat fits and they lose 12–0 in Auckland. The next match in Christchurch is lost 28–12 and the final Test of the tour back in Auckland is also lost, 32–16.

GOLF: July 22

Sevriano Ballesteros wins The Open at St Andrews with a 276 for a two shots win over Bernhard Langer and last year's winner Tom Watson.

OLYMPIC GAMES: July 28–August 11

The spectacular money-making 23rd Olympics could never stage-manage dramas as memorable as those which happened on the field of competition. Mary Decker, America's golden girl, collided with Britain's recently adopted Zola Budd in the 3000m. Decker, of whom so much was expected, crashed to the ground clutching her side and was carried from the track by her husband Richard Slaney to tearfully blame Budd for the incident. For the first time a positive drugs test led to the Finn Martti Vainio being disqualified after coming second in the 10,000m. Meanwhile Carl Lewis continued to deliver. He won the 100m and 200m, the long jump and collected a gold for the 4 × 100m relay. British successes were Tessa Sanderson in the javelin, Daley Thompson won the decathlon, Sebastian Coe won 800m silver and gold in the 1500m. In the swimming pool Neil Cochran collected two bronze medals, first in the 200m medley then with teammates Paul Easter, Paul Howe and Andrew Astbury in the 4 × 200m freestyle relay. Sarah Hardcastle won bronze in the women's 800m freestyle. Britain's only boxing medal was a bronze for Robert Wells. The gold was won by Tyrell Biggs who went on to fight Mike Tyson, run into problems over drugs and was beaten by British heavyweight hopeful Gary Mason in October 1989. Weightlifter David Mercer collected bronze in the middle heavyweight category while Neil Eckersley and Kerrith Brown won bronzes in judo. Brown was to reach the winner's podium again in the Seoul Olympics in 1988 but was stripped of his medal after failing a drugs test. Neil Adams collected a silver at halfmiddleweight. Britain won the coxed fours rowing gold and picked up bronze in sailing in the Flying Dutchman class. Equestrian sports provided silver for the three day eventing team and for the grand prix jumping team while Virginia Holgate collected the individual three day eventing bronze. Malcolm Cooper continued to excel at shooting and was Britain's first gold medal winner of the games in the small bore rifle, combined, 3 positions. Alister Allan won the bronze. The British hockey team laid the foundations for a golden future when they surprisingly picked up the bronze medal.

RUGBY LEAGUE: August 5
At Mount Hagen Great Britain overcame Papua-New Guinea 38–20.

MOTOR RACING: October 21
Niki Lauda in a McLaren wins the world championship for the third time in Estoril, Portugal but really Lauda belonged to the 70s. This era was dominated by a softly-spoken, deep-thinking Frenchman, dubbed The Professor, who won his third world championship in 1989 after one of the most acrimonious seasons in memory. But as Alain Prost collected the title and headed for his new team, Ferrari, he could reflect on a period when, for the best part of it, he seemed destined to always be the bridesmaid.

In 1983 he had been beaten to the world championship by Piquet who had a winning margin of just two points. This time Lauda beat him to the title by a half-point in the last race of the season. Lauda had defied death after a terrible crash in 1976, retired and returned to prove he could still do it. Just when questions were being asked as to whether Prost could go all the way, he produced the answer. He won the championship driving a McLaren-TAG in 1985 and 1986 and repeated the success in a McLaren-Honda in 1989. That was a bitter-sweet triumph for Prost who had spent the season battling with his team-mate Ayrton Senna. Senna, the defending world champion, and Prost were supposed to be given equal status in the team. But early in the season Prost felt Senna had gone back on a deal over race tactics. While Senna incurred the wrath of other drivers, notably Nigel Mansell, Prost felt he was not getting the best deal from his team and he resigned in July 1989, signing for Ferrari two months later.

CRICKET: November 26

In the winter sun of India, English cricket, unexpectedly, recovered. The tour could not have got off to a worse start; Mrs Gandhi was assassinated the morning the team arrived in Delhi and the the first Test was lost to the leg-spin of Sivaramakrishnan. And only hours after the England team had been entertained by Percy Norris, the British Deputy High Commissioner to Western India, Mr Norris was murdered. But in the second Test, through the impetuosity of the Indians and the steady virtues of their own spinners Pocock and Edmonds, at last, David Gower had something to smile about.

BOXING: December 9

It was revealed that a cartel of the four leading figures were covertly sharing the bulk of the profits of the sport in Britain between them. The four – Mickey Duff, Jarvis Astaire, Mike Barrett and the manager, Terry Lawless – signed a secret contract in 1979 to split equally the profits from their various boxing activities. The revelations caused an uproar and the British Boxing Board of Control decided to investigate the matter. The board eventually cleared the four of any wrongdoing. However, the cartel never recovered from this bodyblow. By the end of the decade Mike Barrett had quit the cartel, and other entrepreneurs were flourishing in what used to be the preserve of the cartel.

ROLL OF HONOUR

AMERICAN FOOTBALL: Superbowl: Los Angeles Raiders 38 Washington Redskins 9.

CRICKET: County championship: Essex. John Player League: Essex. NatWest Trophy: Middlesex. Benson & Hedges Cup: Lancashire.

CYCLING: Tour de France, Men: Laurent Fignon (France). Women: M. Martin (US).

DARTS: World Championship: Eric Bristow.

GOLF: US Masters: Ben Crenshaw. US PGA: Lee Trevino. US Open: Fuzzy Zoeller. The Open (St Andrews): Seve Ballesteros.

HORSE RACING: Flat:
1000 Guineas: Pebbles. 2000 Guineas: El Gran Senor. The Derby: Secreto (Jockey: Christy Roche. Trainer: David O'Brien). The Oaks: Sun Princess. St Leger: Sun Princess. Champion jockey Steve Cauthen, 130 wins. Top trainer Henry Cecil, £551,939.

National Hunt: Grand National: Hallo Dandy (Jockey: Neale Doughty. Trainer: Gordon Richards). Cheltenham Gold Cup: Burrough Hill Lad. Champion Hurdle: Dawn Run. Champion jockey John Francome, 131 wins. Top trainer Michael Dickinson, £266,146.

MOTOR RACING: Niki Lauda (Austria) in a McLaren-TAG. Constructors' Cup: McLaren-Porsche.

RUGBY LEAGUE: Challenge Cup: Widnes. Championship: Hull Kingston Rovers.

RUGBY UNION: Grand Slam and Triple Crown: Scotland. County Championship: Middlesex. Pilkington Cup: Bath 10 Bristol 9. Schweppes Welsh Cup: Cardiff 24 Neath 19.

SKIING: Overall champion, Men: Pirmin Zurbriggen (Switzerland). Women: Erika Hess (Switzerland).

SNOOKER: World Championship: Steve Davis 18 Jimmy White 16.

SOCCER: First Division Title: Liverpool (80pts). Runners-up: Southampton. FA Cup: Everton 2 Watford 0. Milk Cup: Liverpool 1 Everton 0 (after replay 0–0). Scotland: Premier League Title: Aberdeen (57pts). Runners-up: Celtic. Scottish Cup: Aberdeen 2 Celtic 1. Scottish League Cup: Rangers 3 Celtic 2. European Cup: Liverpool 1 AS Roma 1, Liverpool win 4–2 on penalties. European Cup Winners' Cup: Juventus 2 FC Porto 1. UEFA Cup: Tottenham beat Anderlecht on penalties. (H) 1–1 (A) 1–1. European Championship (Paris): France 2 Spain 0.

SPEEDWAY: World Champion: Erik Gundersen (Denmark). British League: Ipswich.

SQUASH: World Open Championship: Jahangir Khan (Pakistan).

TENNIS: Wimbledon: Men: John McEnroe (US) beat Jimmy Connors (US) 6–1, 6–1, 6–2. Women: Martina Navratilova (US) beat Chris Evert-Lloyd (US) 7–6, 6–2. US Open: John McEnroe, Martina Navratilova. French Open: Ivan Lendl (Cze), Martina Navratilova. Australian Open: Mats Wilander (Sweden), Chris Evert-Lloyd. Davis Cup: Sweden. Wightman Cup: US beat Britain 5–2.

CANON LEAGUE 1983–84

DIVISION 1

		Home					Away					
	P	W	D	L	F	A	W	D	L	F	A	Pts
1 Liverpool	42	14	5	2	50	12	8	9	4	23	20	80
2 Southampton	42	15	4	2	44	17	7	7	7	22	21	77
3 Nottingham F	42	14	4	3	47	17	8	4	9	29	28	74
4 Manchester U	42	14	3	4	43	18	6	11	4	28	23	74
5 QPR	42	14	4	3	37	12	8	3	10	30	25	73
6 Arsenal	42	10	5	6	41	29	8	4	9	33	31	63
7 Everton	42	9	9	3	21	12	7	5	9	23	30	62
8 Tottenham H	42	11	4	6	31	24	6	6	9	33	41	61
9 West Ham U	42	10	4	7	39	24	7	5	9	21	31	60
10 Aston Villa	42	14	3	4	34	22	3	6	12	25	39	60
11 Watford	42	9	7	5	36	31	7	2	12	32	46	57
12 Ipswich T	42	11	4	6	34	23	4	4	13	21	34	53
13 Sunderland	42	8	9	4	26	18	5	4	12	16	35	52
14 Norwich C	42	9	8	4	34	20	3	7	11	14	29	51
15 Leicester C	42	11	5	5	40	30	2	7	12	25	38	51
16 Luton T	42	7	5	9	30	33	7	4	10	23	33	51
17 WBA	42	10	4	7	30	25	4	5	12	18	37	51
18 Stoke C	42	11	4	6	30	23	2	7	12	14	40	50
19 Coventry C	42	8	5	8	33	33	5	6	10	24	44	50
20 Birmingham C	42	7	7	7	19	18	5	5	11	20	32	48
21 Notts Co	42	6	7	8	31	36	4	4	13	19	36	41
22 Wolverhampton W	42	4	8	9	15	28	2	3	16	12	52	29

DIVISION 2

		Home					Away					
	P	W	D	L	F	A	W	D	L	F	A	Pts
1 Chelsea	42	15	4	2	55	17	10	9	2	35	23	88
2 Sheffield W	42	16	4	1	47	16	10	6	5	25	18	88
3 Newcastle U	42	16	2	3	51	18	8	6	7	34	35	80
4 Manchester C	42	13	3	5	43	21	7	7	7	23	27	70
5 Grimsby T	42	13	6	2	36	15	6	7	8	24	32	70
6 Blackburn R	42	9	11	1	35	19	8	5	8	22	27	67
7 Carlisle U	42	10	9	2	29	13	6	7	8	19	28	64
8 Shrewsbury T	42	13	5	3	34	18	4	5	12	15	35	61
9 Brighton & HA	42	11	6	4	42	17	6	3	12	27	43	60
10 Leeds U	42	13	4	4	33	16	3	8	10	22	40	60
11 Fulham	42	9	6	6	35	24	6	6	9	25	29	57

		Home					Away					
	P	W	D	L	F	A	W	D	L	F	A	Pts
12 Huddersfield T	42	8	6	7	27	20	6	9	6	29	29	57
13 Charlton Ath	42	13	4	4	40	26	3	5	13	13	38	57
14 Barnsley	42	9	6	6	33	23	6	1	14	24	30	52
15 Cardiff C	42	11	3	7	32	27	4	3	14	21	39	51
16 Portsmouth	42	8	3	10	46	32	6	4	11	27	32	49
17 Middlesbrough	42	9	8	4	26	18	2	5	13	15	29	49
18 Crystal Palace	42	8	5	8	18	18	4	6	11	24	34	47
19 Oldham Ath	42	10	6	5	33	27	3	2	16	14	46	47
20 Derby Co	42	9	5	7	26	26	2	4	15	10	46	42
21 Swansea C	42	7	4	10	20	28	0	4	17	16	57	29
22 Cambridge U	42	4	7	10	20	33	0	5	16	8	44	24

DIVISION 3

		Home					Away					
	P	W	D	L	F	A	W	D	L	F	A	Pts
1 Oxford U	46	17	5	1	58	22	11	6	6	33	28	95
2 Wimbledon	46	15	5	3	58	35	11	4	8	39	41	87
3 Sheffield U	46	14	7	2	56	18	10	4	9	30	35	83
4 Hull C	46	16	5	2	42	11	7	9	7	29	27	83
5 Bristol R	46	16	5	2	47	21	6	8	9	21	33	79
6 Walsall	46	14	4	5	44	22	8	5	10	24	39	75
7 Bradford C	46	11	9	3	46	30	9	2	12	27	35	71
8 Gillingham	46	13	4	6	50	29	7	6	10	24	40	70
9 Millwall	46	16	4	3	42	18	2	9	12	29	47	67
10 Bolton W	46	13	4	6	36	17	5	6	12	20	43	64
11 Orient	46	13	5	5	40	27	5	4	14	31	54	63
12 Burnley	46	12	5	6	52	25	4	9	10	24	36	62
13 Newport Co	46	11	9	3	35	27	5	5	13	23	48	62
14 Lincoln C	46	11	4	8	42	29	6	6	11	17	33	61
15 Wigan Ath	46	11	5	7	26	18	5	8	10	20	38	61
16 Preston NE	46	12	5	6	42	27	3	6	14	24	39	56
17 Bournemouth	46	11	5	7	38	27	5	2	16	25	46	55
18 Rotherham U	46	10	5	8	29	17	5	4	14	28	47	54
19 Plymouth Arg	46	11	8	4	38	17	2	4	17	18	45	51
20 Brentford	46	8	9	6	41	30	3	7	13	28	49	49
21 Scunthorpe U	46	9	9	5	40	31	0	10	13	14	42	46
22 Southend U	46	8	9	6	34	24	2	5	16	21	52	44
23 Port Vale	46	10	4	9	33	29	1	6	16	18	54	43
24 Exeter C	46	4	8	11	27	39	2	7	14	23	45	33

DIVISION 4

			Home				Away				
	P	W	D	L	F	A	W	D	L	F	A	Pts
1 York C	46	18	4	1	58	16	13	4	6	38	23	101
2 Doncaster R	46	15	6	2	46	22	9	7	7	36	32	85
3 Reading	46	17	6	0	51	14	5	10	8	33	42	82
4 Bristol C	46	18	3	2	51	17	6	7	10	19	27	82
5 Aldershot	46	14	6	3	49	29	8	3	12	27	40	75
6 Blackpool	46	15	4	4	47	19	6	5	12	23	33	72
7 Peterborough U	46	15	5	3	52	16	3	9	11	20	32	68
8 Colchester U	46	14	7	2	45	14	3	9	11	24	39	67
9 Torquay U	46	13	7	3	32	18	5	6	12	27	46	67
10 Tranmere R	46	11	5	7	33	26	6	10	7	20	27	66
11 Hereford U	46	11	6	6	31	21	5	9	9	23	32	63
12 Stockport Co	46	12	5	6	34	25	5	6	12	26	39	62
13 Chesterfield	46	10	11	2	34	24	5	4	14	25	37	60
14 Darlington	46	13	4	6	31	19	4	4	15	18	31	59
15 Bury	46	9	7	7	34	32	6	7	10	27	32	59
16 Crewe Alex	46	10	8	5	35	27	6	3	14	21	40	59
17 Swindon T	46	11	7	5	34	23	4	6	13	24	33	58
18 Northampton T	46	10	8	5	32	32	3	6	14	21	46	53
19 Mansfield T	46	9	7	7	44	27	4	6	13	22	43	52
20 Wrexham	46	7	6	10	34	33	4	9	10	25	41	48
21 Halifax T	46	11	6	6	36	25	1	6	16	19	64	48
22 Rochdale	46	8	9	6	35	31	3	4	16	17	49	46
23 Hartlepool U	46	7	8	8	31	28	3	2	18	16	57	40
24 Chester C	46	7	5	11	23	35	0	8	15	22	47	34

SCOTTISH LEAGUE 1983–84

PREMIER DIVISION

			Home				Away				
	P	W	D	L	F	A	W	D	L	F	A	Pts
1 Aberdeen	36	14	3	1	46	12	11	4	3	32	9	57
2 Celtic	36	13	5	0	46	15	8	3	7	34	26	50
3 Dundee U	36	11	3	4	38	14	7	8	3	29	25	47
4 Rangers	36	7	8	3	26	18	8	4	6	27	23	42
5 Hearts	36	5	9	4	23	23	5	7	6	15	24	36
6 St Mirren	36	8	6	4	34	23	1	8	9	21	36	32
7 Hibernian	36	7	4	7	21	21	5	3	10	24	34	31
8 Dundee	36	6	1	11	28	42	5	4	9	22	32	27
9 St Johnstone	36	6	1	11	19	33	4	2	12	17	48	23
10 Motherwell	36	2	5	11	15	36	2	2	14	16	39	15

DIVISION 1

	P	W	D	L	F	A	W	D	L	F	A	Pts
			Home						Away			
1 Morton	39	10	6	3	36	21	11	6	3	39	25	54
2 Dumbarton	39	13	4	3	37	19	7	7	5	29	25	51
3 Partick Th	39	11	5	4	37	20	8	3	8	30	30	46
4 Clydebank	39	10	5	5	38	29	6	8	5	24	21	45
5 Brechin C	39	11	4	4	33	22	3	10	7	23	36	42
6 Kilmarnock	39	10	4	5	31	17	6	2	12	26	36	38
7 Falkirk	39	8	5	7	27	25	8	1	10	19	29	38
8 Clyde	39	6	8	5	28	23	6	5	9	25	27	37
9 Hamilton A	39	6	8	5	27	22	5	6	9	16	24	36
10 Adrieonians	39	10	3	7	20	21	3	7	9	25	32	36
11 Meadowbank Th	39	8	4	8	29	35	4	6	9	20	34	34
12 Ayr U	39	5	8	6	29	32	5	4	11	27	38	32
13 Raith R	39	6	6	8	33	30	4	5	10	20	32	31
14 Alloa	39	7	5	7	24	24	1	5	14	17	40	26

DIVISION 2

	P	W	D	L	F	A	W	D	L	F	A	Pts
			Home						Away			
1 Forfar Ath	39	16	4	0	45	13	11	5	3	28	18	63
2 East Fife	39	11	3	6	31	21	9	4	6	26	21	47
3 Berwick R	39	11	5	4	35	13	5	6	8	22	25	43
4 Stirling A	39	9	5	6	23	18	5	9	5	28	24	42
5 Arbroath	39	10	3	6	32	25	8	3	9	19	21	42
6 Queen of the S	39	11	6	2	29	15	5	4	11	22	31	42
7 Stenhousemuir	39	10	5	4	30	25	4	6	10	17	32	39
8 Stranraer	39	9	7	3	25	16	4	5	11	22	31	38
9 Dunfermline Ath	39	7	7	5	25	16	6	3	11	19	29	36
10 Queen's Park	39	10	4	6	35	28	4	4	11	23	35	36
11 East Stirling	39	4	4	11	23	37	6	7	7	31	29	31
12 Montrose	39	7	3	10	17	28	5	4	10	19	31	31
13 Cowdenbeath	39	5	5	10	21	29	5	4	10	23	29	29
14 Albion R	39	3	7	9	24	37	5	4	11	22	39	27

BRITANNIC ASSURANCE CHAMPIONSHIP 1984

		P	W	L	Tie	D	Bt	Bl	Pts
							Bonus		
1	Essex (1)	24	13	3	0	8	64	83	355
2	Nottinghamshire (14)	24	12	3	0	9	68	81	341
3	Middlesex (2)	24	8	7	0	9	63	78	269
4	Leicestershire (4)	24	8	2	0	14	60	78	266
5	Kent (7)	24	8	3	2	11	45	65	254
6	Sussex (11)	24	7	6	1	10	54	79	249
7	Somerset (10)	24	6	7	0	11	60	78	234
8	Surrey (8)	24	6	6	0	12	62	72	230
9	Warwickshire (5)	24	6	7	0	11	71	60	227
10	Worcestershire (16)	24	5	5	0	14	66	74	220
11	Northamptonshire (6)	24	5	9	1	9	58	56	202
12	Derbyshire (9)	24	4	6	0	14	72	66	202
13	Glamorgan (15)	24	4	2	0	18	65	71	200
14	Yorkshire (17)	24	5	4	0	15	59	55	194
15	Hampshire (3)	24	3	13	0	8	58	62	168
16	Lancashire (12)	24	1	9	0	14	49	72	137
17	Gloucestershire (12)	24	1	10	0	13	56	61	133

1983 positions are shown in brackets.

Sussex's total includes 12 points for a win in a match reduced to one innings.

JOHN PLAYER LEAGUE 1984

		P	W	L	Tie	NR	Pts
1	Essex (6)	16	12	3	1	0	50
2	Nottinghamshire (15)	16	10	5	0	1	42
3	Sussex (4)	16	9	4	0	3	42
4	Lancashire (8)	16	10	6	0	0	40
5	Middlesex (8)	16	9	5	1	1	40
	Worcestershire (11)	16	9	5	0	2	40
7	Warwickshire (15)	16	7	6	0	3	34
8	Surrey (11)	16	7	7	0	2	32
9	Glamorgan (10)	16	6	8	0	2	28
	Hampshire (5)	16	7	9	0	0	28
	Kent (3)	16	6	8	0	2	28

		P	W	L	Tie	NR	Pts
12	Northamptonshire (15)	16	6	9	0	1	26
13	Gloucestershire (14)	16	5	9	0	2	24
	Leicestershire (11)	16	4	8	0	4	24
	Somerset (2)	16	5	9	0	2	24
	Yorkshire (1)	16	6	10	0	0	24
17	Derbyshire (6)	16	4	11	0	1	18

1983 positions in brackets.

OLYMPIC GAMES: LOS ANGELES LEADING MEDAL WINNERS

	G	S	B	Tot
United States	83	61	31	175
Romania	20	16	17	53
West Germany	17	19	23	59
China	15	8	9	32
Italy	14	6	12	32
Canada	10	18	16	44
Japan	10	8	14	32
New Zealand	8	1	2	11
Yugoslavia	7	4	7	18
Korea	6	6	7	19
Great Britain	5	11	21	37
France	5	7	16	28
Netherlands	5	2	6	13
Australia	4	8	12	24
Finland	4	2	6	12

BOXING by HARRY MULLAN

THE DAY after Marvin Hagler defeated Thomas Hearns in the greatest fight of the eighties, I was standing in the check-in queue at McCarran Airport, Las Vegas. Behind me was a stocky, nondescript black man wearing sunglasses, a shabby denim suit and cap, and carrying a holdall. He looked as if he had come to check the central heating, or repair the boiler.

It took me fully ten seconds to realise that it was Hagler, and that in the holdall were the championship belts and the gloves which, a few hours earlier, had added another $8m to his bank balance.

But then Hagler always was the self-effacing type, the kind of man who could draw a crowd of 20,000 and then lose himself in it. Sugar Ray Leonard had the showbiz glamour, Robert Duran the posturing machismo, Mike Tyson the air of brooding menace. Hagler needed none of those props; he was a working professional fighter, and a better one pound-for-pound than any of those luminaries.

He personified the honest-to-goodness grafter, a blue-collar champion who did his job, collected his cheque and went home, shunning the fuss, the fans and the phonies. He dominated the middleweight division for nearly a decade, winning the title from Alan Minter on a night at Wembley in 1980 when the racism which is always latent in British boxing bubbled over and shamed the sport. Over the next seven years he beat off all comers until Leonard, aided by what I considered to be biased scoring, dethroned him in Las Vegas. It was Hagler's 13th defence of the title, one short of Carlos Monzon's all-time record, and the loss was only his third in 67 fights.

The injustice of that decision gnawed at Hagler. He valued his championship above anything in his life, and when it was taken away from him he went haywire. The drugs and alcohol in which he sought solace cost him his marriage and his peace of mind. Leonard, typically, was unrepentant when he learned of the catastrophic toll defeat had taken. 'I set out to mess up his life, and that's what I did', he said chillingly, forfeiting with a single sentence the affection and respect which his monumental talent merited.

Hagler was a throwback fighter, one of the old-school professionals who battled his way up through the ranks and never cut a corner in his life. Joe Frazier offered a memorable summary of Hagler's struggle for recognition when he told him: 'You've got three strikes against you – you're black, you're a southpaw, and you're good.' Frazier might have added that Marvin was also stubborn, proud, and fiercely independent, qualities which would not allow him or his loyal managers, the Petronelli brothers, to sign their souls away to one of the major promoters or television networks and thereby smooth their path to the title. As a consequence, Hagler reached the top years later than he should have.

It took him seven years to win the championship, and as long to lose it. On that April night in 1985 when he faced Hearns in the outdoor arena at Caesar's Palace, I doubt if a finer middleweight ever walked . . . and that includes the legends like Harry Greb, Ray Robinson and Carlos Monzon.

Classic fights happen once in a generation, when two great fighters reach their peak simultaneously. This was one of those nights, and even now I tingle to recall it. Hearns had been a thrilling welterweight champion until Ray Leonard found his measure in this same Caesar's ring in 1981. Since then the lanky puncher from Detroit had won a version of the light-middleweight title, and now he sought to become a three-time champion at Hagler's expense.

The combination of Hearns's potential for the dramatic with Hagler's cold and ruthless professionalism meant instant box office appeal, and between them the pair generated more than $30m. Hagler was guaranteed $5.3m, Hearns $5.2m, but closed-circuit and ancillary rights boosted their take to over $8m apiece.

That worked out at around $1m per minute . . . and they were worth every cent. I watched the fight from the ringside, near enough to the action to reach up and touch their boots, and the sense of being so close to one of the epic events in the game's history was overwhelming.

There was genuine antipathy between them, dating back to the cancellation of the match when it had first been scheduled three years previously. 'I don't like Marvin', Hearns announced. 'Never have, never will. I just want to tell you something: get there early and sit tight. Don't blink. You might miss the fight.'

He was almost right: the first round was an absolute explosion of violence, of an intensity and ferocity I had never before seen in a ring. The pair smashed thunderous, yet educated blows at each other, all of them designed to 'destruct and destroy', as Hagler's catch-phrase had it. There were no range-finding jabs, no gradual warming into the fight: every punch would have annihilated a lesser man.

Until then, I had considered myself to be a fairly blasé fight reporter who had long since passed through the awe-struck and wide-eyed 'fan' stage, but this level of excitement was unbearable; I felt my chest tighten, and struggled for breath, fearing an imminent heart attack. The action unfolded directly above me, as Hearns stood with his back to the ropes trading mighty hooks. The round seemed interminable, and I prayed for the bell to ring ... but there was yet more drama to come. With 30 seconds to go, blood spurted from a long vertical cut on Hagler's forehead, running down into his eyes.

It was a bad cut, and he knew it: now there was no possibility of a tactical campaign. He had to get Hearns out of there, and he came out blazing for the second round. But Hearns fired back, and a countering right split open a second cut, this time under Hagler's right eye. Hagler drove Hearns to the ropes, arms pumping, but by the end of the round he seemed to have punched himself out. The blows were landing, but they lacked snap and venom.

Hearns must have thought he had survived the crisis, and when referee Richard Steele led Hagler to the corner early in the third to inspect his injuries, the title was there for the taking. 'Can you see?', Steele asked the blood-smeared champion. 'I'm hitting him, aren't I?' was the laconic reply.

Moments later, a single punch settled it. A right hook caught Hearns flush and he lost control of his legs, staggering drunk-enly backwards and turning almost a full circle. Hagler ran after him, and three more clubbing rights left Hearns spread-eagled and motionless. He did not stir until Steele's count had reached 'six', and then somehow hauled himself upright. But Steele had seen enough, and wrapped his arms around the beaten fighter.

As it ended, I glanced over my shoulder at Sugar Ray Robin-son, seated directly behind me. The old champion was smiling, and nodding his approval of a performance he could not have bettered himself.

Keep Tyson, Leonard and the rest: Hagler was my Man of the Eighties, and that night he showed me why.

ATHLETICS by *CLIFF TEMPLE*

IN ATHLETICS, two names, greatly contrasting competitors, will be forever synonymous with the changing face of the sport during the eighties: Zola Budd and Ben Johnson.

For it was a decade in which, for the sake of circumstances and televised entertainment, a teenage girl could be paid $125,000 to take part in a race she had no hope of winning. But it was also a time when you could begin to cautiously hope and believe that maybe, after all, the drug-takers were not as immune to detection as everyone, including themselves, had previously thought.

Budd was a shy, introspective South African whose magnificent running talent was destined never to bloom as long as she lived in the Republic. But in 1984, her father and her coach managed to circumnavigate a minor inconvenience, like the world ban on South Africans competing internationally, by securing for Zola a British passport with the connivance of the British government and *The Daily Mail*.

They apparently believed that not only was the girl capable of winning a gold medal in the forthcoming Los Angeles Olympics (she wasn't), but that if she did so wearing a Union Jack the British public would stand up and cheer Maggie and the *Mail* for making it happen, having imported young Zola to England like a box of Cape apples.

Unfortunately, Zola attracted trouble, and not only from the anti-apartheid demonstrators who followed her everywhere. In the Los Angeles 3,000 metres, she accidentally tripped America's sweetheart Mary Decker (who wouldn't have won either, but don't tell the crowd), and it was the over-hyped 'rematch' at Crystal Palace in 1985 which netted an out-of-form Budd $125,000 to submit to public execution at the hands of Decker (a mere $75,000) for the sake of American TV.

That appearance money could be openly discussed at all was an eighties development too. Paying it wasn't. The brown envelopes in the car park had seemed here to stay, until the world governing body, the International Amateur Athletic Federation (IAAF), decided at its 1982 congress in Athens that an approved system of appearance money should be introduced before it lost control of the sport altogether. That money would be paid into an athlete's individual trust fund, supervised by his national federation.

Advertising contracts were permitted too, and soon Sebastian Coe was on our ITV screens every night with a steaming cup of Horlicks. There were rumours the East Germans, desperate for some middle distance runners of similar stature, were even trying to import the stuff.

It was a decade of stirring deeds on the track, and misguided actions off it, as the futility of the sporting boycott as a political weapon became clear. The Olympics of 1980 and 1984, held in Moscow and Los Angeles, were victims of tit-for-tat absences by the world super-powers, and Black Africa absented itself from the 1986 Commonwealth Games in Edinburgh, to what avail?

But the huge success of the 1988 Seoul Olympics, and the financial profit accrued, despite the boycott of Los Angeles in 1984, restored the Games to a sporting occasion which the world's cities would once again feverishly compete to host. Already battle lines are being drawn for hosting the 2004 Games.

A significant innovation in 1983 was the first IAAF World Athletics Championships, held with maximum precision and enthusiasm in that athletically inspirational city of Helsinki. It also sounded a warning to the Olympic movement that there was now a viable alternative at last.

Previously the 'world championships' had been the Olympics themselves. But if those games were to deteriorate further, then track and field now had another vehicle ready and waiting for it, while the rest of the Olympic sports, so dependent on the athletics showpiece to sustain the Games, might face a bleak future.

The second edition of the World Championships, held in Rome in 1987, ought to have reaffirmed that strength. But instead it will be remembered primarily for a scandalous incident in which the Italian long jump judges deliberately mismeasured a leap by Giovanni Evangelisti to give him (and Italy) an undeserved bronze medal. While Evangelisti knew nothing of the conspiracy it is hard to be as charitable with the top Italian officials. Even the excitable President of the IAAF, Dr Primo Nebiolo, while not being directly implicated, instead of being outraged appeared to do his best to cover up and play down the incident, and refused to discuss it with the media.

If the incident was bad enough in a sport renowned for the fairness of its competition officials, the subsequent attempted cover-up was worse and the fact that at least one of the leading Italian officials directly involved in the cheating is still intimately involved in IAAF affairs is an element of the scandal which is dragging on into the nineties. The medal, fortunately, was eventually re-awarded to the American Larry Myricks.

But elsewhere the scandal meant drugs. Throughout the decade, rumours abounded over who was on what, and from time to time a positive test would be announced. The most poetically just discovery was Martti Vainio, the tall Finnish distance runner, who was placed second in the Los Angeles Olympic 10,000m. Even before the Games ended he had been disqualified for steroid use, which baffled him as he had not touched the forbidden drug for months. But in an extended attempt to cheat, he had also 'blood doped' which entailed taking, storing and re-injecting a quantity of his own blood to supercharge his volume of red-oxygen-carrying cells.

As he later realised, when his blood was originally removed he still had steroid traces. So they were restored along with his blood just before the Games. But while the IAAF kept hammering the importance of its drug testing programme, the punishments remain ludicrous. Vainio, the deliberate cheat, was lining up again at the IAAF World Cross Country championships just 18 months later, having served his suspension. Several years later the minimum ban was finally increased ... to two years.

Yet the biggest drug scandal, perhaps the biggest sporting scandal of the decade, came near the end of the eighties. It started simply as the showdown at the Seoul Olympics for the title of World's Fastest Human: the 100m final, primarily featuring American Carl Lewis (winner of four Olympic golds in 1984) and Ben Johnson, the Jamaican-born Canadian who had beaten Lewis for the 1987 World 100m title in a world record of 9.83 sec.

In Seoul, however, the odds were on the smoother Lewis, who looked much better in the qualifying rounds and had convincingly beaten the muscular Johnson when they met several months earlier in Zurich, in a race which their bank managers would not allow them to miss.

In the Olympic final though, the one race everyone wanted to see, a new Johnson burst from the blocks, never giving Lewis a chance and winning in another world record 9.78. Three days later, Johnson's disqualification was announced following the discovery of a steroid, Stanazol, in his doping sample. He was stripped of the title, medal and record, and banished in shame. Never had a more prominent athlete, in a such a universally viewed athletics event, been caught so dramatically. In the Olympic village perhaps a hundred, or 500, other athletes slept fitfully that night.

The eighties end with athletics trying to cleanse its soul through the Canadian Dubin Inquiry into drugs, held in Toronto from January to October 1989. Altogether 122 witnesses, including Johnson himself, provided 15,000 pages of sworn evidence in 91 days of hearings, during which they talked candidly for the first time about the nature of the problem. There were signs too on the track that athletes were being more careful, or sparing, about drugs; in some events performances levelled right off.

A new IAAF programme of out-of-competition testing, with athletes liable to be drug tested at short notice anywhere in the world and thus unable to steer clear of tests simply by avoiding competition, gives renewed hope that the drugs menace could be slowed dramatically, if not completely halted. Meanwhile, talks continue about the possibility of a big-money rematch between Lewis and Johnson in late September 1990, when Johnson becomes eligible for competition after two years suspension.

But if athletics really does allow Johnson to earn a sum estimated in millions of dollars, purely as a result of his deliberate attempt to cheat his way to Olympic glory, then the sport has still got some conscience searching to undertake in the nineties.

Coxed pairs at Henley Regatta, 1985.

Pirmin Zurbriggen, World Cup Champion 1984, 1987, 1988.

1985

SNOOKER: January

Drugs dominated. During the final of the British Open in January, Silvino Francisco privately confronted his opponent, Kirk Stevens, and accused him of being on drugs. Francisco won the match and the fracas seemed to have disappeared until the world championships when the story came out in a tabloid. 'He was as high as a kite' says Francisco, the headline screamed. The WPBSA fined Francisco £6,500 and two world ranking points. But the rumpus did not go away. In the summer Stevens admitted that he was hopelessly addicted to cocaine. The Board ignored this. Then in October it was revealed that Rex Williams, the Board's chairman, took beta-blockers because of a medical condition. Unfortunately for Williams, beta-blockers were a drug known to be used by certain athletes to reduce stress and steady the arm. Williams went on TV and said: 'It's like taking a glass of scotch.' The Board refused to ban beta-blockers and split from the Sports Council's drug-testing scheme and set up their own. Within two years snooker had to fall in line and ban beta-blockers. By then, Rex Williams had resigned as chairman, Francisco's punishment had been reduced on appeal and Williams and John Virgo, the vice-chairman, had settled out of court in a libel action brought against them by Francisco.

CRICKET: January

This was the year of the great illusion for England. In January England beat India in Madras, Foster taking 11 for 163, Fowler and Gatting scoring double centuries and England winning by nine wickets. After a draw in the fifth Test England won the series 2–1, the first time that a team touring India had come from behind to win a series.

CHESS: February 15

The International Chess Federation abandon the five month battle for the world championship between Anatoly Karpov and challenger Gary Kasparov on the grounds it 'had exhausted the physical if not the psychological resources, not only of the participants but of all those connected with the match'. Kasparov was furious but was to get the title he so desperately wanted later.

RUGBY LEAGUE: March 1

After the miseries of their tour to the Southern hemisphere Great Britain discover winning again when they thrash France at Leeds 50–4 but it is short lived relief when just over two weeks later they are beaten 24–16 by France in Perpignan.

ATHLETICS: April 21

The London marathon, still booming, is won by Britain's Steve Jones. Ingrid Kristiansen wins the women's race.

SNOOKER: April 28

The World Championship at The Crucible in Sheffield comes to an extraordinary end. Irishman Dennis Taylor has never been ahead in the best of 35 frame final against defending champion Steve Davis. Taylor however manages to cling to Davis's shirt-tails but all looks lost when in the final frame Davis has, by his standards, a simple looking black to pot for the title. Astonishingly he misses and Taylor steps up to take the title. High drama which kept the BBC happy as it reported record viewing figures as the final went on past midnight.

SOCCER: May 11

At the time it was to be described as one of soccer's blackest days but more horrors were to follow. Bradford already promoted to the second division are celebrating their last home match of the season against Lincoln City. Fire breaks out in the packed main stand and 53 people die in the rush to escape the blaze. In only a few minutes the wooden stand is a 40ft wall of flame. In the aftermath questions are asked about locked gates at the back of the stand which delayed the evacuation and an inquiry is set up under the auspices of Mr Justice Popplewell. A discarded cigarette is thought to be the cause of the fire. In Birmingham a boy is killed as rival fans clash and a wall collapses.

MOUNTAINEERING: May 14

At last Chris Bonington, aged 50, reaches the top when he climbs Everest.

SOCCER: May 18

Kevin Moran of Manchester United becomes the first player to be sent off in a Cup Final. Spurred on by playing with only ten men United beat Everton 1–0 in extra time through a Norman Whiteside goal. It is a bitter disappointment for Everton who have won the League and the European Cup Winners' Cup beating Rapid Vienna in Rotterdam 3–1. They are the last English club to win a European trophy in the 80s. In Scotland the 100th Cup Final is won by Celtic. Trailing to a goal from Dundee United's Stuart Beedie, Davie Provan and Frank McGarvey score for Celtic in the last 13 minutes.

SOCCER: May 28

Rioting fans leave 39 dead in Heysel, Belgium. Liverpool are facing Juventus in the European Cup when some of their supporters charge at the Italian fans. A wall and fence collapses crushing them to death. As rescuers try to help some fans continue to fight. After a delay the match starts but a dejected looking Liverpool, who are also about to see manager Bob Paisley step down and make way for player-manager Kenny Dalglish, lose 1–0. The next day British teams are banned from Belgium and the following day the FA bans English clubs from Europe for the following season.

HORSE RACING: June 5

There are 18 runners in the Derby which is won by 9–4 favourite Slip Anchor, ridden by Steve Cauthen. Second is Shirley Heights and third Law Society.

BOXING: June 8

In the middle of Queen's Park Rangers football ground Barry McGuigan wins the WBA featherweight championship on a points decision from Panamanian Eusebio Pedroza. Pedroza had been champion for seven years and this was the 20th defence of his title. For McGuigan it was the chance to become a boxing legend but it was all to go horribly wrong when he fought in the Nevada desert heat against an unfancied American, Steve Cruz. Disenchantment and management wrangles were to follow, then came the failed attempt to climb back.

CRICKET: June 13–18

The first Test of the Ashes series at Headingley is won by England by five wickets. Andrew Hilditch hits 119 for Australia but a big hundred of 175 from Tim Robinson gives England the foundations for victory. In the second Test at Lord's Allan Border scores 196 and England are beaten by four wickets. The third Test at Trent Bridge and the fourth Test at Old Trafford are drawn. But from then on it is downhill for the Australians as they lose by an innings and 118 runs at Edgbaston in August. Robinson hits 145, Gower 215 and Gatting 100. Richard Ellison bags match figures of ten for 104. In the sixth Test at The Oval Gooch scores 196 and Gower 157 as England win by an innings and 94 runs. Gower's hold on the Australians is as vice-like as the wheel clamp put on the tourists' coach on their first day in the country.

TENNIS: June 24–July 7

The 17-year-old West German Boris Becker becomes the first unseeded player to win Wimbledon. Having left the championships a year earlier in a wheelchair after injuring himself, he returned to sweep aside everyone. In the final he beat a very nervous Kevin Curren 6–3, 6–7, 7–6, 6–4 to herald the West German era in tennis. West Germany reached their first Davis Cup final since 1970 but lost 3–2 to Sweden. In a repeat final in 1988 West Germany made amends, winning 4–1. Predictably Martina Navratilova won the women's Wimbledon title and £117,000·when she beat familiar adversary Chris Evert-Lloyd 4–6, 6–3. 6–2.

CRICKET: July 20

Leicestershire beat Essex in the Benson & Hedges Cup final thanks to a stout 86 from Peter Willey. Set to chase 213, Leicestershire score the runs with three overs to spare.

GOLF: July 21

Britain's Sandy Lyle wins The Open at Sandwich, beating Payne Stewart of the US by one shot. He was the first British winner of The Open for 16 years when Tony Jacklin triumphed.

ATHLETICS: July 27

The Gateshead runner Steve Cram wins the Golden Mile in Oslo shaving a second off Sebastian Coe's record time with a run of 3min 46.32secs. Eight days later, in Hungary, he grabs another world record with a run of 4min 51.39 for the 2,000m.

SAILING: August 11

Gales forced 100 yachts in the Fastnet race to retire. But the destruction was not as bad as 1979, when 18 competitors died and 25 of the entries sank.

ATHLETICS: August 15

Zola Budd running in an invitation race at Crystal Palace wins the 5,000m in 14min 48.07 to knock 10 seconds off Ingrid Kristiansen's previous world's best over the distance.

CRICKET: September 7

Needing 18 runs from the last over Nottinghamshire are beaten by one run in the NatWest Trophy final after Derek Randall is caught from the final ball of the match. Essex, thanks to 110 from Brian Hardie, made 280 for 2 from 60 overs. Nottinghamshire's spirited reply left them at 279 for five.

SOCCER: September 10

Scotland manager Jock Stein collapsed and died at the World

Cup qualifying match at Ninian Park against Wales. Scotland came from behind to earn a 1–1 draw to keep alive their hopes in the competition. Stein's death happened at the end of the match. Stein had been Celtic's manager when they became the first British club to win the European Cup in 1967.

CRICKET: September 11–13

Middlesex draw with Essex at Lord's to win the County Championship and £20,000. Hampshire, who finished 15th the previous year, are the runners up.

CRICKET: September 15

With one ball to spare Essex beat Yorkshire by two wickets to successfully defend their Sunday League title and take first prize of £17,000, with Sussex the runners up.

GOLF: September 15

After 28 years the Americans are forced to hand over the Ryder Cup when a European team consisting of seven Britons, four Spaniards and a West German, win by 16.5 to 11.5. Victory is sealed for Tony Jacklin's team by Scotland's Sam Torrance who beat Andy North at the 18th on The Belfry course.

RUGBY LEAGUE: October 19

New Zealand beat Great Britain 22–24. A vast improvement for Britain who win the next match 25–8 thanks to tries from Garry Schofield. But on November 9 it is stalemate as the two sides draw their World Cup match at Elland Road, 6–6.

CHESS: November 9

Gary Kasparov and Anatoly Karpov meet again to decide the World Championship which had earlier been called off. This time the match runs the duration and Kasparov wins.

ROLL OF HONOUR

AMERICAN FOOTBALL: Superbowl: San Francisco 49ers 38 Miami Dolphins 16.

ATHLETICS: World Cup, Men: United States 123pts, USSR 115 pts, East Germany 114pts. Women: East Germany 121pts, USSR 105.5pts, Europe 86pts. European Cup, Men: USSR. Women: USSR.

CRICKET: County championship: Middlesex. John Player League: Essex. NatWest Trophy: Essex. Benson & Hedges Cup: Leicestershire.

CYCLING: Tour de France: Bernard Hinault (France). Women: Maria Canins (Italy).

DARTS: World Championship: Eric Bristow.

GOLF: US Masters: Bernhard Langer (West Germany). US PGA: Hubert Green. US Open: Andy North. The Open (Sandwich): Sandy Lyle (GB). Ryder Cup (The Belfry): Europe 16.5 US 11.5.

HORSE RACING: Flat:

1000 Guineas: Oh So Sharp. 2000 Guineas: Shaheed. The Derby: Slip Anchor (Jockey: Steve Cauthen. Trainer: Henry Cecil). The Oaks: Oh So Sharp. St Leger: Oh So Sharp. Champion jockey Steve Cauthen, 195 wins. Top trainer: Henry Cecil, £1,148,206.

National Hunt: Grand National: Last Suspect (Jockey: Hywel Davies. Trainer: Tim Forster). Cheltenham Gold Cup: Forgive'N'Forget. Champion Hurdle: See You Then. Champion jockey John Francome, 101 winners. Top trainer Fred Winter, £218,978.

MOTOR RACING: Alain Prost in a McLaren-TAG. Constructors' Cup: McLaren-TAG.

RUGBY LEAGUE: Challenge Cup: Wigan. Championship: St Helens.

RUGBY UNION: No Grand Slam. Triple Crown: Ireland. County Championship: Middlesex. Pilkington Cup: Bath 24 London Welsh 15. Schweppes Welsh Cup: Llanelli 15 Cardiff 14.

SKIING: Overall champion, Men: Marc Girardelli (Luxembourg). Women: Michela Figini (Switzerland).

SNOOKER: Dennis Taylor 18 Steve Davis 17.

SOCCER: First Division Title: Everton (90pts). Runners-up: Liverpool. FA Cup: Manchester United 1 Everton 0. Milk Cup: Norwich City 1 Sunderland 0. Scotland Premier League Title: Aberdeen (59pts). Runners-up: Celtic. Scottish Cup: Celtic 2 Dundee United 1. Scottish League Cup: Rangers 1 Dundee United 0. European Cup: Juventus 1 Liverpool 0. Cup Winners' Cup: Everton 3 Rapid Vienna 1. UEFA Cup: Real Madrid beat Videoton 3–1 on agg. (H) 3–0 (A) 0–1.

SPEEDWAY: World Champion: Erik Gundersen (Denmark). British League: Oxford.

SQUASH: World Open Championship, Men: Jahangir Khan (Pakistan). Women: Susan Devoy (New Zealand).

TABLE TENNIS: World Championship, Men: Jiang Jialiang (China). Women: Cao Yan Hua (China).

TENNIS: Wimbledon: Men: Boris Becker (West Germany) beat Kevin Curren (US) 6–3, 6–7, 7–6, 6–4. Women: Martina Navratilova (US) beat Chris Evert-Lloyd (US) 4–6, 6–3, 6–2. US Open:

Ivan Lendl (Cze), Hana Mandlikova (Cze). French Open: Mats Wilander (Sweden), Chris Evert-Lloyd. Australian Open: Stefan Edberg (Sweden), Martina Navratilova. Davis Cup: Sweden. Wightman Cup: US beat Britain 7–0.

YACHTING: Admiral's Cup: West Germany.

CANON LEAGUE 1984-85

DIVISION 1

		Home					Away					
	P	W	D	L	F	A	W	D	L	F	A	Pts
1 Everton	42	16	3	2	58	17	12	3	6	30	26	90
2 Liverpool	42	12	4	5	36	19	10	7	4	32	16	77
3 Tottenham H	42	11	3	7	46	31	12	5	4	32	20	77
4 Manchester U	42	13	6	2	47	13	9	4	8	30	34	76
5 Southampton	42	13	4	4	29	18	6	7	8	27	29	68
6 Chelsea	42	13	3	5	38	20	5	9	7	25	28	66
7 Arsenal	42	14	5	2	37	14	5	4	12	24	35	66
8 Sheffield W	42	12	7	2	39	21	5	7	9	19	24	65
9 Nottingham F	42	13	4	4	35	18	6	3	12	21	30	64
10 Aston Villa	42	10	7	4	34	20	5	4	12	26	40	56
11 Watford	42	10	5	6	48	30	4	8	9	33	41	55
12 WBA	42	11	4	6	36	23	5	3	13	22	39	55
13 Luton T	42	12	5	4	40	22	3	4	14	17	39	54
14 Newcastle U	42	11	4	6	33	26	2	9	10	22	44	52
15 Leicester C	42	10	4	7	39	25	5	2	14	26	48	51
16 West Ham U	42	7	8	6	27	23	6	4	11	24	45	51
17 Ipswich T	42	8	7	6	27	20	5	4	12	19	37	50
18 Coventry C	42	11	3	7	29	22	4	2	15	18	42	50
19 QPR	42	11	6	4	41	30	2	5	14	12	42	50
20 Norwich C	42	9	6	6	28	24	4	4	13	18	40	49
21 Sunderland	42	7	6	8	20	26	3	4	14	20	36	40
22 Stoke C	42	3	3	15	18	41	0	5	16	6	50	17

DIVISION 2

		Home					Away					
	P	W	D	L	F	A	W	D	L	F	A	Pts
1 Oxford U	42	18	2	1	62	15	7	7	7	22	21	84
2 Birmingham C	42	12	6	3	30	15	13	1	7	29	18	82
3 Manchester C	42	14	4	3	42	16	7	7	7	24	24	74
4 Portsmouth	42	11	6	4	39	25	9	8	4	30	25	74
5 Blackburn R	42	14	3	4	38	15	7	7	7	28	26	73
6 Brighton & HA	42	13	6	2	31	11	7	6	8	23	23	72
7 Leeds U	42	12	7	2	37	11	7	5	9	29	32	69
8 Shrewsbury T	42	12	6	3	45	22	6	5	10	21	31	65
9 Fulham	42	13	3	5	35	26	6	5	10	33	38	65
10 Grimsby T	42	13	1	7	47	32	5	7	9	25	32	62
11 Barnsley	42	11	7	3	27	12	3	9	9	15	30	58

		Home					Away					
	P	W	D	L	F	A	W	D	L	F	A	Pts
12 Wimbledon	42	9	8	4	40	29	7	2	12	31	46	58
13 Huddersfield T	42	9	5	7	28	29	6	5	10	24	35	55
14 Oldham Ath	42	10	4	7	27	23	5	4	12	22	44	53
15 Crystal Palace	42	8	7	6	25	27	4	5	12	21	38	48
16 Carlisle U	42	8	5	8	27	23	5	3	13	23	44	47
17 Charlton Ath	42	8	6	6	34	30	3	5	13	17	33	45
18 Sheffield U	42	7	6	8	31	28	3	8	10	23	38	44
19 Middlesbrough	42	6	8	7	22	26	4	2	15	19	31	40
20 Notts Co	42	6	5	10	25	32	4	2	15	20	41	37
21 Cardiff C	42	5	3	13	24	42	4	5	12	23	37	35
22 Wolverhampton W	42	5	4	12	18	32	3	5	13	19	47	33

DIVISION 3

		Home					Away					
	P	W	D	L	F	A	W	D	L	F	A	Pts
1 Bradford C	46	15	6*	2	44	23	13	4	6	33	22	94
2 Millwall	46	18	5	0	44	12	8	7	8	29	30	90
3 Hull C	46	16	4	3	46	20	9	8	6	32	29	87
4 Gillingham	46	15	5	3	54	29	10	3	10	26	33	83
5 Bristol C	46	17	2	4	46	19	7	7	9	28	28	81
6 Bristol R	46	15	6	2	37	13	6	6	11	29	35	75
7 Derby Co	46	14	7	2	40	20	5	6	12	25	34	70
8 York C	46	13	5	5	42	22	7	4	12	28	35	69
9 Reading	46	8	7	8	31	29	11	5	7	37	33	69
10 Bournemouth	46	16	3	4	42	16	3	8	12	15	30	68
11 Walsall	46	9	7	7	33	22	9	6	8	25	30	67
12 Rotherham U	46	11	6	6	36	24	7	5	11	19	31	65
13 Brentford	46	13	5	5	42	27	3	9	11	20	37	62
14 Doncaster R	46	11	5	7	42	33	6	3	14	30	41	59
15 Plymouth Arg	46	11	7	5	33	23	4	7	12	29	42	59
16 Wigan Ath	46	12	6	5	36	22	3	8	12	24	42	59
17 Bolton W	46	12	5	6	38	22	4	1	18	31	53	54
18 Newport Co	46	9	6	8	30	30	4	7	12	25	37	52
19 Lincoln C	46	8	11	4	32	20	3	7*13		18	31	51
20 Swansea C	46	7	5	11	31	39	5	6	-12	22	41	47
21 Burnley	46	6	8	9	30	24	5	5	13	30	49	46
22 Orient	46	7	7	9	30	36	4	6	13	21	40	46
23 Preston NE	46	9	5	9	33	41	4	2	17	18	59	46
24 Cambridge U	46	2	3	18	17	48	2	6	15	20	47	21

* Includes one match abandoned at 0–0 after 40 minutes. Result stands.

DIVISION 4

		Home					Away					
	P	W	D	L	F	A	W	D	L	F	A	Pts
1 Chesterfield	46	16	6	1	40	13	10	7	6	24	22	91
2 Blackpool	46	15	7	1	42	15	9	7	7	31	24	86
3 Darlington	46	16	4	3	41	22	8	9	6	25	27	85
4 Bury	46	15	6	2	46	20	9	6	8	30	30	84
5 Hereford U	46	16	2	5	38	21	6	9	8	27	26	77
6 Tranmere R	46	17	1	5	50	21	7	2	14	33	45	75
7 Colchester U	46	13	7	3	49	29	7	7	9	38	36	74
8 Swindon T	46	16	4	3	42	21	5	5	13	20	37	72
9 Scunthorpe U	46	14	6	3	61	33	5	8	10	22	29	71
10 Crewe Alex	46	10	7	6	32	28	8	5	10	33	41	66
11 Peterborough U	46	11	7	5	29	21	5	7	11	25	32	62
12 Port Vale	46	11	8	4	39	24	3	10	10	22	35	60
13 Aldershot	46	11	6	6	33	20	6	2	15	23	43	59
14 Mansfield T	46	10	8	5	25	15	3	10	10	16	23	57
15 Wrexham	46	10	6	7	39	27	5	3	15	28	43	54
16 Chester C	46	11	3	9	35	30	4	6	13	25	42	54
17 Rochdale	46	8	7	8	33	30	5	7	11	22	39	53
18 Exeter C	46	9	7	7	30	27	4	7	12	27	52	53
19 Hartlepool U	46	10	6	7	34	29	4	4	15	20	38	52
20 Southend U	46	8	8	7	30	34	5	3	15	28	49	50
21 Halifax T	46	9	3	11	26	32	6	2	15	16	37	50
22 Stockport Co	46	11	5	7	40	26	2	3	18	18	53	47
23 Northampton T	46	10	1	12	32	32	4	4	15	21	42	47
24 Torquay U	46	5	11	7	18	24	4	3	16	20	39	41

SCOTTISH LEAGUE 1984–85

PREMIER DIVISION

		Home					Away					
	P	W	D	L	F	A	W	D	L	F	A	Pts
1 Aberdeen	36	13	4	1	49	13	14	1	3	40	13	59
2 Celtic	36	12	3	3	43	12	10	5	3	34	18	52
3 Dundee U	36	13	2	3	47	18	7	5	6	20	15	47
4 Rangers	36	7	6	5	21	14	6	6	6	26	24	38
5 St Mirren	36	10	2	6	29	24	7	2	9	22	32	38
6 Dundee	36	9	3	6	25	19	6	4	8	23	31	37
7 Hearts	36	6	3	9	21	26	7	2	9	26	38	31

	P	W	D	L	F	A	W	D	L	F	A	Pts
			Home						Away			
8 Hibernian	36	5	4	9	23	30	5	3	10	15	31	27
9 Dumbarton	36	4	4	10	17	29	2	3	13	12	35	19
10 Morton	36	3	1	14	18	44	2	1	15	11	56	12

DIVISION 1

	P	W	D	L	F	A	W	D	L	F	A	Pts
			Home						Away			
1 Motherwell	39	11	4	4	34	14	10	4	6	28	22	50
2 Clydebank	39	11	4	4	31	16	6	10	4	26	21	48
3 Falkirk	39	9	3	7	36	31	10	4	6	29	23	45
4 Hamilton A	39	8	5	7	23	24	8	6	5	25	25	43
5 Airdrieonians	39	11	1	7	43	33	6	7	7	27	26	42
6 Forfar Ath	39	9	7	4	27	18	5	6	8	27	31	41
7 Ayr U	39	9	6	5	31	25	6	3	10	26	27	39
8 Clyde	39	9	5	6	31	26	5	6	8	16	22	39
9 Brechin C	39	7	5	8	25	28	7	4	8	24	29	37
10 East Fife	39	6	6	8	26	25	6	6	7	29	31	36
11 Partick Th	39	8	5	6	28	22	5	4	11	22	33	35
12 Kilmarnock	39	8	8	4	23	23	4	2	13	19	38	34
13 Meadowbank Th	39	5	5	9	25	33	6	5	9	25	33	32
14 St Johnstone	39	4	4	11	23	33	6	1	13	28	45	25

DIVISION 2

	P	W	D	L	F	A	W	D	L	F	A	Pts
			Home						Away			
1 Montrose	39	11	5	3	29	21	11	4	5	28	19	53
2 Alloa	39	9	6	4	29	17	11	4	5	29	23	50
3 Dunfermline Ath	39	7	9	4	34	20	10	6	3	27	16	49
4 Cowdenbeath	39	10	5	4	36	17	8	6	6	32	22	47
5 Stenhousemuir	39	9	6	5	27	25	6	9	4	18	18	45
6 Stirling Alb	39	8	7	4	33	22	7	6	7	29	25	43
7 Raith R	39	9	1	9	30	25	9	5	6	39	32	42
8 Queen of the S	39	6	7	7	27	25	4	7	8	15	31	34
9 Albion R	39	7	2	11	27	39	6	6	7	22	33	34
10 Queen's Park	39	7	5	7	24	19	5	4	11	24	36	33
11 Stranraer	39	7	2	11	30	33	6	4	9	22	34	32
12 East Stirling	39	5	8	7	21	22	3	7	9	17	31	31
13 Berwick R	39	5	7	7	18	20	3	5	12	18	29	28
14 Arbroath	39	6	5	9	22	28	3	2	14	13	38	25

BRITANNIC ASSURANCE CHAMPIONSHIP 1985

		P	W	L	D	Bt	Bl	Pts
1	Middlesex (3)	24	8	4	12	61	85	274
2	Hampshire (15)	24	7	2	15	66	78	256
3	Gloucestershire (17)	23	7	3	13	51	78	241
4	Essex (1)	23	7	2	14	42	70	224
5	Worcestershire (10)	24	5	6	13	65	68	221
6	Surrey (8)	24	5	5	14	62	76	218
7	Sussex (6)	23	6	1	16	52	57	205
8	Nottinghamshire (2)	24	4	2	18	66	69	199
9	Kent (5)	24	4	5	15	51	71	186
10	Northamptonshire (11)	24	5	4	15	52	51	183
11	Yorkshire (14)	23	3	4	16	58	59	165
12	Glamorgan (13)	24	4	4	16	41	50	163
13	Derbyshire (12)	24	3	9	12	46	69	163
14	Lancashire (16)	24	3	7	14	44	67	159
15	Warwickshire (9)	24	2	8	14	47	74	153
16	Leicestershire (4)	24	2	3	19	48	65	145
17	Somerset (7)	24	1	7	16	70	45	131

(The *Bt* and *Bl* columns are grouped under the heading *Bonus*.)

1984 positions are shown in brackets.

The totals for Worcestershire and Glamorgan include 8 points for levelling the scores in drawn matches. Where sides are equal on points, the one with the most wins has priority.

JOHN PLAYER LEAGUE 1985

		P	W	L	Tie	NR	Pts
1	Essex (1)	16	9	3	1	3	44
2	Sussex (3)	16	10	5	0	1	42
3	Hampshire (9)	16	8	4	0	4	40
4	Derbyshire (17)	16	8	5	0	3	38
5	Northamptonshire (12)	16	7	4	1	4	38
6	Gloucestershire (13)	16	8	8	0	0	32
	Warwickshire (7)	16	7	7	0	2	32
	Yorkshire (13)	16	6	6	0	4	32
	Leicestershire (13)	16	5	5	1	5	32
10	Kent (9)	16	6	7	0	3	30
	Somerset (13)	16	5	6	0	5	30

		P	W	L	Tie	NR	Pts
12 {	Nottinghamshire (2)	16	6	8	0	2	28
	Middlesex (5)	16	5	7	0	4	28
14 {	Glamorgan (9)	16	4	7	1	4	26
	Lancashire (4)	16	3	6	2	5	26
16	Worcestershire (5)	16	5	9	0	2	24
17	Surrey (8)	16	4	9	0	3	22

1984 positions in brackets.

SOCCER by BRIAN GLANVILLE

FOR ME, football in the 1980s is summed up by one devastating image: Heysel Stadium, Brussels, on a May evening in 1985. A group of us English football journalists is sitting in the main grandstand in the Press 'overflow'. The game has still to start. There has been skirmishing on the Z-terraces to our left, where a group of Italian supporters has been driven leftwards, leaving a great, ominous, gap, as though deserted by some migrating tribe. We are waiting still for the European Cup final between Liverpool and Juventus.

Then the large, blond, bearded figure of Eamonn McCabe, the *Observer* sports photographer, appears on the track, right opposite us. He has just come from the Z-terrace end. He looks up at us, draws his finger across his throat, and raises his ten fingers in the air. Once, twice, three times. So there are 30 dead. That is why the loudspeakers have continuously been broadcasting Italian names, appealing to their relatives to come to the stadium offices.

From where we sat, we could see nothing but the beginning of those horrific events, could see only the Italians put to flight across the terracing. We could not see the supporting wall collapse, the sudden, dreadful pyramid of bodies, could not see those bodies being dragged out and eventually taken away.

What would happen now? The hiatus dragged on and on, with its undertow of disaster. The Belgian police, who had done nothing when the fighting first broke out, who had had a good quarter of an hour to intervene before the second, fatal wave of attacks took place, now marched purposefully into the stadium. With grotesque irrelevance, their commander lined up his men in the centre circle and inspected them.

Now trouble broke out at the opposite end, Juventus's, where a bunch of young Italian fans, perhaps the so-called 'Ultras' in their black and white regalia, began feeling their oats, taunting the police, running on to the field to make mischief. Finally, for what it mattered, the game took place. Juventus won by what might be called a 'moral' penalty, Gillespie's cynical foul quite plainly taking place outside the box.

Then it was off, in the small hours, to the airport, standing on an open field amidst great queues of Liverpool supporters, all waiting for our planes.

How many had died? No one knew. Twenty? Fifty? Even more? Figures flew into the chilly air. Someone said the whole of a youth band had been sitting beneath the wall, and had been killed. In fact, mercifully, they hadn't.

Next day, I was meant to fly to Mexico, where England were on tour, but instead stayed in London, to write about the tragedy. On the Friday morning, I cycled to Downing Street: Mrs Thatcher had summoned seven of us reporters. 'I don't like to talk about informing, but we need to get the decent fans to express their disapproval.'

So to the aftermath, the inevitable and lacerating inquests, the lingering memories of boozy Liverpool fans lying about before the game outside the stadium, half-naked in the sunshine, red and white caps on their heads, beer cans in hand. The revelation that many of them had forced their way on to the Z-terraces, over or under the inadequate wire fence; they had been allowed by police to enter with their cans and bottles. The tickets on that terrace had been sold in Belgium, inevitably reaching Italian fans, most of them 'occasionals' quite unused to the dangers of the modern game. But when UEFA, months earlier, had inspected the rickety old stadium, it had been in so perfunctory a way as to be meaningless. Or in the event, direly meaningful.

Another image of the 1980s: April, 1989, the massive San Siro Stadium in Milan. The semi-final game in the European Cup between Milan and Real Madrid has just begun. The referee blows his whistle for a minute's silence, to commemorate the pitiful death of 95 Liverpool supporters, four days before, at Hillsborough. And up on the high terracing, where the 'Ultras' gather, The Red and Black Brigade, Milan's most passionate supporters, there is a sudden outbreak of applause. Then, astonishingly, they all begin to sing the Liverpool anthem 'You'll Never Walk Alone'.

There was Hillsborough, there was Heysel, there was Bradford. These were the years when the birds came cruelly home to roost. On May 11, 1985, 56 people were burned to death at Valley Parade, where Bradford City were playing Lincoln City. It is said that an old man lit a cigarette and dropped his lighted match down a crack in the floorboards of that death-trap of a grandstand, on to a pile of rubbish which had been accumulating for the past 20 years. The club knew all about it. The

Council knew all about it. The Council had told the club to do something about it. The club had done nothing. The Council had let sleeping dogs lie.

Yet by sharp contrast with Hillsborough, where the police eventually were made the culprits, indicted by the official inquiry, there were no proper repercussions for what, in other countries, would surely have led to criminal prosecutions, probably imprisonment. The relatives of the dead were left to sue for their money. A colossal act of negligence went quite unpunished.

Perhaps the saddest thing about these three disasters is that each of them could so easily have been averted, that they presented, jointly, a picture of dilapidation, danger and incompetence which wasn't wholly justified.

At Bradford, there was negligence. Heysel Stadium should never have been used in the first place for such a major, combustible event. Tickets for those terraces should never have been allowed to reach Italian fans. A braver, more effective police force could have quelled the trouble in minutes. Trouble that was in the air, after the savage way Liverpool's fans had been attacked in Rome by Roma's hooligans, following the 1984 European final.

As for Hillsborough, all might have been well had the policeman who led the operation at the same semi-final, a year earlier, only been in charge again. But he wasn't. He had just been moved, and neither club nor police now made provision to keep people off the packed central terrace, at the Leppings Lane end, and on to those on either side of it.

There was football, too, in the 1980s, some of it of marvellous quality. The brilliance of the Italian team which won the 1982 World Cup in Spain after so costive a beginning in Galicia, was memorable. Suddenly and dynamically, Italy came to life, playing the adventurous football for which it had always been capable over long, sterile, cautious years, finding in little Paolo Rossi a player whose new life put life into them.

In turn, they defeated Argentina, Brazil (a coruscating game), Poland, West Germany. In a supposedly defensive era, this was football to be cherished.

Four years later, in Mexico, Diego Maradona both cheated and excelled. He punched a goal against England with what he chose to call The Hand of God, but followed it with a goal of unbelievable quality, spurting, feinting and dribbling his way through the whole England defence before beating Shilton.

'England were still stunned', said an Italian journalist, 'like a man who has just had his wallet stolen.' That may be true, but the goal was still remarkable.

Then, two years later, in West Germany, it was the turn of Holland to show how gloriously football can still be played, despite its blistering present pace, its endless hazards. Ruud Gullit, with his mighty physique, his black dreadlocks, his absolute versatility; power, pace, skill, flair. Marco Van Basten, with his superbly-volleyed goal against Russia in the final.

How much football, for all its problems, still has to offer!

Steve Davis, six times World Champion during the 1980s.

Seve Ballesteros caught in the rain at the 1985 British Open.

1986

CRICKET: *January 2*

A political row over South Africa leads to a last minute cancellation of England's cricket tour to Bangladesh.

SOCCER: *January 16*

The Mr Justice Popplewell's report into violence at soccer matches says 'we can never suppress soccer thugs completely'.

RUGBY LEAGUE: *February 16*

France and Great Britain draw their World Cup match at Avignon 10–10 but on home soil a fortnight later at Wigan Great Britain beat the French 24–10.

SOCCER: *April*

Rangers pulled off the managerial coup of the decade when they lured Graeme Souness from Sampdoria to be their player-manager. Souness has pursued the dream of making Rangers one of the greatest clubs in Europe by instigating the most remarkable burst of transfer activity in Scottish football history. During a spending spree totalling around £12.5m, he has reversed the age-old trend of Scottish stars moving to English clubs by signing men like Chris Woods, Terry Butcher, Gary Stevens and Trevor Steven. The most astonishing Souness deal of all took place in the summer of 1989, when he ended years of religious bigotry at Ibrox by making Maurice Johnston Rangers' first Catholic signing of modern times. Under Souness Rangers have won the championship twice and the League Cup three times.

CRICKET: *April 23*

Jim Laker dies. He was 64. His finest hour had been in the 1956 Test match against the Australians at Old Trafford when he returned match figures of 19 for 90. In the first innings he took nine for 37 and in the second 10 for 53.

SNOOKER *May 5*

Rank outsider and part time night-club crooner Joe Johnson

wins the World Championship when he beats favourite Steve Davis 18–12 in the final. The odds on Johnson winning were 150–1.

SOCCER: *May 10*

Liverpool complete the double when they win the Cup Final 3–1 against arch rivals Everton. Gary Lineker puts Everton ahead but goals from Ian Rush and Craig Johnston win the trophy. A week earlier Kenny Dalglish had scored the goal at Chelsea which had won the Anfield club the championship. In Scotland, Aberdeen with goals from John Hewitt (2) and Billy Stark beat Hearts 3–0.

CRICKET: *May 29*

Ian Botham, after his 'I smoked pot' confession is banned from first class cricket for two months.

SOCCER: *May 31*

The World Cup kicks off in Mexico with holders Italy squandering chances galore and only managing a 1–1 draw with Bulgaria. England make a disappointing start when they lose 1–0 against Portugal and Northern Ireland draw 1–1 with Algeria. Scotland, the last country to arrive in Mexico for the tournament, lose their opening match against Denmark 1–0. England play their second match on June 6 and the future looks bleak as skipper Bryan Robson leaves the pitch with a dislocated shoulder and Ray Wilkins is sent off after throwing the ball at the referee. They draw 0–0 with unfancied Morocco. Northern Ireland play the following day losing 2–1 to Spain. On June 8 Scotland take the lead against West Germany when Gordon Strachan scores in the 18th minute and though they run themselves into the ground, they are unable to stop the Germans who win 2–1. June 11. Gary Lineker scores a hat trick as England beat Poland 3–0 and Morocco become the first African side to make the second round of the World Cup when they beat Portugal 3–1. June 12. Pat Jennings celebrating his 41st birthday and 119th cap, makes some fine saves for Northern Ireland against Brazil but it is the end of the tournament for the Irishman as they lose 3–0. The following day Scotland bow out too when they draw 0–0 with a ten-man Uruguay. June 18. England are through to the quarter finals when they beat Paraguay 3–0, Lineker scores twice and Beardsley gets the other goal. June 22. England lose 2–1 to Argentina as Maradonna helped by 'the hand of God' scores the first goal when his arm, acting like a flipper on a pinball machine, flicks the ball over Shilton's head for the first goal. He scores the second and Lineker gets England's consolation in a spirited fightback. Argentina go on to win the cup beating West Germany 3–2 in the final on June

29. They had led 2–0, squandered that lead only to grab the winner through Jorges Burruchaga six minutes from time. Gary Lineker was the tournament's top scorer with six goals.

RACING: June 4

Shahrastani scored a half length victory in the Derby. Trained by Michael Stoute, Shahrastani was priced at 11–2.

CRICKET: June 5–10

Graham Gooch scores a century in the first Test against India but England are still beaten at Lord's by five wickets. England lose the second Test at Headingley by 279 runs following two batting collapses that set totals of 102 and 128. The third Test at Edgbaston is a draw. Gatting scores 183.

TENNIS: June 22

Martina Navratilova returns to Czechoslovakia to play tennis for the first time since she defected in 1975, then a few days later returns to Wimbledon where she collects the ladies title yet again when she beats Hana Mandlikova. Boris Becker wins the men's title for the second year running when he beats Ivan Lendl in the final. In August John McEnroe attempts his comeback at the US Open after a six-month break in Malibu to help bring up his baby. But McEnroe who has won the tournament four times is knocked out in the first round.

CYCLING: June 27

The gruelling Tour de France is won for the first time by an American when Greg Lemond rides away from Paris with the yellow jersey.

SOCCER: July 4

The Football League decides to reduce the size of the First Division to 20 clubs.

CRICKET: July 12

Middlesex score 199 for seven and beat Kent by two runs to win the Benson & Hedges Cup. A full house paid £258,510 to watch the final.

GOLF: July 17–20

The Open at Turnberry is won by Australian Greg Norman whose 280 is five shots better than runner-up Gordon Brand jnr.

SOCCER: July 18

Sir Stanley Rous dies aged 91. He had been secretary to the FA from 1934–1961 when he became President of FIFA until 1974.

CRICKET: July 24–29

Gooch scores 183 at Lord's as England force a draw against New Zealand in the first Test. In the second Test in Nottingham 110 runs from Number 8 bat John Bracewell gives New Zealand an eight wicket win. In the third Test John Wright hits a dogged 119 to force a draw despite centuries from Gower and Gatting.

CRICKET: September 6

Paul Parker hits 85 as Sussex beat Lancashire in the NatWest Trophy final at Lord's. Lancashire make 242 for eight off their 60 overs. Sussex reply with 243 for three off 58.2 overs.

BOXING: September 7

Lloyd Honeyghan, a no-hoper, stunned undisputed world light-welterweight champion Don Curry in Atlantic City. Such were the odds against Honeyghan that there was little interest in America for the fight but Curry wilted under Honeyghan's punching-blitz and relinquished his title in the sixth round. Honeyghan had always maintained that he could win and on his arrival in Atlantic City declared: 'I can't wait to get Don Curry in the ring and smash his face in.'

CRICKET: September 10–12

Essex gain three batting points against Nottinghamshire to clinch the County Championship and the £22,000 prize. It was their third success in the competition in the last four years.

SOCCER: September 10

England are beaten 1–0 in Stockholm by Sweden in the European Championships while an equaliser from substitute Neil Slatter earns Wales a 1–1 draw with Finland in Helsinki. The Republic of Ireland draw 2–2 with Belgium while Scotland draw 0–0 with Bulgaria. The match at Hampden Park saw Dalglish collect his 101st cap.

CRICKET: September 14

Hampshire beat Lancashire by eight wickets to win the Sunday League title for the third time. It is the last year the competition is sponsored by John Player.

CRICKET: September 23

Geoff Boycott's tempestuous relationship with his county, Yorkshire, continues when he is sacked by them. The 45-year-old Boycott had been his county's leading batsman in the previous season.

CHESS: October 6

Gary Kasparov, who won the world championship from Anatoly Karpov, retains the title when he beats Karpov again, this time in Moscow.

SOCCER: October 9

Sports minister Dick Tracey tells the Football League they have six weeks in which to make positive moves towards the introduction of membership card schemes for all supporters.

SOCCER: October 15

In the European Championships Gary Lineker scores twice as England beat Northern Ireland 3–0 while in Dublin The Republic of Ireland and Scotland are involved in a 0–0 draw.

OLYMPICS: October 17

The destination of the 1992 Olympic Games is decided when Barcelona win the vote in Switzerland. Birmingham, which had staged a late bid for the Games and thought they had a winning package ended up with a disappointing eight votes and later lost to Manchester for the right to make the British bid for the 1996 Games.

RUGBY LEAGUE: October 25

Great Britain, playing at Manchester United's Old Trafford, are beaten 38–16 by Australia. When the series moves to Elland Road on November 8 it is the same story as they are crushed 34–4. Then on November 22 it is off to Wigan where Australia beat them in a World Cup match 24–15.

RACING: November

Sir Gordon Richards dies aged 82. He had been champion jockey 26 times.

SOCCER: November 12

England beat Yugoslavia 2–0 at Wembley in the European Championships. Gary Mabbutt and Viv Anderson score. Davie Cooper scores twice as Scotland beat Luxembourg 3–0 and Northern Ireland draw 0–0 in Turkey.

SQUASH: November

The greatest unbeaten run in sporting history came to an end when Jahangir Khan lost for the first time in more than 5½ years and over 500 matches. He has been almost certainly the best player of all time, a unique mixture of Pakistani stroke making flair and Western discipline in training. The newspapers said he was an overwhelming certainty to win the world title again that year - even when Borg was having his great run at Wimbledon the bookmakers would quote you odds, it was pointed out. But no one would give odds against a Jahangir defeat. No one except Ross Norman. The sinewy New Zealander never relinquished his belief that it was possible to beat the man whose name in Urdu meant conqueror of the world. And in Toulouse Norman brought Jahangir down by three games to one in the final before 3,000 disbelieving spectators surrounding an all-transparent court. Norman had tried more than 30 times to beat Jahangir.

BOXING: November 22

Mike Tyson, to become the awesome master of the heavyweights wins the WBC title when he dispatches the holder, Canadian Trevor Berbick, in two rounds in Las Vegas. He is the youngest champion at 20 and despite a succession of out of the ring problems and a stormy marriage to the actress Robin Givens, is to prove unbeatable in the eighties. The only threat to his title is boredom as there are no challengers to even remotely test him.

SOCCER December 11

Profit from the Mexico World Cup is announced at £30m.

ROLL OF HONOUR

AMERICAN FOOTBALL: Superbowl: Chicago Bears 46 New England Patriots 10.

COMMONWEALTH GAMES: Held in Edinburgh, Scotland. Australia 39 gold medals, England 38, Canada 26.

CRICKET: County championship: Essex. John Player League: Hampshire. NatWest Trophy: Sussex. Benson & Hedges Cup: Middlesex.

CYCLING: Tour de France, Men: Greg Lemond (US). Women: Maria Canins (Italy).

DARTS: World Championship: Eric Bristow.

GOLF: US Masters: Jack Nicklaus. US PGA: Bob Tway. US Open: Ray Floyd. The Open (Turnberry): Greg Norman (Australia).

HOCKEY: World Cup, Men: Australia. Women: Holland.

HORSE RACING: Flat:

1000 Guineas: Midway Lady. 2000 Guineas: Dancing Brave. The Derby: Shahrastani (Jockey: Walter Swinburn. Trainer: Michael Stoute). The Oaks: Midway Lady. St Leger: Moon Madness. Champion jockey Pat Eddery, 177 wins. Top trainer Michael Stoute, £1,266,807.

National Hunt: Grand National: West Tip (Jockey: Richard Dunwoody. Trainer: Michael Oliver). Cheltenham Gold Cup: Dawn Run. Champion Hurdle: See You Then. Champion jockey Peter Scudamore, 91 wins. Top trainer Nicky Henderson, £162,234.

MOTOR RACING: Alain Prost (France) in a McLaren-TAG. Constructors' Cup: Williams-Honda.

RUGBY LEAGUE: Challenge Cup: Castleford. Championship: Warrington.

RUGBY UNION: No Grand Slam or Triple Crown. Joint winners: France and Scotland. County Championship: Warwickshire. Pilkington Cup: Bath 25 Wasps 17. Schweppes Welsh Cup: Cardiff 28 Newport 21.

SKIING: Overall champion, Men: Marc Girardelli (Luxembourg). Women: Maria Walliser (Switzerland).

SNOOKER: World Championship: Joe Johnson 18 Steve Davis 12.

SOCCER: First Division Title: Liverpool (88pts). Runners-up: Everton. FA Cup winners: Liverpool 3 Everton 1. Littlewoods Cup: Oxford United 3 Queen's Park Rangers 0. Scotland: Premier League Title: Celtic (50pts). Runners-up: Hearts. Scottish Cup: Aberdeen 3 Hearts 0. Scottish League Cup: Aberdeen 3 Hibernian 0. European Cup: Steaua Buch beat Barcelona 2–0 on penalties after 0–0 draw. Cup Winners' Cup: Dynamo Kiev 3 Athletico Madrid 0. UEFA Cup: Real Madrid beat Cologne 5–3 H 5–1 (A) 0–2. World Cup (Mexico): Argentina 3 West Germany 2. France 4 Belgium 2 for third place.

SPEEDWAY: World Champion: Hans Neilsen (Denmark). British League: Oxford.

SQUASH: World Open Championship, Men: Ross Norman.

TENNIS: Wimbledon: Men: Boris Becker (West Germany) beat Ivan Lendl (Cze) 6–4 6–3 7–5. Women: Martina Navratilova (US) beat Hana Mandlikova (Cze) 7–6 6–3. US Open: Ivan Lendl, Martina Navratilova. French Open: Ivan Lendl, Chris Evert-Lloyd. No Australian Open.

CANON LEAGUE 1985–86

DIVISION 1

		Home					Away					
	P	W	D	L	F	A	W	D	L	F	A	Pts
1 Liverpool	42	16	4	1	58	14	10	6	5	31	23	88
2 Everton	42	16	3	2	54	18	10	5	6	33	23	85
3 West Ham U	42	17	2	2	48	16	9	4	8	26	24	84
4 Manchester U	42	12	5	4	35	12	10	5	6	35	24	76
5 Sheffield W	42	13	6	2	36	23	8	4	9	27	31	73
6 Chelsea	42	12	4	5	32	27	8	7	6	25	29	71
7 Arsenal	42	13	5	3	29	15	7	4	10	20	32	69
8 Nottingham F	42	11	5	5	38	25	8	6	7	31	28	68
9 Luton T	42	12	6	3	37	15	6	6	9	24	29	66
10 Tottenham H	42	12	2	7	47	25	7	6	8	27	27	65
11 Newcastle U	42	12	5	4	46	31	5	7	9	21	41	63
12 Watford	42	11	6	4	40	22	5	5	11	29	40	59
13 QPR	42	12	3	6	33	20	3	4	14	20	44	52
14 Southampton	42	10	6	5	32	18	2	4	15	19	44	46
15 Manchester C	42	7	7	7	25	26	4	5	12	18	31	45
16 Aston Villa	42	7	6	8	27	28	3	8	10	24	39	44
17 Coventry C	42	6	5	10	31	35	5	5	11	17	36	43
18 Oxford U	42	7	7	7	34	27	3	5	13	28	53	42
19 Leicester C	42	7	8	6	35	35	3	4	14	19	41	42
20 Ipswich T	42	8	5	8	20	24	3	3	15	12	31	41
21 Birmingham C	42	5	2	14	13	25	3	3	15	17	48	29
22 WBA	42	3	8	10	21	36	1	4	16	14	53	24

DIVISION 2

		Home					Away					
	P	W	D	L	F	A	W	D	L	F	A	Pts
1 Norwich C	42	16	4	1	51	15	9	5	7	33	22	84
2 Charlton Ath	42	14	5	2	44	15	8	6	7	34	30	77
3 Wimbledon	42	13	6	2	38	16	8	7	6	20	21	76
4 Portsmouth	42	13	4	4	43	17	9	3	9	26	24	73
5 Crystal Palace	42	12	3	6	29	22	7	6	8	28	30	66
6 Hull C	42	11	7	3	39	19	6	6	9	26	36	64
7 Sheffield U	42	10	7	4	36	24	7	4	10	28	39	62
8 Oldham Ath	42	13	4	4	40	28	4	5	12	22	33	60
9 Millwall	42	12	3	6	39	24	5	5	11	25	41	59
10 Stoke C	42	8	11	2	29	16	6	4	11	19	34	57
11 Brighton & HA	42	10	5	6	42	30	6	3	12	22	34	56

			Home					Away				
	P	W	D	L	F	A	W	D	L	F	A	Pts
12 Barnsley	42	9	6	6	29	26	5	8	8	18	24	56
13 Bradford C	42	14	1	6	36	24	2	5	14	15	39	54
14 Leeds U	42	9	7	5	30	22	6	1	14	26	50	53
15 Grimsby T	42	11	4	6	35	24	3	6	12	23	38	52
16 Huddersfield T	42	10	6	5	30	23	4	4	13	21	44	52
17 Shrewsbury T	42	11	5	5	29	20	3	4	14	23	44	51
18 Sunderland	42	10	5	6	33	29	3	6	12	14	32	50
19 Blackburn R	42	10	4	7	30	20	2	9	10	23	42	49
20 Carlisle U	42	10	2	9	30	28	3	5	13	17	43	46
21 Middlesbrough	42	8	6	7	26	23	4	3	14	18	30	45
22 Fulham	42	8	3	10	29	32	2	3	16	16	37	36

DIVISION 3

			Home					Away				
	P	W	D	L	F	A	W	D	L	F	A	Pts
1 Reading	46	16	3	4	39	22	13	4	6	28	29	94
2 Plymouth Arg	46	17	3	3	56	20	9	6	8	32	33	87
3 Derby Co	46	13	7	3	45	20	10	8	5	35	21	84
4 Wigan Ath	46	17	4	2	54	17	6	10	7	28	31	83
5 Gillingham	46	14	5	4	48	17	8	8	7	33	37	79
6 Walsall	46	15	7	1	59	23	7	2	14	31	41	75
7 York C	46	16	4	3	49	17	4	7	12	28	41	71
8 Notts Co	46	12	6	5	42	26	7	8	8	29	34	71
9 Bristol C	46	14	5	4	43	19	4	9	10	26	41	68
10 Brentford	46	8	8	7	29	29	10	4	9	29	32	66
11 Doncaster R	46	7	10	6	20	21	9	6	8	25	31	64
12 Blackpool	46	11	6	6	38	19	6	6	11	28	36	63
13 Darlington	46	10	7	6	39	33	5	6	12	22	45	58
14 Rotherham U	46	13	5	5	44	18	2	7	14	17	41	57
15 Bournemouth	46	9	6	8	41	31	6	3	14	24	41	54
16 Bristol R	46	9	8	6	27	21	5	4	14	24	54	54
17 Chesterfield	46	10	6	7	41	30	3	8	12	20	34	53
18 Bolton W	46	10	4	9	35	30	5	4	14	19	38	53
19 Newport Co	46	7	8	8	35	33	4	10	9	17	32	51
20 Bury	46	11	7	5	46	26	1	6	16	17	41	49
21 Lincoln C	46	7	9	7	33	34	3	7	13	22	43	46
22 Cardiff C	46	7	5	11	22	29	5	4	14	31	54	45
23 Wolverhampton W	46	6	6	11	29	47	5	4	14	28	51	43
24 Swansea C	46	9	6	8	27	27	2	4	17	16	60	43

DIVISION 4

			Home					Away				
	P	*W*	*D*	*L*	*F*	*A*	*W*	*D*	*L*	*F*	*A*	*Pts*
1 Swindon T	46	20	2	1	52	19	12	4	7	30	24	102
2 Chester C	46	15	5	3	44	16	8	10	5	39	34	84
3 Mansfield T	46	13	8	2	43	17	10	4	9	31	30	81
4 Port Vale	46	13	9	1	42	11	8	7	8	25	26	79
5 Orient	46	11	6	6	39	21	9	6	8	40	43	72
6 Colchester U	46	12	6	5	51	22	7	7	9	37	41	70
7 Hartlepool U	46	15	6	2	41	20	5	4	14	27	47	70
8 Northampton T	46	9	7	7	44	29	9	3	11	35	29	64
9 Southend U	46	13	4	6	43	27	5	6	12	26	40	64
10 Hereford U	46	15	6	2	55	30	3	4	16	19	43	64
11 Stockport Co	46	9	9	5	35	28	8	4	11	28	43	64
12 Crewe Alex	46	10	6	7	35	26	8	3	12	19	35	63
13 Wrexham	46	11	5	7	34	24	6	4	13	34	56	60
14 Burnley	46	11	3	9	35	30	5	8	10	25	35	59
15 Scunthorpe U	46	11	7	5	33	23	4	7	12	17	32	59
16 Aldershot	46	12	5	6	45	25	5	2	16	21	49	58
17 Peterborough U	46	9	11	3	31	19	4	6	13	21	45	56
18 Rochdale	46	12	7	4	41	29	2	6	15	16	48	55
19 Tranmere R	46	9	1	13	46	41	6	8	9	28	32	54
20 Halifax T	46	10	8	5	35	27	4	4	15	25	44	54
21 Exeter C	46	10	4	9	26	25	3	11	9	21	34	54
22 Cambridge U	46	12	2	9	45	38	3	7	13	20	42	54
23 Preston NE	46	7	4	12	32	41	4	6	13	22	48	43
24 Torquay U	46	8	5	10	29	32	1	5	17	14	56	37

SCOTTISH LEAGUE 1985–86

PREMIER DIVISION

			Home					Away				
	P	*W*	*D*	*L*	*F*	*A*	*W*	*D*	*L*	*F*	*A*	*Pts*
1 Celtic	36	10	6	2	27	15	10	4	4	40	23	50
2 Hearts	36	13	5	0	38	10	7	5	6	21	23	50
3 Dundee U	36	10	6	2	38	15	8	5	5	21	16	47
4 Aberdeen	36	11	4	3	38	15	5	8	5	24	16	44
5 Rangers	36	10	4	4	43	18	3	5	10	19	27	35
6 Dundee	36	11	2	5	32	20	3	5	10	13	31	35

		Home					Away				
	P	W	D	L	F	A	W	D	L	F	A	Pts
7 St Mirren	36	9	2	7	26	24	4	3	11	16	39	31
8 Hibernian	36	6	4	8	27	25	5	2	11	22	38	28
9 Motherwell	36	7	3	8	23	23	0	3	15	10	43	20
10 Clydebank	36	4	6	8	18	32	2	2	14	11	45	20

DIVISION 1

		Home					Away				
	P	W	D	L	F	A	W	D	L	F	A	Pts
1 Hamilton A	39	14	3	2	43	17	10	5	5	34	27	56
2 Falkirk	39	6	8	6	26	24	11	3	5	31	15	45
3 Kilmarnock	39	12	4	4	37	17	6	4	9	25	32	44
4 Forfar Ath	39	11	4	4	28	18	6	6	8	23	25	44
5 East Fife	39	8	9	2	31	18	6	6	8	23	28	43
6 Dumbarton	39	8	6	5	32	23	8	5	7	27	29	43
7 Morton	39	10	3	7	32	27	4	8	7	25	36	39
8 Partick Th	39	5	7	8	25	30	5	9	5	28	43	36
9 Airdrieonians	39	7	6	7	30	27	5	5	9	21	23	35
10 Brechin C	39	8	6	5	35	27	5	3	12	23	37	35
11 Clyde	39	7	7	5	28	28	2	10	8	21	31	35
12 Montrose	39	6	9	5	23	21	4	5	10	20	33	34
13 Ayr U	39	6	3	10	19	29	4	8	8	22	31	31
14 Alloa	39	2	8	10	27	39	4	6	9	22	35	26

DIVISION 2

		Home					Away				
	P	W	D	L	F	A	W	D	L	F	A	Pts
1 Dunfermline Ath	39	14	4	1	52	18	9	7	4	39	29	57
2 Queen of the S	39	14	2	3	40	16	9	7	4	31	20	55
3 Meadowbank Th	39	11	7	2	39	20	8	4	7	29	25	49
4 Queen's Park	39	14	3	3	37	15	5	5	9	24	24	46
5 Stirling A	39	10	6	4	31	17	8	2	9	26	26	44
6 St Johnstone	39	11	3	6	37	23	7	3	9	26	32	42
7 Stenhousemuir	39	11	4	4	34	26	5	4	11	21	37	40
8 Arbroath	39	9	5	5	29	26	6	4	10	27	24	39
9 Raith R	39	11	3	6	41	27	4	4	11	26	38	37
10 Cowdenbeath	39	9	4	7	32	26	5	5	9	20	27	37
11 East Stirling	39	7	2	10	26	32	4	4	12	23	37	28
12 Berwick R	39	5	9	6	25	33	2	2	15	20	47	25
13 Albion R	39	4	5	10	19	34	4	3	13	19	52	24
14 Stranraer	39	5	1	13	21	38	4	4	12	20	45	23

BRITANNIC ASSURANCE CHAMPIONSHIP 1986

	P	W	L	D	*Bt*	*Bl*	*Pts*
1 Essex (4)	24	10	6	8	51	76	287
2 Gloucestershire (3)	24	9	3	12	50	65	259
3 Surrey (6)	24	8	6	10	54	66	248
4 Nottinghamshire (8)	24	7	2	15	55	80	247
5 Worcestershire (5)	24	7	5	12	58	72	242
6 Hampshire (2)	23	7	4	12	54	69	235
7 Leicestershire (16)	24	5	7	12	55	67	202
8 Kent (9)	24	5	7	12	42	75	197
9 Northamptonshire (10)	24	5	3	16	53	60	193
10 Yorkshire (11)	24	4	5	15	62	59	193
11 Derbyshire (13)	24	5	5	14	42	70	188
12 { Middlesex (1)	24	4	9	11	47	65	176
{ Warwickshire (15)	24	4	5	15	61	51	176
14 Sussex (7)	23	4	7	12	46	56	166
15 Lancashire (14)	23	4	5	14	41	51	156
16 Somerset (17)	23	3	7	13	52	52	152
17 Glamorgan (12)	24	2	7	15	39	47	118

1985 positions are shown in brackets.

The total for Derbyshire includes 12 points for a win in a one-innings match and that for Yorkshire includes 8 points for levelling the scores in a drawn match.

JOHN PLAYER LEAGUE 1986

	P	W	L	*Tie*	*NR*	*Pts*
1 Hampshire (3)	15	12	3	0	1	50
2 Essex (1)	16	11	4	0	1	46
3 Nottinghamshire (12)	15	10	5	0	1	42
4 Sussex (2)	16	10	6	0	0	40
5 Northamptonshire (5)	15	9	5	0	2	40
6 { Somerset (10)	16	8	6	0	2	36
{ Kent (10)	14	7	5	1	3	36
8 Yorkshire (6)	15	7	6	1	2	34
9 { Derbyshire (4)	16	7	9	0	0	28
{ Warwickshire (6)	15	5	7	2	2	28
{ Middlesex (12)	14	5	7	1	3	28

		P	W	L	Tie	NR	Pts
12	Lancashire (14)	16	6	9	0	1	26
	Glamorgan (14)	15	6	9	0	1	26
	Surrey (17)	15	5	8	1	2	26
15	Leicestershire (6)	15	5	10	0	1	22
16	Worcestershire (16)	16	5	11	0	0	20
17	Gloucestershire (6)	14	3	11	0	2	16

1985 positions in brackets.

RACING by BROUGH SCOTT

So fast the treadmill, indeed the tumbril, turns. In the beginning Shergar was a two-year-old, Scudamore was just a contender, Martin Pipe trained selling hurdlers and Lester Piggott still ruled the riding tree.

Looking ahead, it's the funding and structure of the whole game that seem the biggest issues. But cast an eye back and it's the individual players that fill the eye, a whole thundering herd of memories, mornings in the rain, afternoons in the sun, straining horses and set-eyed men, just mention the name and a whole vivid cameo comes galloping by.

The jumpers last longest, face the greatest risks and so leave the deepest mark. Take Aldaniti's Grand National in 1981. Through the whole decade there was nothing to match the emotion as Bob Champion rode back between the police horses. He had not just conquered Aintree, his victory over cancer said something about life itself.

Twice more in the 80s we had moments that went way out into a wider world: Dawn Run's great Cheltenham victory in the 1986 Gold Cup and Desert Orchid's equally unforgettable triumph through the mud three years later. Both horses rode great tides of emotion and as the crowd roared for them in the depths of that final hill, history knew there could only be one result.

Jumping horses may have a longer innings but it's still brutally hard. Dawn Run was to die in France that summer, by which time Jonjo O'Neill was suffering not just casualty but the cancer ward. Indeed the turnover of people was a relentless theme.

Who would have thought when Michael Dickinson pulled off the decade's outstanding training feat, saddling the first five in the 1983 Gold Cup, that he would end the 1980s largely forgotten, rebuilding his career in America after an abortive spell as private trainer to Robert Sangster?

Even if you might have guessed that the golden genius of John Francome would be succeeded and surpassed in the same span by the superhuman work-rate of Peter Scudamore, no one would have predicted the breakthrough on the training front: that Martin Pipe, the bookie's son from Somerset with no link to any of the Rimells, Winters or Dickinsons, should tear up the record books and make sure nothing was the same again. Despite all sorts of dark, jealous mutterings, Pipe was merely applying his own untutored, indefatigable logic to elements men like Guy Harwood had been practising for years. But maybe it wasn't just coincidence that it was Harwood who came up with the flat racehorse of the decade.

Dancing Brave's performance in the Arc de Triomphe will always remain a flashing jewel in the memory, a blend of devastating athletic power on the part of the horse and extra-ordinary match-winning cool from an inspired Pat Eddery in the saddle. It was our first Arc live to Britain and the rest of the world on Channel 4, and with its success came both the challenge and the headaches for the time ahead. The challenge is to put racing in the vanguard of the sports and leisure business as we approach the new millennium, the problem is to catch the public interest with equine performers of swallow-short careers and owners of such mega-billion funding that viewers and readers cannot relate to them.

In fact Dancing Brave's owner Prince Khalid Abdulla, of Saudi Arabia, has hardly a quarter of the thousand plus horses in training owned world wide by the Maktoum family of Dubai. These investors, and many others from those countries as well as from Abu Dhabi, Bahrain and Oman, are the biggest single input that British racing has ever received, but the danger of uncompetitive, uninteresting monopoly is clear.

For while breeders, trainers, jockeys and stable staff of Arab owned horses cannot believe their luck, while unpublicised gifts to racing charities have done incalculable good, the debt is almost too great.

For all those positive signs won't undo the damage if the public perception of big-time flat racing is something of a millionaire's stitch-up. Specifically if one man, or in the Mak-toum's case, one family, decide to avoid major challengers to keep their horses' reputation intact. To this end the early retirement of Touching Wood, Shareef Dancer, and most of all of Nashwan last year, put public interest at risk.

Those of us who love to applaud a champion begin to bat a bit carefully if we feel that the moment one cheer is given the wretched quadruped will be rushed off to cash in on that bubble of reputation at stud. But like many other of racing's oft-noised problems this difficulty can be overcome if only the racing authorities will face up to the mechanics of balancing the private business of racehorse owning and training with the public entertainment of watching and betting.

For arguments about 'protecting value' are clearly ridiculous for people of such wealth and who have such depth of talent at their disposal. What's more, the benefits of racing top horses through to their natural conclusion could seal a pact with the public that would reverse the present suspicion. British racing has never had such a powerful set of investors, as altruistic a bunch of owners.

Parallel to this opportunity has come the arrival of satellite television into betting shops, the emergence of Ladbrokes, Hills and Corals as super betting chains with world wide ambitions, and a new sense of realism within racing's leadership. Not since the Jockey Club thick-headedly turned down the opportunity of having a say in off-course betting has there been a chance like this.

What has to happen is that the different and often warring sectors of the racing activity have to realise their inter-dependence. Breeders may hate bookmakers and vice versa, trainers and journalists ditto, but the business they are into is just one small part of the larger leisure spectrum. It needs fans and punters and they will only come if the game at the centre of it can compete with other shows on offer.

The 80s have ended with an unprecedented sense of vitality within the game. There is still massive press coverage in the national dailies and on network television which now even embraces wider international events like the Breeders' Cup in America and the Japan Cup in Tokyo. Where else but in Britain could you suggest, as you quite legitimately could with Desert Orchid in 1989, that the most popular sportsperson around was a horse?

But Desert Orchid will gallop into the sunset soon enough. Racing's time is now.

Greyhound racing became increasingly popular during the decade.

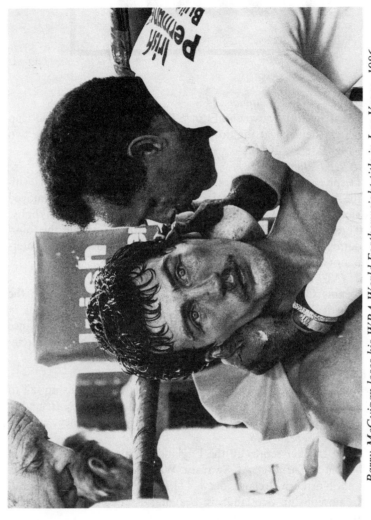

Barry McGuigan loses his WBA World Featherweight title in Las Vegas, 1986.

1987

RUGBY LEAGUE: *January 24*

Great Britain overwhelm France 52–4 at Leeds in a World Cup match then repeat the dose when they win at Carcassonne two weeks later by 20–10.

CRICKET: *January 15*

Despite losing the fifth Test England returned from Australia with the Ashes. Under the captaincy of Mike Gatting they also enjoyed victories in the World Series Cup and the Perth Challenge Trophy. Three successive Test hundreds from Chris Broad laid the foundations for the 2–1 series triumph and Broad was declared International Cricketer of the Year.

SAILING: *February 4*

Dennis Conner having suffered the ignominy of defeat in the America's Cup when he lost the trophy to the Australians in September 1983, recaptures it at Fremantle but the romance and magic of the competition has been destroyed by commercial overkill, bickering and never ending legal rows.

RUGBY UNION: *February 7*

England's high hopes in the Five Nations Championship fall to pieces at the first hurdle when they are beaten 17–0 by Ireland in Dublin while in Paris Wales were losing 16–9 to France.

SOCCER: *February 18*

Gary Lineker scores all the England's goals as they beat Spain 4–2 in a friendly. At Swansea Wales draw 0–0 with Russia and Northern Ireland draw 1–1 in Israel. In the European Championship Scotland are beaten 1–0 at home by Northern Ireland.

RUGBY UNION: *February 21*

Ireland after such a promising start to the Five Nations Championship are beaten 16–12 by Scotland at Murrayfield. Roy Laidlaw and Ieuan Tukalo score the tries while Gavin Hastings kicks a conversion and John Rutherford drops two goals. Donal

Lenihan scored the Irish try while Michael Kiernan added a drop goal, conversion and penalty. England, criticised for a lack of fire against the Irish, showed plenty of spirit at Twickenham against the French but lost 15–19.

SOCCER: February 24

For the first time in the history of the FA Cup there is a 4–4 draw in a replay as Walsall snatch an equaliser against Watford in extra time.

BOXING: March 4

Terry Marsh seemed to be heading for the heights when he beat Joe Louis Manley to take the IBF lightwelterweight title in a circus tent on the outskirts of Basildon. Staged on the night of his wedding anniversary and his small daughter's birthday, Marsh had seemingly set himself up for a lucrative defence. After defending the title against Japan's Akio Kameda Marsh was on course for a big pay day fight against Hector 'Macho' Camacho. Marsh's manager Frank Warren had settled the deal when Marsh confessed that he was an epileptic and was risking his life every time he stepped into the ring. His fighting career was over and he became embroiled in a bitter dispute with Warren. By 1989 Marsh claimed that he was not an epileptic but suffering from a condition brought on by gorging on chocolate and other sweet foods. This attempt to return to the ring under the banner of the UK-IBF was a failure and Marsh, the former schoolboy chess champion who broke the mould of the public's perception of the boxer, was finished.

RUGBY UNION: March 7

England lose again going down 19–12 at Cardiff Arms Park to Wales. The match was marred by violence and led to four English players being banned from the next international. Wade Dooley, Graham Dawe, Garth Chilcott and captain Richard Hill were the men singled out. Mark Wyatt kicked five penalties and Stuart Evans scored the Welsh try while all England's points came from the boot of Marcus Rose. In Paris a pulsating match between Scotland and France tipped France's way 28–22.

SOCCER: March 10

UEFA extends the European ban on English clubs playing in Europe for another year.

RUGBY UNION: March 21

Scotland improve on their sparkling performance in Paris and go one better beating Wales 21–15 thanks to tries from John Beattie and John Jeffrey. Gavin Hastings kicked the conversions and added two penalties while John Rutherford landed a penalty.

Mark Jones scored the Welsh try while Mark Wyatt added a conversion, dropped goal and two penalties. In Dublin France beat Ireland 19–13 to land the Grand Slam – but it was not plain sailing. They trailed 10–0 at half time.

RACING: March

Racehorse owner Jim Joel, 92, missed seeing his horse Maori Venture win the Grand National when he was inflight rather than at the racecourse when the victory was sealed.

RUGBY UNION: April 4

England, despite the suspension of four players, pulled together to earn an unexpected but deserved 21–12 victory over Scotland at Twickenham. They scored a penalty try and Marcus Rose also crossed for a try as well as adding two conversions and three penalties. For Scotland Keith Robertson scored their only try while Hastings kicked the conversion and two penalties. In Cardiff Ireland beat Wales 15–11. Paul Dean and Brendan Mullin scored their tries while Mike Kiernan kicked both conversions and a penalty.

SOCCER: April 5

Charlie Nicholas scores both goals as Arsenal beat Liverpool 2–1 in the Littlewoods Cup at Wembley. Ian Rush opened the scoring for Liverpool and it was the first time in 145 games that he had scored and ended up on the losing side.

SOCCER: April 29

In the European Championship England are held 0–0 in Turkey, Northern Ireland are beaten 2–1 by Yugoslavia in Dublin, Ian Rush scores to earn Wales a 1–1 draw with Czechoslovakia. The Republic of Ireland draw 0–0 with Belgium.

SNOOKER: May 3

In a repeat pairing of last year's final, Steve Davis took his revenge on Joe Johnson winning the title 18–14.

SOCCER: May 4

Everton's 1–0 win over Norwich earns them the League Championship. In Scotland a 1–1 draw for Rangers at Aberdeen earns them their first title in nine years as Celtic surprisingly lose at home for the first time in the season, beaten 2–1 by Falkirk.

SOCCER: May 16

In their first FA Cup Final Coventry beat Tottenham 3–2. The thrilling match is decided in extra time when Gary Mabbutt deflects a shot from Lloyd McGrath into his own net. A crowd of 98,000 paid £1,286,737.50 to see the match. In Scotland favourites Dundee United are surprisingly beaten by St Mirren when Ian Ferguson scores the only goal of the game in extra time.

SOCCER: May 23

Scotland and England are involved in a dull 0–0 draw at Hampden Park.

RUGBY UNION: May 23–June 20

The first World Cup is played in Australia and New Zealand, and England open against Australia losing 19–6 with captain Mike Harrison scoring England's try. A week later England routed Japan 60–7 and secured a quarter finals place with a 34–6 win over the USA. Wales topped their group beating Ireland 13–6, Tonga 29–16 and Canada 40–9. Ireland led by Donal Lenihan were runners up beating Canada 46–19 and Tonga 32–9. Scotland started their campaign with a thrilling 20–20 draw with the French, beat Zimbabwe 60–21, running in 11 tries and then got the better of Romania by 55–28. However they lost in the quarter finals against the all-powerful All Blacks 30–3. Ireland were also knocked out by Australia 33–15. Wales met England and beat them 16–3 to face the All Blacks in the semi-finals where they lost 49–6. The All Blacks, captained by David Kirk, then demolished the French 29–9 in the final on June 20 in Auckland. In the build-up to the final the All Blacks had averaged a staggering 50 points from each of their five matches, their highest score being a 74–13 win over Fiji in which they scored 12 tries, one of them a penalty try.

CRICKET: June 3–9

The first Test at Old Trafford against Pakistan ends in a draw. The match is plagued by bad weather. The second Test at Lord's is drawn but England lose the third at Headingley by an innings and 18 runs where they are dismissed for 136 and 199. The fourth Test is a draw with Gatting scoring a century, as is the fifth where Gatting again scores a hundred.

TENNIS: June 22–July 5

Six in a row as Martina Navratilova beats Steffi Graf in the women's final. But the young West German is to learn from the experience and to close the 80s as the top player, the heir apparent to Navratilova. Ivan Lendl, the world's number one male player, struggled again on grass and lost in the final to Australian Pat Cash. Cash on winning the title did away with protocol and clambered up into the players' box to embrace his coach, friends and family. In the mixed doubles Britain's Jo Durie and Jeremy Bates collected the title.

CRICKET: July 11

Northamptonshire scored 244 for seven in the Benson and Hedges Cup Final as did Yorkshire, but because they had lost one fewer wickets they lifted the trophy. A full house paid £288,221 to see the match.

MOTOR RACING: July 12

The British Grand Prix is won by Nigel Mansell in a Williams-Honda.

GOLF: July 19

The Open at Muirfield is won by Nick Faldo. He took the title by a shot and was in the clubhouse waiting for others to try and overhaul his score when he learned that he was the winner. A week later in the Women's US Open 23-year-old Laura Davies became the first Briton to win the event.

CYCLING: July 26

The Tour de France was won by Irishman Stephen Roche who built up a 40sec lead over Pedro Delgado of Spain which he held in the final run into Paris. Roche for so long overshadowed by fellow countryman Sean Kelly joined last year's winner Greg Lemond as the only two men from outside the continent to win the event.

BOXING: August 1

Mike Tyson brings the three heavyweight titles, the WBA, WBC and the IBF, under one heading when he defeats Tony Tucker to become the undisputed champion of the world.

ATHLETICS: August 30–September 6

Canadian Ben Johnson sets the world record for the 100m at 9.83 when he beats the previous holder Carl Lewis in the world championships in Rome. But Johnson's triumph is to end in disgrace a year later when he is disqualified from the Olympics after failing a drugs test. British champions Steve Cram and Daley Thompson both failed to win a medal but Fatima Whitbread won the women's javelin gold with a throw of 76.64m.

CRICKET: September 7

The NatWest Trophy final carried over to the Monday when Nottinghamshire completed the double beating North-amptonshire by three wickets. Northants made 228 for three and Nottinghamshire replied with 231 for seven.

CRICKET: September 9–11

Nottinghamshire beat Glamorgan by nine wickets but have to wait on the Lancashire v Essex result to see if they have won the title. In the event Lancashire only gained two batting points and Nottinghamshire were champions and £25,000 richer.

RACING: September 13

Despite opposition from churches The Jockey Club approves racing on Sunday.

CRICKET: September 13

Worcestershire win the Sunday League after a nine wicket win over Northamptonshire. It was a remarkable turnaround for a side who finished 16th the previous year and vindication of their decision to sign Ian Botham. They were the first winners of the tournament under the new sponsorship of Refuge Assurance.

GOLF: September 27

Europe retained the Ryder Cup, winning for the first time on US soil. Having built up a lead in the four-ball and foursomes, the Americans staged a charge in the singles. But Eammon Darcy sunk a wicked downhill putt at Muirfield, Ohio to beat Ben Crenshaw and Europe kept the trophy by a 15–13 margin.

RACING: October 23

Lester Piggott is jailed for three years at Ipswich Crown Court after admitting tax evasion totalling £3.1m. Piggott had ridden over 5,000 winners in his career and been in the saddle for nine Derby wins. He retired as a jockey to become a trainer in 1985.

RUGBY LEAGUE: October 24

Great Britain beat Papua-New Guinea 42–0 in a World Cup match at Wigan.

BOXING: October 28

Lloyd Honeyghan loses his world welterweight title to Jorge Vaca. The Mexican is cut after a clash of heads and takes the title by default.

CRICKET: November 8

England lose the World Cup final in Calcutta to Australia by seven runs. David Boon was the Australian man of the match with 75 runs. The tournament co-hosted by India and Pakistan saw both those countries reach the semi finals. Pakistan were beaten by Australia while a century from Graham Gooch ended India's interest in the tournament.

CRICKET: December 9

England captain Mike Gatting is involved in a finger-wagging cheating row with Pakistani umpire Shakoor Rana. The row halts the match and hours are lost as the political wrangle over who should apologise to whom rumbles on. Gatting and the England team eventually get back on the field of play but too much time has been lost and the series ends on a bitter note.

CHESS: December 19

Gary Kasparov as holder of the world championship retains his title after a 12–12 tie with his arch-rival Anatoly Karpov in Seville.

ROLL OF HONOUR

AMERICAN FOOTBALL: Superbowl: New York Giants 39 Denver Broncos 20.

ATHLETICS: European Cup, Men: USSR. Women: East Germany.

CRICKET: County championship: Nottinghamshire. Refuge Assurance League: Worcestershire. NatWest Trophy: Nottinghamshire. Benson & Hedges Cup: Yorkshire.

CYCLING: Tour de France, Men: Stephen Roche (Ireland). Women: Jeannie Longo (France).

GOLF: US Masters: Larry Mize. US PGA: Larry Nelson. US Open: Scott Simpson. The Open (Muirfield): Nick Faldo (GB).Ryder Cup (Muirfield Village, Columbus): Europe 15 US 13.

HORSE RACING: Flat:

1000 Guineas: Miesque. 2000 Guineas: Don't Forget Me. The Derby: Reference Point (Jockey: Steve Cauthen. Trainer: Henry Cecil). The Oaks: Unite. St Leger: Reference Point. Champion jockey Steve Cauthen, 197 wins. Top trainer Henry Cecil, £1,882,116.

National Hunt: Grand National: Maori Venture (Jockey: Steve Knight. Trainer: Andy Turnell). Cheltenham Gold Cup: The Thinker. Champion Hurdle: See You Then. Champion jockey Peter Scudamore, 123 wins. Top trainer Nicky Henderson, £162,234.

MOTOR RACING: Nelson Piquet (Brazil) in a Williams-Honda. Constructors' Cup: Williams-Honda.

RUGBY LEAGUE: Challenge Cup: Halifax. Championship: Wigan.

RUGBY UNION: Grand Slam: France. County Championship: Yorkshire. Pilkington Cup: Bath 19 Wasps 12. Schweppes Welsh Cup: Cardiff 16 Swansea 15. World Cup: New Zealand 29 France 9.

SKIING: Overall champion, Men: Pirmin Zurbriggen (Switzerland). Women: Maria Walliser (Switzerland).

SNOOKER: World Championship: Steve Davis 18 Joe Johnson 14.

SOCCER: First Division Title: Everton (86pts). Runners-up: Liverpool. FA Cup Winners: Coventry City 3 Tottenham 2 (aet). Littlewoods Cup: Arsenal 2 Liverpool 1. Scotland Premier League Title: Rangers (69pts). Runners-up: Celtic. Scottish Cup: St

Mirren 1 Dundee United 0. Scottish League Cup: Rangers 2 Celtic 1. European Cup: FC Porto 2 Bayern Munich 1. Cup Winners' Cup: Ajax 1 Lokomotiv Leipzig 0. UEFA Cup: IFK Gothenburg beat Dundee United 2–1. (H) 1–0 (A) 1–1.

SPEEDWAY: World Champion: Hans Nielsen (Denmark). British League: Coventry.

SQUASH: World Open Championship: Jansher Khan (Pakistan). Women: Susan Devoy (New Zealand).

TABLE TENNIS: World Championships, Men: Jiang Jialiang (China). Women: He Zhili (China).

TENNIS: Wimbledon: Men: Pat Cash (Australia) beat Ivan Lendl (Cze) 7–6 6–2 7–5. Women: Martina Navratilova (US) beat Steffi Graf (West Germany) 7–5 6–3. US Open: Ivan Lendl, Martina ˙ Navratilova. French Open: Ivan Lendl, Steffi Graff. Australian Open: Stefan Edberg (Sweden), Hana Mandlikova (Cze).

YACHTING: America's Cup: *Stars & Stripes* (US) skipper Dennis Conner. Admiral's Cup: New Zealand.

TODAY LEAGUE 1986–87

DIVISION 1

		Home					Away					
	P	W	D	L	F	A	W	D	L	F	A	Pts
1 Everton	42	16	4	1	49	11	10	4	7	27	20	86
2 Liverpool	42	15	3	3	43	16	8	5	8	29	26	77
3 Tottenham H	42	14	3	4	40	14	7	5	9	28	29	71
4 Arsenal	42	12	5	4	31	12	8	5	8	27	23	70
5 Norwich C	42	9	10	2	27	20	8	7	6	26	31	68
6 Wimbledon	42	11	5	5	32	22	8	4	9	25	28	66
7 Luton T	42	14	5	2	29	13	4	7	10	18	32	66
8 Nottingham F	42	12	8	1	36	14	6	3	12	28	37	65
9 Watford	42	12	5	4	38	20	6	4	11	29	34	63
10 Coventry C	42	14	4	3	35	17	3	8	10	15	28	63
11 Manchester U	42	13	3	5	38	18	1	11	9	14	27	56
12 Southampton	42	11	5	5	44	24	3	5	13	25	44	52
13 Sheffield W	42	9	7	5	39	24	4	6	11	19	35	52
14 Chelsea	42	8	6	7	30	30	5	7	9	23	24	52
15 West Ham U	42	10	4	7	33	28	4	6	11	19	39	52
16 QPR	42	9	7	5	31	27	4	4	13	17	37	50
17 Newcastle U	42	10	4	7	33	29	2	7	12	14	36	47
18 Oxford U	42	8	8	5	30	25	3	5	13	14	44	46
19 Charlton Ath	42	7	7	7	26	22	4	4	13	19	33	44
20 Leicester C	42	9	7	5	39	24	2	2	17	15	52	42
21 Manchester C	42	8	6	7	28	24	0	9	12	8	33	39
22 Aston Villa	42	7	7	7	25	25	1	5	15	20	54	36

Charlton won play off to stay in Division 1.

DIVISION 2

		Home					Away					
	P	W	D	L	F	A	W	D	L	F	A	Pts
1 Derby Co	42	14	6	1	42	18	11	3	7	22	20	84
2 Portsmouth	42	17	2	2	37	11	6	7	8	16	17	78
3 Oldham Ath	42	13	6	2	36	16	9	3	9	29	28	75
4 Leeds U	42	15	4	2	43	16	4	7	10	15	28	68
5 Ipswich T	42	12	6	3	29	10	5	7	9	30	33	64
6 Crystal Palace	42	12	4	5	35	20	7	1	13	16	33	62
7 Plymouth Arg	42	12	6	3	40	23	4	7	10	22	34	61
8 Stoke C	42	11	5	5	40	21	5	5	11	23	32	58
9 Sheffield U	42	10	8	3	31	19	5	5	11	19	30	58
10 Bradford C	42	10	5	6	36	27	5	5	11	26	35	55

	P	W	D	L	F	A	W	D	L	F	A	Pts
		Home					*Away*					
11 Barnsley	42	8	7	6	26	23	6	6	9	23	29	55
12 Blackburn R	42	11	4	6	30	22	4	6	11	15	33	55
13 Reading	42	11	4	6	33	23	3	7	11	19	36	53
14 Hull C	42	10	6	5	25	22	3	8	10	16	33	53
15 WBA	42	8	6	7	29	22	5	6	10	22	27	51
16 Millwall	42	10	5	6	27	16	4	4	13	12	29	51
17 Huddersfield T	42	9	6	6	38	30	4	6	11	16	31	51
18 Shrewsbury T	42	11	3	7	24	14	4	3	14	17	39	51
19 Birmingham C	42	8	9	4	27	21	3	8	10	20	38	50
20 Sunderland	42	8	6	7	25	23	4	6	11	24	36	48
21 Grimsby T	42	5	8	8	18	21	5	6	10	21	38	44
22 Brighton & HA	42	7	6	8	22	20	2	6	13	15	34	39

DIVISION 3

	P	W	D	L	F	A	W	D	L	F	A	Pts
		Home					*Away*					
1 Bournemouth	49	19	3	1	44	14	10	7	6	32	26	97
2 Middlesbrough	46	16	5	2	38	11	12	5	6	29	19	94
3 Swindon T	46	14	5	4	37	19	11	7	5	40	28	87
4 Wigan Ath	46	15	5	3	47	26	10	5	8	36	34	85
5 Gillingham	46	16	5	2	42	14	7	4	12	23	34	78
6 Bristol C	46	14	6	3	42	15	7	8	8	21	21	77
7 Notts Co	46	14	6	3	52	24	7	7	9	25	32	76
8 Walsall	46	16	4	3	50	27	6	5	12	30	40	75
9 Blackpool	46	11	7	5	35	20	5	9	9	39	39	64
10 Mansfield T	46	9	9	5	30	23	6	7	10	22	32	61
11 Brentford	46	9	7	7	39	32	6	8	9	25	34	60
12 Port Vale	46	8	6	9	43	36	7	6	10	33	34	57
13 Doncaster R	46	11	8	4	32	19	3	7	13	24	43	57
14 Rotherham U	46	10	6	7	29	23	5	6	12	19	34	57
15 Chester C	46	7	9	7	32	28	6	8	9	29	31	56
16 Bury	46	9	7	7	30	26	5	6	12	24	34	55
17 Chesterfield	46	11	5	7	36	33	2	10	11	20	36	54
18 Fulham	46	8	8	7	35	41	4	9	10	24	36	53
19 Bristol R	46	7	8	8	26	29	6	4	13	23	46	51
20 York C	46	11	8	4	34	29	1	5	17	21	50	49
21 Bolton W	46	8	5	10	29	26	2	10	11	17	32	45
22 Carlisle U	46	7	5	11	26	35	3	3	17	13	43	38

		Home					Away					
	P	W	D	L	F	A	W	D	L	F	A	Pts
23 Darlington	46	6	10	7	25	28	1	6	16	20	49	37
24 Newport Co	46	4	9	10	26	34	4	4	15	23	52	37

Swindon Town promoted after play off.

DIVISION 4

		Home					Away					
	P	W	D	L	F	A	W	D	L	F	A	Pts
1 Northampton T	46	20	2	1	56	20	10	7	6	47	33	99
2 Preston NE	46	16	4	3	36	18	10	8	5	36	29	90
3 Southend U	46	14	4	5	43	27	11	1	11	25	28	80
4 Wolverhampton W	46	12	3	8	36	24	12	4	7	33	26	79
5 Colchester U	46	15	3	5	41	20	6	4	13	23	36	70
6 Aldershot	46	13	5	5	40	22	7	5	11	24	35	70
7 Orient	46	15	2	6	40	25	5	7	11	24	36	69
8 Scunthorpe U	46	15	3	5	52	27	3	9	11	21	30	66
9 Wrexham	46	8	13	2	38	24	7	7	9	32	27	65
10 Peterborough U	46	10	7	6	29	21	7	7	9	28	29	65
11 Cambridge U	46	12	6	5	37	23	5	5	13	23	39	62
12 Swansea C	46	13	3	7	31	21	4	8	11	25	40	62
13 Cardiff C	46	6	12	5	24	18	9	4	10	24	32	61
14 Exeter C	46	11	10	2	37	17	0	13	10	16	32	56
15 Halifax T	46	10	5	8	32	32	5	5	13	27	42	55
16 Hereford U	46	10	6	7	33	23	4	5	14	27	38	53
17 Crewe Alex	46	8	9	6	38	35	5	5	13	32	37	53
18 Hartlepool U	46	6	11	6	24	30	5	7	11	20	35	51
19 Stockport Co	46	9	6	8	25	27	4	6	13	15	42	51
20 Tranmere R	46	6	10	7	32	37	5	7	11	22	35	50
21 Rochdale	46	8	8	7	31	30	3	9	11	23	43	50
22 Burnley	46	9	7	7	31	35	3	6	14	22	39	49
23 Torquay U	46	8	8	7	28	29	2	10	11	28	43	48
24 Lincoln C	46	8	7	8	30	27	4	5	14	15	38	48

Aldershot promoted after play off.

FINE FARE SCOTTISH LEAGUE 1986–87

PREMIER DIVISION

			Home				*Away*					
	P	W	D	L	F	A	W	D	L	F	A	Pts
1 Rangers	44	18	2	2	45	6	13	5	4	40	17	69
2 Celtic	44	16	5	1	57	17	11	4	7	33	24	63
3 Dundee U	44	15	5	2	38	15	9	7	6	28	21	60
4 Aberdeen	44	13	6	3	32	11	8	10	4	31	18	58
5 Hearts	44	13	7	2	42	19	8	7	7	22	24	56
6 Dundee	44	11	6	5	49	31	7	6	9	25	26	48
7 St Mirren	44	9	5	8	23	20	3	7	12	13	31	36
8 Motherwell	44	7	5	10	24	28	4	7	11	19	36	34
9 Hibernian	44	6	8	8	24	30	4	5	13	20	40	33
10 Falkirk	44	4	9	9	17	28	4	1	17	14	42	26
11 Clydebank	44	3	7	12	19	40	3	5	14	16	53	24
12 Hamilton A	44	2	4	16	15	40	4	5	13	24	53	21

DIVISION 1

			Home				*Away*					
	P	W	D	L	F	A	W	D	L	F	A	Pts
1 Morton	44	12	4	6	43	27	12	5	5	45	29	57
2 Dunfermline Ath	44	12	5	5	29	16	11	5	6	32	25	56
3 Dumbarton	44	12	6	4	37	25	11	1	10	30	27	53
4 East Fife	44	10	10	2	34	22	5	11	6	34	33	51
5 Airdrieonians	44	15	2	5	39	22	5	9	8	19	24	51
6 Kilmarnock	44	11	7	4	35	20	6	4	12	27	33	45
7 Forfar Ath	44	7	9	6	38	34	7	6	9	23	29	43
8 Partick Th	44	7	7	8	27	25	5	8	9	22	29	39
9 Clyde	44	6	9	7	26	25	5	7	10	22	31	38
10 Queen of the S	44	7	5	10	24	26	4	7	11	26	45	34
11 Brechin C	44	5	5	12	26	39	6	5	11	18	33	32
12 Montrose	44	7	5	10	24	30	2	6	14	13	44	29

DIVISION 2

		Home					Away				
	P	W	D	L	F	A	W	D	L	F	A	Pts
1 Meadowbank Th	39	14	3	2	37	11	9	6	5	32	27	55
2 Raith R	39	8	10	1	34	19	8	10	2	39	25	52
3 Stirling A	39	11	5	3	27	13	9	7	4	28	20	52
4 Ayr U	39	13	3	4	38	24	9	5	5	32	25	52
5 St Johnstone	39	10	2	7	26	24	6	11	3	33	25	45
6 Alloa	39	9	3	8	26	27	8	4	7	22	23	41
7 Cowdenbeath	39	8	5	6	33	31	8	3	9	26	24	40
8 Albion R	39	6	5	9	28	29	9	4	6	20	22	39
9 Queen's Park	39	5	12	2	27	20	4	7	9	21	29	37
10 Stranraer	39	4	7	9	17	28	5	4	10	24	31	29
11 Arbroath	39	5	5	10	25	33	6	2	11	21	33	29
12 Stenhousemuir	39	5	6	9	21	28	5	3	11	16	30	29
13 E Stirling	39	3	6	11	17	31	3	5	11	16	25	23
14 Berwick R	39	5	3	11	21	31	3	4	13	19	38	23

BRITANNIC ASSURANCE CHAMPIONSHIP 1987

						Bonus		
	P	W	L	Tie	D	Bt	Bl	Pts
1 Nottinghamshire (4)	23	9	1	0	13	68	80	292
2 Lancashire (15)	24	10	4	0	10	55	73	288
3 Leicestershire (7)	24	8	3	0	13	57	75	260
4 Surrey (3)	24	7	4	0	13	65	73	250
5 Hampshire (6)	24	7	3	0	14	59	73	244
6 Derbyshire (11)	24	6	5	1	12	51	70	225
7 Northamptonshire (9)	24	7	4	0	13	48	68	224
8 Yorkshire (10)	23	7	3	0	13	52	58	222
9 Worcestershire (5)	24	5	4	0	15	58	68	206
10 Gloucestershire (2)	24	5	8	1	10	62	50	200
11 Somerset (16)	24	2	3	0	19	61	70	163
12 Essex (1)	24	2	4	0	18	45	77	162
13 Glamorgan (17)	24	3	9	0	12	40	70	158
14 Kent (8)	24	2	7	0	15	53	66	151
15 Warwickshire (12)	24	2	7	0	15	48	67	147
16 Middlesex (12)	23	2	8	0	13	47	60	139
17 Sussex (14)	23	1	8	0	14	47	56	119

1986 positions are shown in brackets.

The total for Northamptonshire includes 12 points for a win in a one-innings match and that for Essex includes 8 points for levelling the scores in a drawn match.

REFUGE ASSURANCE LEAGUE 1987

		P	W	L	T	NR	Pts
1	Worcestershire (16)	16	11	4	0	1	46
2	Nottinghamshire (3)	13	9	3	0	4	44
3	Gloucestershire (17)	16	9	4	1	2	42
4	Somerset (6)	15	8	4	0	4	40
5	Derbyshire (9)	14	8	4	1	3	40
6	Kent (6)	14	8	5	0	3	38
7	Hampshire (1)	14	6	6	2	2	32
	Surrey (12)	14	6	6	0	4	32
9	Lancashire (12)	13	5	6	0	5	30
10	Middlesex (9)	13	5	7	0	4	28
	Northamptonshire (5)	12	4	6	0	6	28
12	Yorkshire (8)	14	5	8	0	3	26
	Leicestershire (15)	12	3	6	0	7	26
14	Glamorgan (12)	14	5	9	0	2	24
	Sussex (4)	13	4	8	0	4	24
	Essex (2)	13	4	8	0	4	24
17	Warwickshire (9)	12	3	9	0	4	20

1986 positions in brackets.

SAILING by *KEITH WHEATLEY*

LANCASHIRE FOLK used to have a saying to put down the upwardly mobile. 'Clogs to clogs in three generations,' the old cynics would chant, implying that the children of the newly-rich would soon be poor again. If a sporting event as esoteric as an international yacht race can share such a gritty metaphor, then the America's Cup is back in clogs after a brief spell as a glittering star.

Two years spent bogged down in the claims and counter-claims of the American legal system have crippled the Cup. When Californian helmsman Dennis Conner seized the Auld Mug back from the Australians in February 1987, it was the culmination of the greatest regatta in sailing history.

For five months the most talented sailors afloat had battled it out amidst the giant turquoise seas and high winds off Fremantle, Western Australia. Television took tacks and gybes into the world's living rooms. Couch potatoes who would have been sick on the Serpentine shouted encouragement to Harold Cudmore and his crew aboard the British entry, *White Crusader*.

It was the first time ever that sailing – yachting to the traditionalists – had made the big time. Elegant 12-metre yachts pushed soccer off the back page. Bookmakers offered precisely calculated odds on whether the New Zealand skipper, a 23-year-old wunderkind named Chris Dickson, could handle the pressures of an America's Cup final.

Six months later the dream was over. Harmonious, hot-blooded, competition gave way to legal wrangling as the Kiwis sought to exploit a loophole in the Victorian rules of the competition. It would end with Dennis Conner and NZ designer Bruce Farr on the brink of punching each other at a live televised news conference.

Back in 1980 it would have seemed impossible that the Cup should cause a brawl. Fierce backroom politics and high drama on the water had always existed as part of sailing's premier trophy. Yet the atmosphere at Newport, Rhode Island, was not conducive to fist-fights.

Amid the mansions of the Vanderbilts and the Rockefellers it was true that the Cup was becoming more professional. The old bilateral competition between Britain and the USA, growing out of an 1851 schooner race around the Isle of Wight, had begun to evolve into an international event. In 1980 France competed, as did Britain, Sweden and Australia.

On the American side at least one man had begun to realise that 130 years of undefeated possession of the Cup was going to take some maintaining. Dennis Conner had his yacht *Freedom* trialling and tuning for 300 days in the year prior to the regatta. Conner, a brash young Californian, was anathema to the stiff white collars and minds of the New York Yacht Club.

Only one other group began to approach the professionalism of Conner – Australian tycoon Alan Bond and his team. In both 1974 and 1977 they had challenged and failed in pursuit of the Cup. It was the same story in 1980, but each time they came to Newport the skill and depth of experience in the Aussie camp grew.

When they returned in 1983 it was with a secret weapon. The 12-metre class had been used for America's Cup races since the Second World War but had hardly changed since its inception at the turn of the century. The boats were graceful, lovely to look at, and slow.

Australian designer Ben Lexcen, a mercurial self-taught genius as fiery as Bond himself, added wings to the keel of the group's new 12-metre, *Australia II*. They enabled the sleek white yacht to point higher into the wind and manoeuvre more adroitly – vital in the pre-start 'fencing' between the two skippers.

However, Bond's master-stroke was to keep the winged-keel a deadly secret. Each time *Australia II* was hoisted from the water, canvas skirts shrouded the underbody from prying eyes and cameras. Security guards were posted around the dock and 'spy-divers' were caught in the water beneath the keel.

Naturally, the media loved it. A rich man's yacht race had become an international three-ring circus before their very eyes. British tycoon Peter De Savary was simultaneously mounting his first challenge for the Cup with the 12-metre *Victory*. De Savary's showmanship and ability to rile the NYYC almost matched that of Bond and hardly a day passed without some controversy boiling to the surface.

Events on the water were just as exciting. Dennis Conner was once more the defending skipper but his yacht *Liberty* was off-the-pace. Had it not been for catastrophic gear failure then *Australia II* could probably have won the best-of-seven series 4–0.

As it happened, the Australian boat, skippered by John Bertrand, went 3–1 down before beginning to claw back the series. With the scores level at 3–3 the eyes of the world were on Newport for the final race.

On a beautiful sunny day off Rhode Island a light breeze ushered in a new era of sailing. Conner led for the first five legs but, with just four miles to go downwind, Bertrand took an enormous gamble that paid off. He found a workable breeze while *Liberty* sat dead in a private doldrum. *Australia II* crossed the line 43 seconds ahead and Alan Bond had won the America's Cup.

Victory for Bond meant that the Victorian silver ewer, presented by the Royal Yacht Squadron for the 1851 race, was unbolted from its plinth in the NYYC and taken to Perth, Western Australia – home of both Bond and the Royal Perth Yacht Club. Within weeks of the trophy's carnival arrival plans were being laid for the 27th defence of the America's Cup, the first-ever outside the USA.

Despite the enormous growth in the cost of an America's Cup campaign, by now a minimum $10m, an overwhelming 23 challenges poured into RPYC. Not all would materialise but in mid-1986 the world's largest and longest regatta began with 13 challengers and four teams of would-be defenders.

After 400 elimination races taking four months, the stage was set for a Cup final between Conner at the helm of *Stars & Stripes*, and the Australian newcomers aboard *Kookaburra*. Bond had been unsuccessful in his bid to be the Defender, despite building three boats and spending $18m.

Sponsorship paid the bills for this extraordinary sailing fiesta. With television around the world now showing many hours of the Cup racing, blue-chip companies such as Newsweek, Digital and Fosters lager were willing to invest huge sums in an event that was becoming as complex and expensive as Grand Prix racing.

New Zealand were the surprise package. Led by Auckland financier Michael Fay, the Kiwis amazed the world by building the first glass-fibre 12-metres. Every previous boat in the class had been of wood or aluminium. Dubbed 'the plastic fantastics' the yachts were nearly good enough to put Conner out of the Challenger final.

He accused the New Zealanders of cheating and the stage was set for the farce of the past two years. Fay built a 120ft giant of a yacht that complied with the Deed of Gift governing the Cup. Unwilling to be outflanked, Conner responded with a hi-tech catamaran – an inherently faster boat.

The two mismatched yachts raced – by judicial order – off San Diego in September 1988. The result was a hollow 2–0 victory for Conner and the lawyers. Sailors everywhere and the America's Cup itself were the losers.

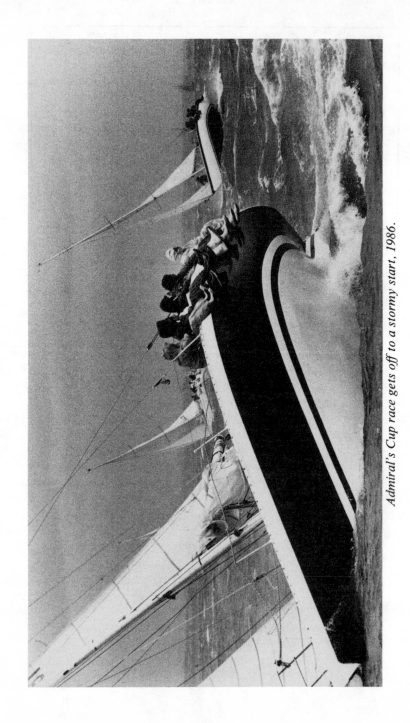

Admiral's Cup race gets off to a stormy start, 1986.

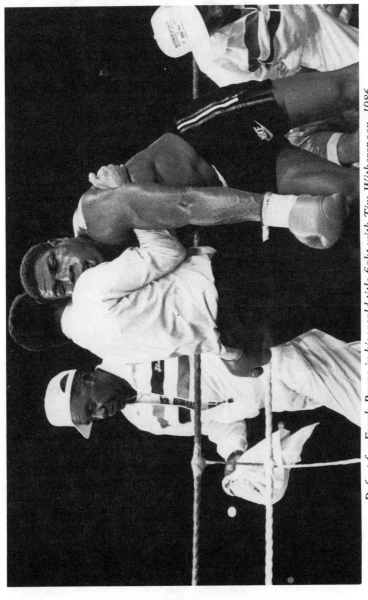

Defeat for Frank Bruno in his world title fight with Tim Witherspoon, 1986.

RUGBY UNION: *January 16*

England put up a surprisingly tough performance in their opening Five Nations Championship match in Paris when they lose to the French 10–9. In Dublin Ireland beat Scotland 22–18.

BOXING: *January 22*

Mike Tyson successfully defends his title by knocking out Larry Holmes, 17 years older, in the fourth round. But the old men will not go away as George Foreman, now known as the Preacher, prepares for a comeback at the end of 1989, and of course Tyson is the one he wants. The old masters never seem to learn to quit gracefully, but then money never did pin itself to dignity.

RUGBY LEAGUE: *January 24*

Great Britain win 28–14 in Avignon against France.

ATHLETICS: *February 4*

Zola Budd is banned from the world cross country championships in New Zealand.

RUGBY UNION: *February 6*

After their impressive performance in Paris England come down to earth when they are beaten 11–3 at Twickenham by Wales who score two tries through Adrian Hadley and a Jonathan Davies dropped goal. Scotland beat France 23–12, mainly thanks to Gavin Hastings who scored a try and four penalties.

CRICKET: *February 4*

England lose by 22 runs to Australia in a day-night match in Melbourne. Australia totalled 235.

RUGBY LEAGUE: *February 6*

Great Britain beat France at Leeds 30–12.

WINTER OLYMPICS: *February 13–29*

Martin Bell has the best ever finish for a Briton in the blue riband men's downhill event finishing eighth. It is won by Switzerland's Pirmin Zurbriggen who edged out fellow countryman Peter Muller by 0.51 sec. France's Frank Piccard collected the bronze.

Away from the winner's podium interest revolved around Cheltenham plasterer Eddie Edwards. The self-styled Eddie the Eagle became a winning loser finishing last in the 70m ski jump but had sponsors and the media queuing up for his thoughts. He finished some 20m behind the person second to last. The competition ended on February 29 with an ice spectacular. The Soviet Union topped the medals table with 11 golds, nine silvers and nine bronzes. East Germany's Katrina Witt left a lasting memory from her free skating performance while Yvonne van Gennip, a Dutch speed skater, won three golds.

CRICKET: February 18

England draw with New Zealand in Christchurch but bowler Graham Dilley is fined for swearing.

RUGBY UNION: February 20

Ireland lose 25–6 as the French record their second win of the championships while Wales build on their victory over England with a 25–20 win over Scotland thanks to tries from Davies, Watkins and Evans, two Thorburn conversions and a penalty goal and two Davies drop goals. Scotland's scorers were Calder and Duncan with tries and Gavin Hastings with four penalties.

RUGBY UNION: March 5

Wales continued to relive their golden days with a 12–9 win over Ireland in Dublin. In a battling performance they came back from a 9–3 deficit thanks to a Moriarty try, a Thorburn conversion and penalty and a Davies drop goal. Kingston scored the Irish try, converted by Kiernan who also landed a penalty. In Scotland two penalties from Jonathan Webb and a Rob Andrew drop goal gave England a 9–6 win. Gavin Hastings kicked two penalties for Scotland.

ATHLETICS: March 16

After being criticised for attending a race meeting in South Africa Zola Budd withdraws from the British international cross country team. A month later the Budd debate leads to a call from the International Amateur Athletic Federation for Budd to be suspended for a year. A failure to ban her could lead to Britain not taking part in the Seoul Olympics. On April 18 the possible crisis was averted when Budd was banned from taking part in competitions by the International Amateur Athletics Association.

RACING: March 17

Richard Dunwoody on the David Nicholson trained Charter Party wins the Cheltenham Gold Cup.

RUGBY UNION: March 19

Wales looking for their first Grand Slam in 10 years took on

France for the Five Nations Championship decider. Wales went down 10–9 despite some thrilling rugby and a try from Evans and a Thorburn conversion and penalty. France scored through Lescarboura and two Lafond penalties. Ireland took a hammering from a revitalised England who defied all their recent form to run in six tries, more than they had scored in four previous championship seasons. Leading the way was winger Chris Oti who scored three, Rory Underwood two and Gary Rees as England won 35–3.

BOXING: March 21

Mike Tyson, fighting in Tokyo, takes less than two rounds to destroy the challenge of Tony Tubbs. Tyson is a big hero in Japan where the warrior cult is still big business.

RUGBY LEAGUE: March 27

Martin Offiah scores three tries as Widnes beat St Helens 16–6 and need only a draw in their last match of the season to win the First Division Championship. In the event they beat Hunslet five days later 66–14, running in 12 tries.

CRICKET: March 28

Ian Botham, having been fined after a rumpus on a plane in Australia, is not to be fined over the incident by the TCCB. At the end of the month Botham starts his modern-day Hannibal journey for charity.

BOXING: March 29

Lloyd Honeyghan puts the record straight by regaining his world welterweight title when he knocks out Jorge Vaca at Wembley.

SNOOKER: March 31

Former world champion Cliff Thorburn is banned from two tournaments after failing a drugs test, fined £10,000 and docked two world ranking points.

BOAT RACE: April 2

Oxford win.

MOTOR RACING: April 3

Alain Prost wins the Brazilian Grand Prix.

CRICKET: April 6

Imran Khan inspires Pakistan to a nine wicket victory over the West Indies at Georgetown in Guyana. The Pakistan captain took seven for 80 in the first innings and followed that up with four for 41 as Pakistan ended a home run which went back 10 years. They did it with a day to spare.

RACING: April 9

Brendan Powell on Rhyme'N'Reason wins the Grand National which is worth £68,740.50 to the winning owner Juliet Reed.

GOLF: April 10

Sandy Lyle became the first Briton to win the US Masters and claim the coveted green jacket when he beat American Mark Calcavecchia by one shot in Augusta. Lyle who had led from the second round had to dig deep into his reserves to seal the victory. On the 18th of the final round and needing a birdie, he drove into a bunker and only a seven iron out of the sand, some 150 yards from the pin, put him back on course. The ball landed eight feet from the flag and Lyle sank the putt to collect the title.

ATHLETICS: April 17

The London Marathon is won by Henryk Jorgensen from Denmark.

RUGBY LEAGUE: April 30

A crowd of 94,273 pay £1,102,247 to see Wigan beat Halifax 32–12 to win the Challenge Cup Final at Wembley.

RACING: April 30

Walter Swinburn on the Aga Khan's Doyoun wins the 2,000 Guineas at Newmarket.

SNOOKER: May 2

Steve Davis collected £95,000 for retaining his world title when he beat Terry Griffiths 18–11 in the final of the world championships. Griffiths always struggled and was 5–1 down before clawing himself back into the game at 8–8. But he was eventually overawed by Davis.

CRICKET: May 6

Worcestershire batsman Graeme Hick etched himself a place in the record books with an unbeaten 405 at Taunton. He was only 19 short of Archie MacLaren's record score, also made at Taunton, of 424 made for Lancashire in 1895. Worcestershire captain Phil Neale declared the innings unaware Zimbabwe-born Hick had the English record in his sights. On May 28 Hick became only the eighth batsman to reach 1,000 runs in May when he scored 172 against the West Indies.

SOCCER: May 14

Lawrie Sanchez scores the goal that gives Wimbledon a surprise 1–0 FA Cup Final win over Liverpool and Wimbledon goalkeeper Dave Beasant is the first to save a penalty in a final at Wembley when he defies John Aldridge in the 61st minute. In Scotland Celtic complete the League and Cup double when they beat Dundee United 2–1 in the final, thanks to two goals from Frank McAvennie.

CRICKET: May 19

England beat the West Indies by six wickets in a one-day international at Edgbaston.

SOCCER: May 21

In the first England v Scotland match at Wembley on a Saturday for seven years, a Peter Beardsley goal gives England victory. The day is marred by crowd trouble with over 200 arrests made outside the stadium. In a World Cup qualifying match Northern Ireland beat Malta 3–0 at Windsor Park.

RACING: June 1

The Derby is won by the Aga Khan's Kayhasi, ridden by Ray Cochrane. The win is worth £296,500. Five days after the race, Lester Piggott, the Derby's most successful jockey and now in prison for tax evasion, is stripped of his OBE.

TENNIS: June 4

Steffi Graf wins the French title beating Natalia Zvereva 6–0 6–0. It is the first time since 1911 that a Grand Slam title has been won without a set being dropped. The men's title is won by Mats Wilander of Sweden.

GOLF: June 5

Sandy Lyle wins the British Masters at Woburn.

CRICKET: June 7

England make sure that the Test series cannot be another 'black-wash' when they draw the first Test of the summer series thanks to a second innings century by Graham Gooch. In the first innings Gooch had shared an opening partnership of a 100 with Chris Broad. But the summer is about to fall apart for England when three days later Mike Gatting is sacked as captain after inviting a barmaid back to his room for drinks. He departs with the words, 'No player should put himself in a position whereby the image of England is damaged in any way', ringing in his ears. The choice of who should lead England leads to the summer's least funny and longest running farce. John Emburey is appointed, to be replaced on July 14 by Chris Cowdrey, who in turn makes way for Graham Gooch, who when injured in the final Test leaves the pitch for treatment and England in the hands of Derek Pringle, making it five captains in five Tests.

RACING: June 15

Pat Eddery on Magic Life, owned by Stavros Niarchos, wins the Gold Cup.

SOCCER: June 12–25

The European Championships kick off in West Germany and England lose their opening game in Stuttgart against the Republic of Ireland 1–0. Ray Houghton is the scorer. There are 107 arrests following crowd trouble. Three days later and England are knocked out. Holland beat them 3–1 with Marco Van Basten scoring a hat-trick. The only bright spot is Peter Shilton's milestone as he collects his 100th cap. Ronnie Whelan scores as the Republic of Ireland draw 1–1 with Russia. On June 16, and following the crowd troubles, the FA withdraws the application for English clubs to return to European soccer. England's grim tournament is completed as they are beaten 3–1 by Russia and the Republic of Ireland go down 1–0 to Holland; 381 British supporters have been arrested. In the final Holland beat Russia 2–0 with Marco Van Basten and Ruud Gullit scoring.

CRICKET: June 21

England lose the second Test at Lord's.

TENNIS: June 20–July 4

Steffi Graf beats Martina Navratilova to win Wimbledon. She loses the first set 5–7 but takes the next two 6–2 6–1. The men's final is delayed by rain and not settled until the Monday when Stefan Edberg beat Boris Becker 4–6 7–6 6–4 6–2.

GOLF: June 20

Nick Faldo loses the US Open in a play-off when Curtis Strange beats him by four shots.

BOXING: June 28

Mike Tyson knocks out Michael Spinks in 91 seconds. Spinks, never knocked down before in his career, is sent reeling, recovers but Tyson shows him no mercy as he retains his heavyweight title.

MOTOR RACING: July 3

Alain Prost wins the French Grand Prix.

SOCCER: July 4

The United States is awarded the World Cup for 1994.

CRICKET: July 7

Exceptional bowling from Stephen Jeffries earns Hampshire the Benson & Hedges Cup. His spell of five for 13 from ten overs sends Derbyshire crashing to 117 all out. Hampshire knock off the runs in 32 overs for the loss of three wickets. Gate receipts are £338,989.

MOTOR RACING: July 10

In a rain and shine British Grand Prix which plays havoc with the drivers' choice of tyres, Ayrton Senna takes the chequered flag despite an heroic drive by Nigel Mansell who ends the race 23.3 secs behind the McLaren driver.

SOCCER: July 10

An ITV offer to ten clubs to screen League and Littlewoods Cup matches threatens a breakaway and formation of a Super League. Three days later the money on the table from the television company is raised to £52m. Six days after that and following a Football League injunction to stop five clubs privately dealing with the television companies, the Super League threat recedes as 80 per cent of the television money will go to the First Division clubs and the rest to be shared out throughout the League.

ATHLETICS: July 16
Running in Indianapolis Florence Griffith-Joyner sets the women's 100m record at 10.49 secs.

GOLF: July 18
Seve Ballesteros ends four years without a major championship when he wins the Open with a dazzling final round of 65 which puts him two shots ahead of Zimbabwean Nick Price.

CYCLING: July 21
Tour de France race leader Pedro Delgado fails a drugs test. Protesting his innocence Delgado is allowed to continue in the race while a retest is carried out. Delgado goes on to win the Tour even though the second test also proves positive. However the International Cycling Union says that as the drug Benemide found in the Delgado test has not been banned by them, the win will stand.

CRICKET: July 26
It's the same old story for England as they lose the fourth Test.

ATHLETICS: August 6
Sebastian Coe finds the decade catching up with him as he flops in the Olympic trials in Birmingham. Dreams of a third 1500m lie in tatters as the selectors have decided to award places to first and second with only the third spot at their discretion. Bidding for it are Steve Cram, the fastest man over the distance for the year, and Peter Elliott who won silver in the previous year's World Championship. Plans to find a way of awarding Coe a wild card place are finally ditched on the 23rd of the month.

SOCCER: August 8
Sports minister Colin Moynihan warns that he wants a football membership card scheme to be introduced in a year.

MOTOR RACING: August 14
Enzo Ferrari dies aged 80. Since starting his world-famous marque in 1940 his cars have won 13 world titles.

CRICKET: August 19
Graeme Hick scores the fastest century of the season from 79 balls as Worcestershire play Surrey at The Oval.

SWIMMING: August 28
Adrian Moorhouse sets the world record for 100m breaststroke in Bonn with a time of 1min 01.71secs.

CRICKET: September 3

Middlesex win the NatWest trophy by three wickets. A full house paid £353,017 to see them restrict Worcestershire to 161–9 from their 60 overs before replying with 162–7 from 55.3 overs. However the seemingly straightforward win was not achieved easily and there was a scare when skipper Mike Gatting was run out without facing a ball.

TENNIS: September 10

Steffi Graf completes the Grand Slam after beating Gabriela Sabatini 6–3 3–6 6–1 to claim the US Open. It is only the second time in the four championships she has dropped a set. She is the 5th Grand Slam winner and the first since Margaret Court in 1970.

SOCCER: September 14

Neil Webb scores the only goal at Wembley as England beat Denmark. In the World Cup qualifying matches Northern Ireland and the Republic of Ireland draw 0–0, Scotland win 2–1 in Norway while Ruud Gullit scores as Holland beat Wales 1–0 in Amsterdam. Scotland beat Norway 2–1 in Oslo in a World Cup qualifying match.

CRICKET: September 16

Worcestershire demolish Glamorgan by an innings and 76 runs to win the championship by one point from Kent. Attempts to sabotage their charge by pouring oil on the pitch fail and Hick closes the season with 197. They collect £35,000 and the trophy to add to the Sunday League title already retained.

OLYMPICS: September 17–October 2

Ben Johnson wins the 100m in 9.79 seconds but is stripped of the title six days later after failing a drugs test. Traces of Stanazol are found in his system. Britain's Linford Christie, who had finished third, is promoted to the silver medal position. The drugs issue casts a shadow over the Games and Britain's Kerrith Brown, a bronze medal winner in judo, is stripped of his prize after failing a test. Nine athletes are disqualified during the Games. Florence Griffith-Joyner wins the women's 100m and 200m while Britain's Daley Thompson, reigning Olympic champion, finishes fourth in the decathlon. Liz McCoglan, Fatima Whitbread and Colin Jackson win silver in the track and field events while Mark Rowland and Yvonne Murray collect bronze. Britain wins 4 × 100m silver. Adrian Moorhouse wins Britain's swimming gold in the 100m breaststroke. But the stars of the pool are East German Kristen Otto and American Matt Biondi, both of whom won five golds. Malcolm Cooper repeats his success of four years ago by taking the small bore rifle gold while his team-mate Allister Allan goes one better by taking the silver. On the water Steve Redgrave and Andy Holmes win gold in the coxless pairs, then go on to add a bronze. Mike McIntyre and Bryn Vaile collect star class yachting gold. The hockey team, with Imran Sherwani scoring twice, defeats West Germany for gold to give a final medal tally of five golds, ten silver and nine bronzes.

SOCCER: October 8
Newcastle and England legend Jackie Milburn dies. He was 64.

RACING: October 9
Lester Piggott is given parole.

GOLF: October 16
Ireland win the Dunhill Cup at St Andrews beating Australia 2–1.

SOCCER: October 17
The trial of 26 fans over the tragedy at Heysel begins.

SOCCER: October 19
In the World Cup qualifying stages goal-shy England draw 0–0 with Sweden at Wembley. Wales draw 2–2 with Finland in Swansea while Northern Ireland are beaten 1–0 in Hungary. Scotland draw 1–1 with Yugoslavia at Hampden Park.

SNOOKER: October 23
Steve Davies wins the Rothmans Grand Prix.

RACING: October 24
Lester Piggott is released after serving 12 months of a three year sentence.

RUGBY UNION: November 5
England beat Australia at Twickenham 28–19.

BOXING: November 8
Sugar Ray Leonard, 32, wins the world welterweight title for the fifth time in Las Vegas.

CRICKET: November 13
Viv Richards scores his 100th 100 in a Test match in Sydney against Australia.

SOCCER: November 16
England, playing with an experimental side, draw 1–1 in a friendly with Saudi Arabia.

RUGBY UNION: November 18
Australia recover from their upsets in England, which not only included defeat by the national side but also by London Division, to destroy Scotland at Murrayfield 32–13.

CRICKET: November 25
Peter May resigns as chairman of England's cricket selectors.

TENNIS: December 6

Boris Becker wins the US Masters final in New York beating Ivan Lendl.

ATHLETICS: December 12

David Jenkins was jailed for seven years in California on charges of supplying steroids but was released in June 1989 after a federal judge said that he had supplied information which led to 20 other people being caught. On his release from prison Jenkins, the former 400m runner, said 'I wish I'd never heard of steroids'.

SOCCER: December 21

Northern Ireland are crushed 4–0 by Spain in Seville in a World Cup qualifying match.

RACING: December 26

Desert Orchid wins the King George VI steeplechase at Kempton.

CRICKET: December 29

The West Indies tour to Australia helps Malcolm Marshall to become the ninth member of the 300 wicket-takers club.

ROLL OF HONOUR

AMERICAN FOOTBALL: Superbowl: Washington Redskins 42 Denver Broncos 10.

CRICKET: County championship: Worcester. Refuge Assurance League: Worcestershire. NatWest Trophy: Middlesex. Benson & Hedges Cup: Hampshire.

CYCLING: Tour de France: Pedro Delgado (Spain). Women: Jeannie Longo (France).

GOLF: US Masters: Sandy Lyle (GB). US PGA: Jeff Sluman. US Open: Curtis Strange. The Open (Royal Lytham): Seve Ballesteros (Spain).

HORSE RACING: Flat: 1000 Guineas: Ravinella. 2000 Guineas: Doyoun. The Derby: Kayhasi (Jockey: Ray Cochrane. Trainer: Luca Cumani). The Oaks: Diminuendo. St Leger: Minister Son. Champion jockey Pat Eddery, 183 wins. Top trainer Henry Cecil, £1,186,122.

National Hunt: Grand National: Rhyme'N'Reason (Jockey: Brendon Powell. Trainer: David Elsworth). Cheltenham Gold Cup: Charter Party. Champion Hurdle: Celtic Shot. Champion jockey Peter Scudamore, 132 wins. Top trainer David Elsworth, £344,210.

MOTOR RACING: Ayrton Senna (Brazil) in a McLaren-Honda. Constructors' Cup: McLaren-Honda.

RUGBY LEAGUE: Challenge Cup: Wigan. Championship: Widnes.

RUGBY UNION: Championship: France. Triple Crown: Wales. County championship: Lancashire. Pilkington Cup: Harlequins 28 Bristol 22. Schweppes Welsh Cup: Llanelli 28 Neath 13.

SKIING: Overall champion, Men: Pirmin Zurbriggen (Switzerland). Women: Michela Figini (Switzerland).

SNOOKER: World Championship: Steve Davis 18 Terry Griffiths 11.

SOCCER: First Division Title: Liverpool (90pts). Runners-up: Manchester United. FA Cup Winners: Wimbledon 1 Liverpool 0. Littlewoods Cup: Luton Town 3 Arsenal 2. Scotland: Premier League Title: Celtic (72pts). Runners-up: Hearts. Scottish Cup: Celtic 2 Dundee United 1. Scottish League Cup: Rangers 3 Aberdeen 3 (Rangers won 5–3 on penalties). European Cup: PSV Eindhoven 0 Benfica 0 (PSV Eindhoven won 6–5 on penalties). Cup Winners' Cup: Mechelen 1 Ajax 0. UEFA Cup: Bayer Leverkusen beat Espanol on penalties after aggregate score 3–3. (H) 3–0 (A) 0–3. European Championships (Munich): Holland 2 USSR 0.

SPEEDWAY: World Champion: Erik Gundersen (Denmark). British League: Coventry.

SQUASH: World Open Championship, Men: Jahangir Khan (Pakistan). Women: Susan Devoy (New Zealand).

TENNIS: Wimbledon: Men: Stefan Edberg (Sweden) beat Boris Becker (West Germany) 4–6 7–6 6–4 6–2. Women: Steffi Graf (West Germany) beat Martina Navratilova (US) 5–7 6–2 6–1. US Open: Mats Wilander (Sweden), Steffi Graf. French Open: Mats Wilander, Steffi Graf. Australian Open: Mats Wilander, Steffi Graf. Davis Cup: West Germany. Wightman Cup: US beat Britain 7–0.

YACHTING: America's Cup: *Stars & Stripes* (US) skipper Dennis Conner.

BARCLAYS LEAGUE 1987–88

DIVISION 1

		P	W	D	L	F	A	W	D	L	F	A	Pts
			Home					*Away*					
1	Liverpool	40	15	5	0	49	9	11	7	2	38	15	90
2	Manchester U	40	14	5	1	41	17	9	7	4	30	21	81
3	Nottingham F	40	11	7	2	40	17	9	6	5	27	22	73
4	Everton	40	14	4	2	34	11	5	9	6	19	16	70
5	QPR	40	12	4	4	30	14	7	6	7	18	24	67
6	Arsenal	40	11	4	5	35	16	7	8	5	23	23	66
7	Wimbledon	40	8	9	3	32	20	6	6	8	26	27	57
8	Newcastle U	40	9	6	5	32	23	5	8	7	23	30	56
9	Luton T	40	11	6	3	40	21	3	5	12	17	37	53
10	Coventry C	40	6	8	6	23	25	7	6	7	23	28	53
11	Sheffield W	40	10	2	8	27	30	5	6	9	25	36	53
12	Southampton	40	6	8	6	27	26	6	6	8	22	27	50
13	Tottenham H	40	9	5	6	26	23	3	6	11	12	25	47
14	Norwich C	40	7	5	8	26	26	5	4	11	14	26	45
15	Derby Co	40	6	7	7	18	17	4	6	10	17	28	43
16	West Ham U	40	6	9	5	23	21	3	6	11	17	31	42
17	Charlton Ath	40	7	7	6	23	21	2	8	10	15	31	42
18	Chelsea	40	7	11	2	24	17	2	4	14	26	51	42
19	Portsmouth	40	4	8	8	21	27	3	6	11	15	39	35
20	Watford	40	4	5	11	15	24	3	6	11	12	27	32
21	Oxford U	40	5	7	8	24	34	1	6	13	20	46	31

DIVISION 2

		P	W	D	L	F	A	W	D	L	F	A	Pts
			Home					*Away*					
1	Millwall	44	15	3	4	45	23	10	4	8	27	29	82
2	Aston Villa	44	9	7	6	31	21	13	5	4	37	20	78
3	Middlesbrough	44	15	4	3	44	16	7	8	7	19	20	78
4	Bradford C	44	14	3	5	49	26	8	8	6	25	28	77
5	Blackburn R	44	12	8	2	38	22	9	6	7	30	30	77
6	Crystal Palace	44	16	3	3	50	21	6	6	10	36	38	75
7	Leeds U	44	14	4	4	37	18	5	8	9	24	33	69
8	Ipswich T	44	14	3	5	38	17	5	6	11	23	35	66
9	Manchester C	44	11	4	7	50	28	8	4	10	30	32	65
10	Oldham Ath	44	13	4	5	43	27	5	7	10	29	37	65
11	Stoke C	44	12	6	4	34	22	5	5	12	16	35	62

			Home				Away				
	P	W	D	L	F	A	W	D	L	F	A	Pts
12 Swindon T	44	10	7	5	43	25	6	4	12	30	35	59
13 Leicester C	44	12	5	5	35	20	4	6	12	27	41	59
14 Barnsley	44	11	4	7	42	32	4	8	10	19	30	57
15 Hull C	44	10	8	4	32	22	4	7	11	22	38	57
16 Plymouth Arg	44	12	4	6	44	26	4	4	14	21	41	56
17 Bournemouth	44	7	7	8	36	30	6	3	13	20	38	49
18 Shrewsbury T	44	7	8	7	23	22	4	8	10	19	32	49
19 Birmingham C	44	7	9	6	20	24	4	6	12	21	42	48
20 WBA	44	8	7	7	29	26	4	4	14	21	43	47
21 Sheffield U	44	8	6	8	27	28	5	1	16	18	46	46
22 Reading	44	5	7	10	20	25	5	5	12	24	45	42
23 Huddersfield T	44	4	6	12	20	38	2	4	16	21	62	28

Middlesbrough promoted after play-offs.

DIVISION 3

			Home				Away				
	P	W	D	L	F	A	W	D	L	F	A	Pts
1 Sunderland	46	14	7	2	51	22	13	5	5	41	26	93
2 Brighton & HA	46	15	7	1	37	16	8	8	7	32	31	84
3 Walsall	46	15	6	2	39	22	8	7	8	29	28	82
4 Notts Co	46	14	4	5	53	24	9	8	6	29	25	81
5 Bristol C	46	14	6	3	51	30	7	6	10	26	32	75
6 Northampton T	46	12	8	3	36	18	6	11	6	34	33	73
7 Wigan Ath	46	11	8	4	36	23	9	4	10	34	38	72
8 Bristol R	46	14	5	4	43	19	4	7	12	25	37	66
9 Fulham	46	10	5	8	36	24	9	4	10	33	36	66
10 Blackpool	46	13	4	6	45	27	4	10	9	26	35	65
11 Port Vale	46	12	8	3	36	19	6	3	14	22	37	65
12 Brentford	46	9	8	6	27	23	7	6	10	26	36	62
13 Gillingham	46	8	9	6	45	21	6	8	9	32	40	59
14 Bury	46	9	7	7	33	26	6	7	10	25	31	59
15 Chester C	46	9	8	6	29	30	5	8	10	22	32	58
16 Preston NE	46	10	6	7	30	23	5	7	11	18	36	58
17 Southend U	46	10	6	7	42	33	4	7	12	23	50	55
18 Chesterfield	46	10	5	8	25	28	5	5	13	16	42	55
19 Mansfield T	46	10	6	7	25	21	4	6	13	23	38	54
20 Aldershot	46	12	3	8	45	32	3	5	15	19	42	53
21 Rotherham U	46	8	8	7	28	25	4	8	11	22	41	52

		Home					Away					
	P	W	D	L	F	A	W	D	L	F	A	Pts
22 Grimsby T	46	6	7	10	25	29	6	7	10	23	29	50
23 York C	46	4	7	12	27	45	4	2	17	21	46	33
24 Doncaster R	46	6	5	12	25	36	2	4	17	15	48	33

Walsall promoted after play-offs.

DIVISION 4

		Home					Away					
	P	W	D	L	F	A	W	D	L	F	A	Pts
1 Wolverhampton W	46	15	3	5	47	19	12	6	5	35	24	90
2 Cardiff C	46	15	6	2	39	14	9	7	7	27	27	85
3 Bolton W	46	15	6	2	42	12	7	6	10	24	30	78
4 Scunthorpe U	46	14	5	4	42	20	6	12	5	34	31	77
5 Torquay U	46	10	7	6	34	16	11	7	5	32	25	77
6 Swansea C	46	9	7	7	35	28	11	3	9	27	28	70
7 Peterborough U	46	10	5	8	28	26	10	5	8	24	27	70
8 Leyton Orient	46	13	4	6	55	27	6	8	9	30	36	69
9 Colchester U	46	10	5	8	23	22	9	5	9	24	29	67
10 Burnley	46	12	5	6	31	22	8	2	13	26	40	67
11 Wrexham	46	13	3	7	46	26	7	3	13	23	32	66
12 Scarborough	46	12	8	3	38	19	5	6	12	18	29	65
13 Darlington	46	13	6	4	39	25	5	5	13	32	44	65
14 Tranmere R*	46	14	2	7	43	20	5	7	11	18	33	64
15 Cambridge U	46	10	6	7	32	24	6	7	10	18	28	61
16 Hartlepool U	46	9	7	7	25	25	6	7	10	25	32	59
17 Crewe Alex	46	7	11	5	25	19	6	8	9	32	34	58
18 Halifax T**	46	11	7	5	37	25	3	7	13	17	34	55
19 Hereford U	46	8	7	8	25	27	6	5	12	16	32	54
20 Stockport Co	46	7	7	9	26	26	5	8	10	18	32	51
21 Rochdale	46	5	9	9	28	34	6	6	11	19	42	48
22 Exeter C	46	8	6	9	33	29	3	7	13	20	39	46
23 Carlisle U	46	9	5	9	38	33	3	3	17	19	53	44
24 Newport Co	46	4	5	14	19	36	2	2	19	16	69	25

Swansea City promoted after play-offs.
  * 2 pts deducted for failing to meet a fixture.
 ** 1 pt deducted for fielding an unregistered player.

FINE FARE SCOTTISH LEAGUE 1987–88

PREMIER DIVISION

	P	W	D	L	F	A	W	D	L	F	A	Pts
			Home						*Away*			
1 Celtic	44	16	5	1	42	11	15	5	2	37	12	72
2 Hearts	44	13	8	1	37	17	10	8	4	37	15	62
3 Rangers	44	14	4	4	49	17	12	4	6	36	17	60
4 Aberdeen	44	11	7	4	27	11	10	10	2	29	14	59
5 Dundee U	44	8	7	7	29	24	8	8	6	25	23	47
6 Hibernian	44	8	8	6	18	17	4	11	7	23	25	43
7 Dundee	44	9	5	8	31	25	8	2	12	39	39	41
8 Motherwell	44	10	2	10	25	31	3	8	11	12	25	36
9 St Mirren	44	5	11	6	22	28	5	4	13	19	36	35
10 Falkirk	44	8	4	10	26	35	2	7	13	15	40	31
11 Dunfermline Ath	44	6	6	10	23	35	2	4	16	18	49	26
12 Morton	44	3	7	12	19	47	0	3	19	8	53	16

DIVISION 1

	P	W	D	L	F	A	W	D	L	F	A	Pts
			Home						*Away*			
1 Hamilton Acad	44	12	5	5	36	24	10	7	5	31	15	56
2 Meadowbank Th	44	12	4	6	41	26	8	8	6	29	25	52
3 Clydebank	44	13	2	7	32	25	8	5	9	27	36	49
4 Forfar Ath	44	9	9	4	44	28	7	7	8	23	30	48
5 Raith R	44	10	4	8	45	33	9	3	10	36	43	45
6 Airdrieonians	44	11	4	7	34	28	5	9	8	31	40	45
7 Queen of the S	44	8	7	7	23	28	6	8	8	33	39	43
8 Partick Th	44	9	6	7	32	27	7	3	12	28	37	41
9 Clyde	44	8	5	9	40	38	9	1	12	33	37	40
10 Kilmarnock	44	8	6	8	30	30	5	5	12	25	30	37
11 East Fife	44	8	5	9	34	34	5	5	12	27	42	36
12 Dumbarton	44	4	8	10	23	30	8	4	10	28	40	36

DIVISION 2

		Home					Away					
	P	W	D	L	F	A	W	D	L	F	A	Pts
1 Ayr U	39	15	2	2	52	14	12	5	3	43	17	61
2 St Johnstone	39	14	5	1	40	11	11	4	4	34	13	59
3 Queen's Park	39	10	6	4	30	20	11	3	5	34	24	51
4 Brechin C	39	12	3	5	33	20	8	5	6	23	20	48
5 Stirling Albion	39	12	4	4	34	23	6	6	7	26	28	46
6 East Stirling	39	8	5	6	25	23	7	8	5	26	24	43
7 Alloa	39	10	4	6	30	19	6	4	9	20	27	40
8 Montrose	39	6	4	9	21	25	6	7	7	24	26	35
9 Arbroath	39	8	6	5	32	24	2	8	10	22	42	34
10 Stenhousemuir	39	5	6	8	19	25	7	3	10	30	33	33
11 Cowdenbeath	39	6	7	7	30	36	4	6	9	21	30	33
12 Albion R	39	6	5	8	21	33	4	6	10	24	42	31
13 Berwick R	39	3	4	13	18	38	3	0	16	14	39	16
14 Stranraer	39	2	6	11	22	42	2	2	16	12	42	16

BRITANNIC ASSURANCE CHAMPIONSHIP 1988

					Bonus		
	P	W	L	D	Bt	Bl	Pts
1 Worcestershire (9)	22	10	3	9	55	75	290
2 Kent (14)	22	10	5	7	57	72	289
3 Essex (12)	22	9	5	8	61	69	282
4 Surrey (4)	22	7	5	10	57	72	241
5 Nottinghamshire (1)	22	8	8	6	34	71	229
6 Warwickshire (15)	22	6	8	8	48	74	218
7 Middlesex (16)	22	7	3	12	49	54	215
8 Leicestershire (3)	22	6	3	13	56	63	215
9 Lancashire (2)	22	6	7	9	41	67	212
10 Gloucestershire (10)	21	6	7	8	52	59	207
11 Somerset (11)	22	5	6	11	48	65	201
12 Northamptonshire (7)	22	5	7	10	48	71	199
13 Yorkshire (8)	22	4	6	12	48	65	177
14 Derbyshire (6)	22	4	3	15	53	54	171
15 Hampshire (5)	22	4	6	12	33	69	166
16 Sussex (17)	22	3	11	8	37	65	150
17 Glamorgan (13)	21	1	8	12	42	53	111

1987 positions are shown in brackets.

The total for Nottinghamshire includes 12 points for a win in a one-innings match, and those for Essex, Lancashire and Somerset include 8 points for levelling the scores in a drawn match.

REFUGE ASSURANCE LEAGUE

	P	W	L	Tie	NR	Pts
1 Worcestershire (1)	15	12	3	0	1	50
2 Gloucestershire (3)	14	10	4	0	2	44
3 Lancashire (9)	15	10	4	0	2	44
4 Middlesex (10)	15	9	3	0	4	44
5 { Surrey (7)	15	8	5	1	2	38
Glamorgan (14)	15	8	5	1	2	38
7 Kent (6)	14	7	6	0	3	34
8 Yorkshire (12)	15	7	7	0	2	32
9 Hampshire (7)	15	7	8	0	1	30
10 { Essex (14)	15	6	8	1	1	28
Warwickshire (17)	14	6	8	0	2	28
12 { Somerset (4)	15	6	9	0	1	26
Derbyshire (5)	16	5	8	1	2	26
Northamptonshire (10)	14	4	9	0	3	22
14 { Sussex (14)	15	4	9	2	1	22
Leicestershire (12)	14	4	9	0	3	22
17 Nottinghamshire (2)	14	3	11	0	2	16

1987 positions in brackets.

OLYMPIC GAMES: SEOUL LEADING MEDAL WINNERS

	G	S	B	Tot
Soviet Union	55	31	46	132
East Germany	37	35	30	102
United States	36	31	27	94
South Korea	12	10	11	33
West Germany	11	14	15	40
Hungary	11	6	6	23
Bulgaria	10	12	13	35
Romania	7	11	6	24
France	6	4	6	16
Italy	6	4	4	14
China	5	11	12	28

	G	*S*	*B*	*Tot*
Great Britain	5	10	9	24
Kenya	5	2	2	9
Japan	4	3	7	14
Australia	3	6	5	14

MOTOR RACING by NORMAN HOWELL

THIS YEAR will be the eleventh that Alain Prost has donned flame-proof overalls, pulled on his helmet and strapped himself into a Formula 1 racing car. He has lined up on the grid 153 times, winning a record 39 times and becoming world champion three times.

Formula 1 is a sport riddled with statistics, and hundreds of figures could be reeled out to attempt to explain the greatness of this diminutive Frenchman with the gnarled looks of a rugby scrum half who has dominated the pinnacle of motor racing for the past decade. But mere figures could not do justice to this man.

When he drove for Renault in the early 80s, the mechanics nicknamed him 'Le professeur' because of his extraordinary punctiliousness in all matters relating to the car, its engine, chassis, and set up. The soubriquet has stuck and Prost, though barely 35, has acquired near-legendary status within the hard, business-like world of Formula 1.

He is the man who seems not to race to win at all costs. He prefers to see the 16-race season as a whole, a war to be planned out meticulously, a battle plan that involves him in as little risk as is possible in this sport.

He has been accused of lacking 'bottle', an extraordinary accusation which has been levelled either by uncomprehending members of the media looking for quick sensation, or by former drivers who resent his resistance to be a macho driver at all costs.

Of course Prost has courage, he also has the necessary bloody-mindedness to take on Ayrton Senna, his biggest rival over the past two years. At Suzuka, in Japan last year, Prost muscled his way past the Brazilian, hitherto the fastest off the grid, and proceeded to give him a driving lesson for most of the race. When Senna finally caught up, Prost appeared to make an error of judgement, easing to the left and allowing the Brazilian to see a 'gap' to drive through and overtake.

But as soon as Senna took the inside line to pass his team mate, Prost veered into him and both cars locked wheels and came to a halt. The manoeuvre was so smoothly executed that it took an aerial shot of the accident before anyone realised that it was indeed Prost who had lured Senna into a trap and into the loss of the World Championship. As an added twist to his scheme, Prost locked his car into gear, so as to make it near-impossible for the Brazilian to re-start.

Normally Prost does not engage in these sorts of incidents, though like all great champions he has proved again and again that meanness is an important factor in the winner's make-up. Shyness is a more fundamental trait of the man.

A gentle yet haunted look often crosses his features, he talks softly when interviewed, giving considered answers and expressing himself comfortably in three languages. But the steel is always barely beneath the surface. He gave notice of being different in 1979 when he was offered an end-of-season race with McLaren. He had just won that year's Formula 3000 championship and was hanging around the paddock as so many young, able but teamless drivers do. Alain Prost, aged 24, said no to a dream drive.

He was already shrewd enough to realise that it was not as good a drive as it might have looked on the surface. He had never sat in a F1 car and he would have been on a hiding to nothing. Instead he took the car for testing at the Paul Ricard circuit and on the strength of that he was offered a proper drive for the whole of the following year.

From McLaren he went to Renault. His time there was not a happy one. Never one to express patriotic feelings he suffered at the hand of René Arnoux, his team mate, who broke an agreement and went on to win a race. This is something that has happened more than once to him, and for this he has been accused of being naive.

That may be so, but it also adds a human touch to a champion who has also been regarded as metronomic in his driving; his effortless skill and flowing style have not been deemed quite right by the 'experts'. His belief in his team mate has already cost him a world championship and caused him a lot of heartache, but there is nothing to show he will not do it again.

From Renault he went back to McLaren, a team he left at the end of last year to claim his place at Ferrari, the only other team he could have gone to where he could still feel an incentive to prove himself. On the way he drove with Niki Lauda and learnt from Jim Clark and Jackie Stewart, the drivers he most admired – all effortless craftsmen of F1, never straining the car, hardly ever involved in incidents.

Like Senna he is a Christian, but unlike the Brazilian he is quiet about his belief, owning up only to a 1985 meeting with the Pope, which he described as one of the highlights of his life.

His quietness extends to his life in the paddock, where unlike some of the other drivers, he keeps a low profile, spending most of his time playing cards with the same three French partners.

He is intensely private about his life away from the race track. His home in Switzerland is his sanctuary, where only a handful of outsiders are allowed in. When at home he relaxes by watching football and tennis or indeed playing golf, a game he was introduced to by Jacques Lafitte. But the man is a racing driver, a winner. He has said that life is a game, and in that he wants to be the best. Otherwise life, the game, is not interesting. That is a sentiment they will share and understand at Ferrari.

James Hunt, a shrewd judge of men, sums him up thus: 'Prost is as quick as anybody, he's really super quick. His setting up is outstanding, his race tactics are superlative, his physical and mental understanding exceptional.'

Martina Navratilova on her way to victory in the 1987 Wimbledon final.

The British biathlon team at the Winter Olympics, Lake Placid 1988.

BOXING: *February 5*

Lloyd Honeyghan loses his WBC welterweight title to Marlon Starling at Caesar's Palace. The fight, hyped by a war of words between Honeyghan and Starling, was stopped in the ninth round.

RUGBY UNION: *February 4*

The Five Nations Championship kicks off with England and Scotland drawing 12–12 at Twickenham and Ireland beating Wales 19–13 at Cardiff Arms Park.

RACING: *February 7*

Peter Scudamore rides his 150th winner of the season and seven days later makes it his 1,000th winner of his career when he wins at Newton Abbot on Avionne. His 100th winner on December 20th of 1988 was achieved six weeks faster than the previous fastest 100 by Jonjo O'Neill in 1978.

SOCCER: *February 8*

A Richard Gough goal five minutes into injury time gives Scotland a 3–2 win over Cyprus in a World Cup qualifying game but Northern Ireland are beaten 2–0 at home by Spain. Bryan Robson scores the winner as England beat Greece 2–1 in a friendly. Wales draw 3–3 with Israel.

RUGBY UNION: *February 18*

England make up for the disappointment of the draw against Scotland by beating Ireland 16–3 in Dublin. France demolish Wales 31–12.

BOXING: *February 27*

At long last, the postponements and the talk are over and it is down to business but Frank Bruno's efforts to relieve Mike Tyson of his world heavyweight title end in the fifth round. Bruno, always a no-hoper in the contest, walked away with £1m for his trouble and the knowledge that after a knock down in the first round he caught Tyson with a punch which hurt the champion. Not only richer, his pride as a fighter was still intact.

RUGBY UNION: March 4

England's season gets better and better when they beat France 11–0 at Twickenham. Scotland beat Ireland 37–21 at Murrayfield.

CRICKET: March 8

Ted Dexter is appointed the new chairman of England's cricket selectors. He enters the stage full of bravado and promises of better things to come, blissfully unaware of the summer of disasters that are to come.

SOCCER: March 8

Goals by John Barnes and Bryan Robson earn England a 2–0 win in Albania in a World Cup qualifying game while Mo Johnston scores both Scottish goals in their 2–0 win over France at Hampden Park. Hungary and Northern Ireland draw 0–0.

BOXING: March 8

Duke McKenzie retains his IBF flyweight title after stopping Tony DeLuca, of the US, in the fourth round of their bout at the Albert Hall.

RACING: March 17

The legend of Desert Orchid is in the making when he becomes the first grey to win the Cheltenham Gold Cup.

RUGBY UNION: March 19

England's Welsh nightmare continues. Tipped to at last break that sequence of no win at Cardiff Arms Park since 1963, England, overwhelming favourites, manage to lose again 12–9.

BOAT RACE: March 25

Oxford score a two and a half length victory over Cambridge despite conceding 11lbs per man and being the outsiders for the race.

MOTOR RACING: March 29

Nigel Mansell's first Grand Prix drive for Ferrari brings victory in the opening race of the season in Brazil.

SAILING: March 29

A New York judge quashed the US America's Cup victory of 1988 and handed it to New Zealand after ruling that the catamaran, *Stars & Stripes*, skippered by Dennis Conner, violated the spirit of the race.

SQUASH: April

Martine le Moignan, a tall left-hander from Guernsey, created one of the women's games biggest upsets in the world open final by bringing down the title holder Susan Devoy 3–1 in Holland. But the New Zealander won her sixth successive British Open title by beating le Moignan 3–1 in the Wembley final one month later and ended the decade as still the world's number one ranked player. The English could only make an impact in women's events and won the team title in Holland which they took from Australia in 1985 in Dublin and retained in 1987 in Australia.

CRICKET: April 5

David Gower is recalled to lead England for the whole of the Ashes series.

RACING April 6

The seemingly invincible Desert Orchid, partnered by Simon Sherwood, fell at the 12th in the Martell Cup Chase at Aintree, ending a run of nine wins.

RACING: April 8

The Grand National is won by outsider Little Polveir, priced at 28–1.

GOLF: April 9

Nick Faldo picked up where Sandy Lyle left off when he won the Masters on the second hole of a play-off with Scott Hoch. Faldo and Hoch shot 283 and were followed by Australian Greg Norman and Ben Crenshaw on 284.

SOCCER: April 9

For the third year running the Littlewoods Cup holders lose the trophy in the final. Two goals from Nigel Clough help Nottingham Forest to a 3–1 victory over Luton Town.

SOCCER: April 11

UEFA lift their ban on English clubs playing in Europe providing the government support the move.

BOXING: April 12

One of the sport's most stylish fighters, Sugar Ray Robinson, dies. He was 67. Sugar Ray was five times world middleweight champion and welterweight champion. Jake La Motta, the Raging Bull, who fought Sugar Ray six times, said, 'He opened everything that was closed and closed everything that was open'.

SNOOKER: April 14–May 1

The World Championship starts in Sheffield and Steve Davis is the inevitable finalist where he faces John Parrott. Parrott is ruthlessly swept aside 18–3 and Davis pockets the winner's cheque for £105,000.

SOCCER: April 15

The Hillsborough disaster. Ninety-five Liverpool fans are crushed to death in the Leppings Lane end of the ground during the FA Cup semi-final between Liverpool and Nottingham Forest, another 200 are injured. The match is abandoned after six minutes. Lord Justice Taylor will head an inquiry into the disaster. Matches are postponed as soccer suffers from shock and Liverpool are in two minds over whether to continue in the FA Cup competition. The disaster is the worst in British sporting history and shows that the lessons of Bradford had not been learned. The focus shifts to the abysmal state of England's sporting stadiums as the question of safety hangs like a cloud over soccer.

ATHLETICS: April 23

The ninth London marathon is run with 27,000 contestants, some serious but most just doing it for fun. The outcome is that they raise £9m for charity. Kenyan Douglas Wakiihuri wins in 2hours 09min 03secs.

SOCCER: April 26

England beat Albania 5–0 at Wembley in a World Cup qualifying match with goals from Lineker, Beardsley 2, Waddle and Gascoigne. Scotland, with goals by Johnston and McCoist, beat Cyprus 2–1, an own goal earns the Republic of Ireland a 1–0 home win over Spain and Northern Ireland win 2–0 in Malta. Clarke and O'Neill are their scorers. In a friendly at Wrexham Wales are beaten 2–0 by Sweden.

RACING: April 27

Peter Scudamore rides his 200th winner of the season. The last time 200 winners were ridden was by Sir Gordon Richards in 1952 with 231.

SOCCER: April 28

Of the 24 Liverpool fans charged with manslaughter over the Heysel Stadium disaster 14 are found guilty in Brussels and sentenced to three years with half the term suspended and fined £1,000. They were given a fortnight to appeal. Ten others were released on grounds of insufficient evidence.

RUGBY UNION: April 29

In their fifth Twickenham final Bath overcome Leicester 10–6 to win the Pilkington Cup and complete a cup and league double. They snatch victory with a late try and make it a sad final appearance for the Leicester and England full-back Dusty Hare who is retiring from the game having amassed a world record 7,177 points.

SOCCER: May 7

The ill-fated Liverpool v Nottingham Forest FA Cup semi-final is played with Liverpool emerging 3–1 winners.

BOXING: May 10

Herol Graham fails to wrest the WBA middleweight title from Mike McCallum of Jamaica, after a bruising encounter at the Albert Hall which is settled on a points decision.

SOCCER: May 20

The FA Cup final is won by Liverpool. They beat Everton 3–2

after extra time. The familiar Liverpool names of Aldridge and Rush, 2, are on the score sheet. Both Everton's goals were scored by McCall. In Scotland Celtic beat Rangers 1–0, Joe Miller scoring.

SOCCER: May 26

Needing to win by two goals to take the championship, Arsenal end Liverpool's 24 match run without defeat by doing just that. The winner comes only seconds from the end of the match.

SOCCER: May 31

Wales' World Cup hopes are dashed as they draw 0–0 with West Germany in a qualifying match at Cardiff Arms Park, the first soccer match in Britain to be played in an all-seat stadium.

BOXING: May 31

Barry McGuigan, who threatened to have a dazzling career as an all-time boxing great, says goodbye to the ring after he is beaten by Jim McDonnell in a superfeatherweight contest. The fight was stopped in the fourth round after McGuigan suffered a bad cut.

SOCCER: June 3

Gary Lineker, John Barnes and Neil Webb score as England beat Poland 3–0 at Wembley in a World Cup qualifying match. It was Peter Shilton's 108th cap, equalling Bobby Moore's record. The following day the Republic of Ireland beat Hungary 2–0 in Dublin in the same competition.

SOCCER: June 7

England draw 1–1 with Denmark in Copenhagen in a match to celebrate 100 years of Danish soccer.

RACING: June 7

Willie Carson riding 5–4 favourite Nashwan wins The Derby.

BOXING: June 7

Dave McAuley, a chef from Larne, beat holder Duke McKenzie on points for the IBF flyweight title at the Wembley Arena.

TENNIS: June 11

Michael Chang caused a sensation when he became the youngest winner of a Grand Slam event. He beat Stefan Edberg 6–1 3–6 4–6 6–4 6–2 in the final of the French Open. Along the way Chang, of the US, had also beaten Ivan Lendl. There was a surprise in the ladies tournament as well. Steffi Graf also fell to a 17-year-old, Spain's Arantxa Sanchez-Vicario 7–6 3–6 7–5.

CRICKET: June 13

Another summer of discontent is taking shape for England as they lose the first Test against the Australians by 210 runs. Gower won the toss and made the wrong choice while Australian batsmen

Steve Waugh and Mark Taylor hit an undefeated 177 and 136. When England batted they ran into the formidable form of Terry Alderman. From such a humbling beginning was the rest of the season to be fashioned.

GOLF: June 18

Curtis Strange made the first successful defence of the US Open since Ben Hogan. He shot 278 on the Oak Hill course at Rochester to take the title. Britain's Ian Woosnam was one shot behind.

TENNIS: June 26–July 9

Boris Becker gained revenge for his Wimbledon defeat a year earlier by Stefan Edberg while Steffi Graf bounced back from the shock of Paris to demolish Martina Navratilova and make the prospect of her winning another Wimbledon title highly unlikely. The tournament was noted for the return of John McEnroe who lasted through to the quarter finals.

CRICKET: June 27

England lose the second Test at Lord's by six wickets. Steve Waugh remains unbeaten in the series scoring another undefeated century of 152. The third Test at Edgbaston is drawn although England are always struggling. At least they have the consolation of at last getting Steve Waugh out. He is bowled by Test debutant Angus Fraser. However Dean Jones scored 157.

RUGBY UNION: July 1

The British Lions took a mauling in the first Test in Sydney when they were completely outplayed by Australia and lost 30–12. A week later in Brisbane the Lions, spurred on by pride and a magnificent individual try by Jeremy Guscott, managed a late rally to beat Australia 19–12.

CRICKET: July 15

A last ball four by Eddie Hemmings off John Lever earned Nottinghamshire the Benson & Hedges Cup at Lord's, denying Essex. Essex made 243 for seven, with Alan Lilley hitting an undefeated 95. In reply Nottinghamshire made 244 for seven.

RUGBY UNION: July 15

The Lions won a sensational victory in Sydney by 19–18 to turn a tour that looked set for disaster into a glorious triumph. A horrendous mistake by David Campese gave the Lions a lifeline which they never let slip.

GOLF: July 23

A final round of 81 earned Mark Calcavecchia a play-off place in the Open at Royal Troon where he beat Greg Norman and Wayne Grady over the four holes to win the 118th Open.

ATHLETICS: July 30

Cuban Javier Sotomayor became the first man to clear 8ft in the high jump.

CRICKET: August 1

England lose the Ashes when they fall to their third defeat of the series at Old Trafford by nine wickets. Robin Smith is the light in England's darkness hitting 143. But the defeat is overshadowed by the announcement on the same day of a rebel squad of English cricketers to go to South Africa. They are to be led by Mike Gatting and include Test regulars Graham Dilley and Neil Foster. Phil DeFreitas and Roland Butcher are also signed up but both withdraw.

SWIMMING: August

Adrian Moorhouse earned a place alongside West German 'Alba-tross' Michael Gross – a living legend – when he won his fourth successive gold at the European championships in Bonn in August 1989. In the 100m heats Moorhouse broke the world record, the first Briton to do so since David Wilkie 13 years earlier. Nick Gillingham equalled the world record in the 200m breaststroke but his place in the swimming hall of fame only lasted two days. The American Mike Barrowman set a new record for the event in the Pan-Pacific Games. Among the women there were a number of schoolgirl prodigies like Sarah Hardcastle who threatened to deliver more than they did. It was all left to British swimming's femme fatale Sharron Davies, who after quitting the sport after the 1980 Olympics, made a return at the ripe old age of 26 in 1989 and immediately won a place in the Commonwealth Games team.

ATHLETICS: August 5–6

Great Britain won the European Cup at Gateshead when a team led by Linford Christie scored 115pts. East Germany were second and the USSR third.

CRICKET: August 10–14

Australia win the fifth Test match at Trent Bridge by an innings and 180 runs after Australian openers Greg Marsh and Mark Taylor bat through the first day for 301. They are broken at 329 with Marsh on 138 and Taylor makes 219. Robin Smith provides the resistance with 101. The sixth Test at the Oval ends in a draw.

GOLF: August 16–17

A Great Britain and Ireland team win the Walker Cup for the first time on American soil when they lift the trophy in Atlanta.

CRICKET: August 27

Lancashire beat Surrey by three wickets to collect the Sunday League title.

ATHLETICS: September 4
After their European success the Great Britain team came third
in the World Cup in Barcelona confirming that the Gateshead
result was not a fluke. They finished behind the US and Europe.
CRICKET: September 2
A majestic six from Neil Smith helped Warwickshire to a surprise
win over Middlesex in the NatWest Final at Lord's.
CRICKET: September 13–16
Worcestershire retain the County Championship after their match
at Glamorgan is ruined by rain, but the win was never totally
convincing as they finished less than 25 points ahead of Essex
who had 25 points deducted for a sub-standard pitch at Southend,
which was controlled by the local council and totally out of their
hands.
GOLF: September 25
The Ryder Cup is retained as Europe and the US draw at The
Belfry.
RUGBY UNION: November 18
The All Blacks are within sight of an unbeaten tour of Wales and
Ireland following their demolition of Ireland 23–6 at Lansdowne
Road. The Irish playing with fire were eventually worn down by
the pounding power of the New Zealand pack. They eventually
head home with a 100 per cent record after overcoming the
Barbarians at Twickenham.
BOXING: November 30
Frank Warren was gunned down as he got out of his chauffeur-
driven Bentley to attend a show in Barking. Warren made an
amazing recovery and two weeks later was back on his feet holding
a press conference.
SNOOKER: December 3
Stephen Hendry beat Steve Davis 16–12 to collect the UK Open
title at Preston and £100,000. In the process he became the youngest player, at 20, to win the event, usurping Davis from the
position.
BOXING: December 7
Boxer Sugar Ray Leonard made an estimated $30 million during
the year collecting between $17 and $18 million for his dull points
win over the aging Roberto Duran in Las Vegas. His other fight,
with Thomas Hearns, paid him about $13 million. These earnings
made him the first fighter in history to earn $100 million in lifetime
purses. Muhammad Ali's biggest payday was $8 million against
Larry Holmes in 1980, and that gave him $60 million for his
career. 'Some day, they'll say, Poor Sugar Ray Leonard. He came

along too soon. The most he ever made for a fight was $20 million', said promoter Bob Arum.

SOCCER: December 9

On a glittering stage and featuring stars from screen, stage and opera the World Cup draw for 1990 is made in Italy. England are drawn in the same group as Holland and it is the only time the two sides will meet in the competition unless they contest the final. England are priced at 12–1 to win the trophy with the Republic of Ireland 40–1 and Scotland 50–1.

RUGBY UNION: December 13

Cambridge win the sell-out Varsity Match at Twickenham 22–13.

ROLL OF HONOUR

AMERICAN FOOTBALL: Superbowl: San Francisco 49ers 20 Cincinnati Bengals 16.

ATHLETICS: World Cup, Men: United States (133pts), Europe (127pts) Great Britain (119pts). Women: East Germany (124pts), USSR (106pts), Americas (94pts). European Cup, Men: Great Britain. Women: East Germany.

CRICKET: County championship: Worcestershire. Refuge Assurance League: Lancashire. NatWest Trophy: Warwickshire. Benson & Hedges Cup: Nottinghamshire.

CYCLING: Tour de France: Greg Lemond (US). Women: Jeannie Longon (France).

DARTS: World Championship: Jocky Wilson.

GOLF: US Masters: Nick Faldo (GB). US PGA: Payne Stewart. US Open: Curtis Strange. The Open (Royal Troon): Mark Calcavecchia (after play-off). Ryder Cup (The Belfry): Europe 14 US 14.

HORSE RACING: Flat: 1000 Guineas: Musical Bliss. 2000 Guineas: Nashwan. The Derby: Nashwan (Jockey: Willie Carson. Trainer: Dick Hern). The Oaks: Aliysa. St Leger: Michelozzo. Champion jockey Pat Eddery, 171 wins. Top trainer Michael Stoute, £1,469,180.

National Hunt: Grand National: Little Polveir (Jockey: Jimmy Frost. Trainer: Toby Balding). Cheltenham Gold Cup: Desert Orchid. Champion Hurdle: Beech Road. Champion jockey Peter Scudamore, 221 wins. Top trainer Martin Pipe, £589,460.

MOTOR RACING: Alain Prost in a McLaren-Honda. Constructors' Cup: McLaren-Honda.

RUGBY LEAGUE: Challenge Cup: Wigan. Championship: Widnes.

RUGBY UNION: Championship: France. County Championship: Durham. Pilkington Cup: Bath 10 Leicester 6. Schweppes Welsh Cup: Neath 14 Llanelli 13.

SKIING: Overall champion, Men: Marc Girardelli (Luxembourg). Women: Vreni Schneider (Switzerland).

SNOOKER: World Championship: Steve Davis 18 John Parrott 3.

SOCCER: First Division Title: Arsenal (76pts). Runners-up: Liverpool. FA Cup winners: Liverpool 3 Everton 2. Littlewoods Cup: Nottingham Forest 3 Luton Town 1. Scotland: Premier League Title: Rangers (56pts). Runners-up: Aberdeen. Scottish Cup: Celtic 1 Rangers 0. Scottish League Cup: Rangers 3 Aberdeen 2. European Cup: AC Milan 4 Steaua Bucharest 0. Cup Winners' Cup: Barcelona 2 Sampdoria 0. UEFA CUP: Napoli beat VFB Stuttgart 5–4 on aggregate. (H) 2–1 (A) 3–3.

SPEEDWAY: World Champion: Hans Nielsen (Denmark). British League: Coventry.

SQUASH: World Open Championship, Men: Jansher Khan. Women: Martine Le Moignan (GB).

TABLE TENNIS: World Championship, Men: Jan-Ove Waldner (Sweden). Women: Qiao Hong (China).

TENNIS: Wimbledon, Men: Boris Becker (West Germany) beat Stefan Edberg (Sweden) 6–0 7–6 6–4. Women: Steffi Graf (West Germany) beat Martina Navratilova 6–2 6–7 6–1. US Open: Boris Becker, Steffi Graf. French Open: Michael Chang (US), Arantxa Sanchez-Vicario (Spain). Australian Open: Ivan Lendl (Cze), Steffi Graf. Davis Cup: West Germany. Wightman Cup: US beat Britain 7–0.

YACHTING: America's Cup: *Stars & Stripes* (US) skipper Dennis Conner. Admiral's Cup: Great Britain.

BARCLAYS LEAGUE 1988–89

DIVISION 1

		Home					Away					
	P	W	D	L	F	A	W	D	L	F	A	Pts
1 Arsenal	38	10	6	3	35	19	12	4	3	38	17	76
2 Liverpool	38	11	5	3	33	11	11	5	3	32	17	76
3 Nottingham F	38	8	7	4	31	16	9	6	4	33	27	64
4 Norwich C	38	8	7	4	23	20	9	4	6	25	25	62
5 Derby Co	38	9	3	7	23	18	8	4	7	17	20	58
6 Tottenham H	38	8	6	5	31	24	7	6	6	29	22	57
7 Coventry C	38	9	4	6	28	23	5	9	5	19	19	55
8 Everton	38	10	7	2	33	18	4	5	10	17	27	54
9 QPR	38	9	5	5	23	16	5	6	8	20	21	53
10 Millwall	38	10	3	6	27	21	4	8	7	20	31	53
11 Manchester U	38	10	5	4	27	13	3	7	9	18	22	51
12 Wimbledon	38	10	3	6	30	19	4	6	9	20	27	51
13 Southampton	38	6	7	6	25	26	4	8	7	27	40	45
14 Charlton Ath	38	6	7	6	25	24	4	5	10	19	34	42
15 Sheffield W	38	6	6	7	21	25	4	6	9	13	26	42
16 Luton T	38	8	6	5	32	21	2	5	12	10	31	41
17 Aston Villa	38	7	6	6	25	22	2	7	10	20	34	40
18 Middlesbrough	38	6	7	6	28	30	3	5	11	16	31	39
19 West Ham U	38	3	6	10	19	30	7	2	10	18	32	38
20 Newcastle U	38	3	6	10	19	28	4	4	11	13	35	31

DIVISION 2

		Home					Away					
	P	W	D	L	F	A	W	D	L	F	A	Pts
1 Chelsea	46	15	6	2	50	25	14	6	3	46	25	99
2 Manchester C	46	12	8	3	48	28	11	5	7	29	25	82
3 Crystal Palace	46	15	6	2	42	17	8	6	9	29	32	81
4 Watford	46	14	5	4	41	18	8	7	8	33	30	78
5 Blackburn R	46	16	4	3	50	22	6	7	10	24	37	77
6 Swindon T	46	13	8	2	35	15	7	8	8	33	38	76
7 Barnsley	46	12	8	3	37	21	8	6	9	29	37	74
8 Ipswich T	46	13	3	7	42	23	9	4	10	29	38	73
9 WBA	46	13	7	3	43	18	5	11	7	22	23	72
10 Leeds U	46	12	6	5	34	20	5	10	8	25	30	67
11 Sunderland	46	12	8	3	40	23	4	7	12	20	37	63
12 Bournemouth	46	13	3	7	32	20	5	5	13	21	42	62
13 Stoke C	46	10	9	4	33	25	5	5	13	24	47	59
14 Bradford C	46	8	11	4	29	22	5	6	12	23	37	56
15 Leicester C	46	11	6	6	31	20	2	10	11	25	43	55

		Home					Away					
	P	W	D	L	F	A	W	D	L	F	A	Pts
16 Oldham Ath .	46	9	10	4	49	32	2	11	10	26	40	54
17 Oxford U	46	11	6	6	40	34	3	6	14	22	36	54
18 Plymouth Arg	46	11	4	8	35	22	3	8	12	20	44	54
19 Brighton & HA	46	11	5	7	36	24	3	4	16	21	42	51
20 Portsmouth	46	10	6	7	33	21	3	6	14	20	41	51
21 Hull C	46	7	9	7	31	25	4	5	14	21	43	47
22 Shrewsbury	46	4	11	8	25	31	4	7	12	15	36	42
23 Birmingham C	46	6	4	13	21	33	2	7	14	10	43	35
24 Walsall	46	3	10	10	27	42	2	6	15	14	38	31

Crystal Palace promoted after play-offs.

DIVISION 3

		Home					Away					
	P	W	D	L	F	A	W	D	L	F	A	Pts
1 Wolverhampton W	46	18	4	1	61	19	8	10	5	35	30	92
2 Sheffield U	46	16	3	4	57	21	9	6	8	36	33	84
3 Port Vale	46	15	3	5	46	21	9	9	5	32	27	84
4 Fulham	46	12	7	4	42	28	10	2	11	27	39	75
5 Bristol R	46	9	11	3	34	21	10	6	7	33	30	74
6 Preston NE	46	14	7	2	56	31	5	8	10	23	29	72
7 Brentford	46	14	5	4	36	21	4	9	10	30	40	68
8 Chester C	46	12	6	5	38	18	7	5	11	26	43	68
9 Notts Co	46	11	7	5	37	22	7	6	10	27	32	67
10 Bolton W	46	12	8	3	42	23	4	8	11	16	31	64
11 Bristol C	46	10	3	10	32	25	8	6	9	21	30	63
12 Swansea C	46	11	8	4	33	22	4	8	11	18	31	61
13 Bury	46	11	7	5	27	22	5	6	12	28	45	61
14 Huddersfield T	46	10	8	5	35	25	7	1	15	28	48	60
15 Mansfield T	46	10	8	5	32	22	4	9	10	16	30	59
16 Cardiff C	46	10	9	4	30	16	4	6	13	14	40	57
17 Wigan Ath	46	9	5	9	28	22	5	9	9	27	31	56
18 Reading	46	10	6	7	37	29	5	5	13	31	43	56
19 Blackpool	46	10	6	7	36	29	4	7	12	20	30	54
20 Northampton T	46	11	2	10	41	34	5	4	14	25	42	54
21 Southend U	46	10	9	4	33	26	3	6	14	23	49	54
22 Chesterfield	46	9	5	9	35	35	5	2	16	16	51	49
23 Gillingham	46	7	3	13	25	32	5	1	17	22	49	40
24 Aldershot	46	7	6	10	29	29	1	7	15	19	49	37

Port Vale promoted after play-offs.

DIVISION 4

		Home					Away					
	P	W	D	L	F	A	W	D	L	F	A	Pts
1 Rotherham U	46	13	6	4	44	18	9	10	4	32	17	82
2 Tranmere R	46	15	6	2	34	13	6	11	6	28	30	80
3 Crew Alex	46	13	7	3	42	24	8	8	7	25	24	78
4 Scunthorpe U	46	11	9	3	40	22	10	5	8	37	35	77
5 Scarborough	46	12	7	4	33	23	9	7	7	34	29	77
6 Leyton Orient	46	16	2	5	61	19	5	10	8	25	31	75
7 Wrexham	46	12	7	4	44	28	7	7	9	33	35	71
8 Cambridge U	46	13	7	3	45	25	5	7	11	26	37	68
9 Grimsby T	46	11	9	3	33	18	6	6	11	32	41	66
10 Lincoln C	46	12	6	5	39	26	6	4	13	25	34	64
11 York C	46	10	8	5	43	27	7	5	11	19	36	64
12 Carlisle U	46	9	6	8	26	25	6	9	8	27	27	60
13 Exeter C	46	14	4	5	46	23	4	2	17	19	45	60
14 Torquay U	46	15	2	6	32	23	2	6	15	13	37	59
15 Hereford U	46	11	8	4	40	27	3	8	12	26	45	58
16 Burnley	46	12	6	5	35	20	2	7	14	17	41	55
17 Peterborough U	46	10	3	10	29	32	4	9	10	23	42	54
18 Rochdale	46	10	10	3	32	26	3	4	16	24	56	53
19 Hartlepool U	46	10	6	7	33	33	4	4	15	17	45	52
20 Stockport Co	46	8	10	5	31	20	2	11	10	23	32	51
21 Halifax T	46	10	7	6	42	27	3	4	16	27	48	50
22 Colchester U	46	8	7	8	35	30	4	7	12	25	48	50
23 Doncaster R	46	9	6	8	32	32	4	4	15	17	46	49
24 Darlington	46	3	12	8	28	38	5	6	12	25	38	42

Leyton Orient promoted after play-offs.

B & Q SCOTTISH LEAGUE 1988–89

PREMIER DIVISION

		Home					Away					
	P	W	D	L	F	A	W	D	L	F	A	Pts
1 Rangers	36	15	1	2	39	11	11	3	4	23	15	56
2 Aberdeen	36	10	7	1	26	10	8	7	3	25	15	50
3 Celtic	36	13	1	4	35	18	8	3	7	31	26	46
4 Dundee U	36	6	8	4	20	16	10	4	4	24	10	44

		Home					Away					
	P	W	D	L	F	A	W	D	L	F	A	Pts
5 Hibernian	36	8	4	6	20	16	5	5	8	17	20	35
6 Hearts	36	7	6	5	22	17	2	7	9	13	25	31
7 St Mirren	36	5	6	7	17	19	6	1	11	22	36	29
8 Dundee	36	8	4	6	22	21	1	6	11	12	27	28
9 Motherwell	36	5	7	6	21	21	2	6	10	14	23	27
10 Hamilton Acad	36	5	0	13	9	42	1	2	15	10	34	14

DIVISION 1

		Home					Away					
	P	W	D	L	F	A	W	D	L	F	A	Pts
1 Dunfermline Ath	39	13	5	2	37	17	9	5	5	23	19	54
2 Falkirk	39	13	3	3	38	10	9	5	6	33	27	52
3 Clydebank	39	12	6	2	50	29	6	6	7	30	26	48
4 Airdrieonians	39	11	6	2	36	16	6	7	7	30	28	47
5 Morton	39	8	5	6	20	20	8	4	8	26	26	41
6 St Johnstone	39	11	4	4	30	16	3	8	9	21	26	40
7 Raith Rovers	39	8	6	6	29	25	7	4	8	21	27	40
8 Partick Th	39	7	6	6	26	24	6	5	9	31	34	37
9 Forfar Ath	39	6	9	5	24	24	4	7	8	28	32	36
10 Meadowbank Th	39	8	4	7	26	26	5	6	9	19	24	36
11 Ayr U	39	8	6	6	39	37	5	3	11	17	35	35
12 Clyde	39	7	6	7	23	26	2	10	7	17	26	34
13 Kilmarnock	39	5	7	7	19	25	5	7	8	28	35	34
14 Queen of the S*	39	1	6	13	20	47	1	2	16	18	52	10

DIVISION 2

		Home					Away					
	P	W	D	L	F	A	W	D	L	F	A	Pts
1 Albion R	39	14	5	1	39	19	7	3	9	26	29	50
2 Alloa	39	12	6	1	42	20	5	5	10	24	28	45
3 Brechin C	39	8	5	6	27	24	7	8	5	31	25	43
4 Stirling Albion	39	10	6	3	31	20	5	6	9	33	35	42
5 East Fife	39	9	8	3	30	20	5	5	9	25	34	41
6 Montrose	39	10	4	5	25	25	5	7	8	29	30	41
7 Queen's Park	39	8	7	4	26	20	2	11	7	24	29	38
8 Cowdenbeath*	39	6	11	2	30	27	7	3	10	18	25	38
9 East Stirling	39	10	3	7	31	31	3	8	8	23	27	37
10 Arbroath	39	5	6	9	29	40	6	9	4	27	23	37
11 Stranraer	39	6	8	6	30	31	6	4	9	28	32	36

| | Home | | | | | | Away | | | | | |
	P	W	D	L	F	A	W	D	L	F	A	Pts
12 Dumbarton	39	10	2	8	28	27	2	8	9	17	28	34
13 Berwick R	39	5	7	7	18	26	5	6	9	32	33	33
14 Stenhousemuir	39	6	8	6	27	24	3	3	13	17	35	29

* 2 points deducted for breach of rules.

BRITANNIC ASSURANCE CHAMPIONSHIP 1989

| | | | | | Bonus | | |
	P	W	L	D	Bt	Bl	Pts
1 Worcestershire (1)	22	12	3	7	44	83	319
2 Essex (3)	22	13	2	7	59	71	313
3 Middlesex (8)	22	9	2	11	50	72	266
4 Lancashire (9)	22	8	5	9	57	65	250
5 Northamptonshire (12)	22	7	8	7	47	63	222
6 { Hampshire (15)	22	6	8	8	55	65	216
{ Derbyshire (14)	22	6	6	10	45	75	216
8 Warwickshire (6)	22	5	4	13	44	75	207
9 Gloucestershire (10)	22	6	11	5	38	70	204
10 Sussex (16)	22	4	4	14	60	68	192
11 Nottinghamshire (5)	22	6	6	10	54	65	190
12 Surrey (4)	22	4	7	11	50	69	183
13 Leicestershire (7)	22	4	8	10	43	74	181
14 Somerset (11)	22	4	6	12	50	54	168
15 Kent (2)	22	3	8	11	53	53	154
16 Yorkshire (13)	22	3	9	10	41	60	149
17 Glamorgan (17)	22	3	6	13	38	59	145

1988 positions in brackets.

Warwickshire's total includes 8 points as the side batting second in a match where the scores finished level. Essex and Nottinghamshire deducted 25 points for sub-standard pitches at Southend and Trent Bridge.

REFUGE ASSURANCE LEAGUE

		P	W	L	Tie	NR	Pts
1	Lancashire (3)	16	12	2	0	2	52
2 {	Worcestershire (1)	16	11	4	0	1	46
	Essex (10)	16	11	4	0	1	46
4 {	Nottinghamshire (17)	16	9	6	0	1	38
	Derbyshire (12)	16	9	6	0	1	38
	Hampshire (9)	16	8	6	1	1	36
6 {	Surrey (5)	16	9	7	0	0	36
	Northamptonshire (14)	16	8	6	0	2	36
9	Middlesex (4)	16	8	7	1	0	34
10	Somerset (12)	16	7	8	1	0	30
	Yorkshire (8)	16	7	9	0	0	28
11 {	Kent (7)	16	7	9	0	0	28
	Sussex (14)	16	6	8	1	1	28
14 {	Leicestershire (14)	16	5	10	0	1	22
	Warwickshire (10)	16	5	10	0	1	22
16 {	Gloucestershire (2)	16	3	13	0	0	12
	Glamorgan (5)	16	2	12	0	2	12

1988 positions in brackets

GOLF by JOHN HOPKINS

IN MOST recent decades, the moments of pure genius from home-bred golfers have totalled only marginally more than the number of woods in a golfer's bag. In the eighties it was different. From a decade that was unrivalled in terms of success by any this century, the problem is not in remembering the few but in selecting one from so many.

I could say that my favourite moment was when Jack Nicklaus stooped to kiss a divot that had fallen from Lanny Wadkins's club. Wadkins had just played the shot that won the US the 1983 Ryder Cup when it had looked to Nicklaus as though he would be the first American captain to lose this event at home - and this just a month or so after Dennis Conner had lost the America's Cup. For Nicklaus it hardly bore thinking about.

Or it was the sight of Nicklaus whose eyesight was failing and whose injured back was suspect, charging through the field, covering the second nine in 30, to win the 1986 US Masters. He was then 46, old enough to be the father of some of the competitors – Sandy Lyle, his playing partner, for one. And he was the father of his caddie, Jackie.

If you have followed British golf from the bleak postwar years through to the dawning of the new age you know what it is to come second. Second was where British players always ended in the Open. Second was where the Ryder, Curtis and Walker Cup teams finished every other year. Coming second became sickening.

So it would be understandable if one's abiding memory of the eighties was of Europeans either singly or in a team achieving victories that had seemed unattainable before. Of Seve Ballesteros toying with the field in the 1980 US Masters and leading by ten strokes at one moment. Of Bernhard Langer storming to victory in the 1985 US Masters. Of Laura Davies defeating the cream of women's professional golf in the 1987 US Open. Of Nick Faldo in April 1989 receiving the victor's green jacket given to the US Masters' champion from none other than Sandy Lyle, who had won it the year before.

No one who was there could possibly forget the heartfelt cheers that rang out at Royal St George's in 1985 when Lyle won the Open, the first Briton since Tony Jacklin in 1969 – and then Faldo followed suit in 1987. Grown men cried at Muirfield Village in 1987 when Europe, having defeated the US in the Ryder Cup at The Belfry two years earlier, defeated them again, for the first time on American soil.

My moment of the decade might be any of these or it might be the sight of Ballesteros hitting a shot with a three wood from a bunker to the green 240 yards away in the 1983 Ryder Cup, the greatest shot I saw hit anywhere in the 80s, though Lyle's bunker shot on the final hole of the 1988 US Masters was almost as good. But brilliant as each of these was, neither is the moment I will cherish above all others.

It is, instead, of the events that unfolded one steamy afternoon in Atlanta, Georgia, in August 1989 as the US fought to retain the Walker Cup.

Jim Milligan was the hero. At the moment this story begins Milligan was two down with four holes to play in the match that would decide the Walker Cup. If he won, Britain and Ireland would win the Cup for the first time ever in the US. Jay Sigel, the experienced American amateur, was charged with defeating Milligan and thereby retaining the Cup for the US.

In previous years the scenario would have gone like this. Milligan would have won the 16th, snatched a half by holing a long putt on the 17th but then would have done no better than a half on the 18th, thereby losing by one hole. He would have tried his best – but he would have lost.

But in the 80s European golf was different. No one feared the Americans any more. They didn't need to. In the professional game three of Europe's best were also three of the world's best. This bred confidence that spread to the amateur game, men and women, as well.

And particularly to people like Milligan, a chippie back home in Scotland, as he faced his moment of truth. Milligan halved the 15th, won the 16th as crowds gathered for his match, the last one on the course. He won the 17th after fluffing one chip by chipping into the hole with his next.

Then Milligan played the 18th as if his nerves were made of steel. A good drive, a safe second shot, a good chip from thick clinging rough that lapped the edge of the green. When Sigel fluffed another short chip Milligan had only to putt close to gain the half that was needed.

This man and this match remain in my mind above all else

from the 1980s, above even Christy O'Connor Junior's brilliant iron to the last green in the 1989 Ryder Cup and Ballesteros's play in the fourth round of the 1988 Open, because Milligan was under such pressure for so long. For an hour he played in front of his team mates knowing that the slightest slip might let them down. He knew that he was expected to lose – and yet he didn't.

His victory could be a metaphor for European golf's performance in the 80s. Milligan brought home the Walker Cup by skill, nerve, resolution and self belief. For what he did that summer's afternoon, his was my moment of the decade.

Ben Johnson leads Carl Lewis (right) over 100 metres finish. Linford Christie (second right) is third in the 1988 Olympics.

John Kirwin on the All Blacks 1989 tour in their match against Cardiff.